JUN 2 8 2018

W9-AXH-217

KICKS

THE GREAT AMERICAN STORY OF SNEAKERS

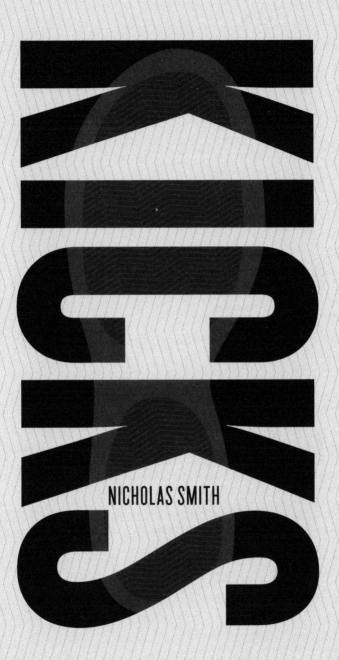

KICKS

NICHOLAS SMITH

CROWN

NEW YORK

All rights reserved.
Published in the United States by Crown, an imprint of
the Crown Publishing Group, a division of Penguin Random House LLC,
New York.
crownpublishing.com

CROWN and the Crown colophon are registered trademarks of
Penguin Random House LLC.
For a list of photo credits, see page 300.

Library of Congress Cataloging-in-Publication Data
Names: Smith, Nicholas, author.
Title: Kicks : the great American story of sneakers / by Nicholas Smith.
Description: First Edition. | New York : Crown Publishing, [2018] |
    Includes bibliographical references.
Identifiers: LCCN 2017040841| ISBN 9780451498113 (Hardcover) |
    ISBN 9780451498120 (Trade Paperback) | ISBN 9780451498137 (eBook)
Subjects: LCSH: Sneakers—United States. | Sneakers—Social aspects—
    United States.
Classification: LCC GV749.S64 S58 2018 | DDC 685/.31—dc23 LC record
    available at https://lccn.loc.gov/2017040841

ISBN 978-0-451-49811-3
Ebook ISBN 978-0-451-49813-7

PRINTED IN THE UNITED STATES OF AMERICA

Book design by Andrea Lau
Jacket design by Christopher Brand
Jacket illustration by Yunosuke Otani

10 9 8 7 6 5 4 3 2 1

First Edition

To my wife, Ghadeer, who still owns more sneakers than I do

You cannot be comfortable on a high heel shoe
the way you would be in sneakers.
But, you know, not everyone wants to be in sneakers.
Sneakers are for different purposes.

—CHRISTIAN LOUBOUTIN

In L.A. we wearing Chucks, not Ballys.

—TUPAC SHAKUR

CONTENTS

PROLOGUE

"**I**t's gotta be the shoes." Most people have heard it, even if they can't remember the source: a 1989 commercial for the Nike Air Jordan IIIs. In the commercial, Spike Lee, playing his alter ego Mars Blackmon from the movie *She's Gotta Have It*, lists all the possible reasons Michael Jordan is "the best player in the universe."

His dunks? asks Lee.

No, Mars, says Jordan.

His shorts? asks Lee.

No, Mars, says Jordan.

His bald head? asks Lee.

No, Mars, says Jordan.

His shoes? asks Lee.

Jordan denies it, but Lee keeps circling back to the shoe guess. In the thirty-second ad, the word "shoes" is spoken ten times.

Before the familiar swoosh appears onscreen, a cheeky

disclaimer informs us that "Mr. Jordan's opinions do not necessarily reflect those of Nike, Inc.," but everyone already knows the
message here: "It's gotta be the shoes."

Nike sold millions of Air Jordans through that ad campaign,
and Lee's most famous line was bound for pop culture immor-
tality. But the ad didn't work just because it was catchy and star-
studded; it was also a clever update of an idea that most of us have
lived with from a young age: the idea that shoes are magical.

Cinderella's glass slipper makes her a princess. Dorothy's
ruby slippers not only transport her back to Kansas but keep the
Wicked Witch of the West at bay. Puss-in-Boots' request for footwear helps him win legitimacy for his master. With his winged
sandals Hermes can fly. The "seven-league boots" of European
folklore let the wearer travel great distances in a single step. A
young orphan's shoes compel her to dance in Hans Christian
Andersen's "The Red Shoes," and in the Grimms' version of
"Snow White," the wicked stepmother dances herself to death in
charmed red-hot iron heels.

Fast-forwarding a few centuries, Lil' Bow Wow finds a pair of
magic sneakers that let him play professional basketball in 2002's
Like Mike, and in the Harry Potter series a teleporting "portkey"
comes in the form of an old boot. And at the end of the first *Sex
and the City* movie, the first thing Carrie Bradshaw uses in her
new apartment-size closet—a fairy tale for anyone familiar with
Manhattan real estate—is the shoe rack.

When Jacob and Wilhelm Grimm were collecting their folk-
tales in the early eighteenth century, footwear sometimes did
mean the difference between life and death, as well as between
rungs of the social ladder. Without owning a reliable pair of boots,
finding work was difficult; sturdy shoes gave the lower-class
wearer the unmagical but useful ability not to starve to death.
Until the mid-1800s, shoes were made entirely by hand in a long

and costly process. The supply was always limited, and shoes were coveted highly enough to inspire generations of storytellers.

Shoes may no longer mean the difference between starving and not, but they still have great symbolic power. It's embedded in our language: to understand each other we must "walk a mile in someone's shoes." A guess about one's character will prove true "if the shoe fits." Someone irreplaceable has "hard shoes to fill." Someone may offer to "eat his shoe" if he's wrong. An uncomfortable reversal means that "the shoe is on the other foot." Before the inevitable, we wait for "the other shoe to drop."

Our contact with shoes as objects is unusually intimate: shoes change, adjust, and warp to fit us like no other piece of clothing. Finding a worn-out vintage rock tee at a Goodwill store might be a hipster's treasure; finding a worn-out pair of sneakers is infinitely less so. Their soles both connect us to our environment and protect us from it. They can be either utilitarian or expressive or both, whatever we choose. Somewhere in these qualities is, maybe, the source of their appeal as, well, more than shoes.

Which takes us back to Jordan and his Nikes. Ever since there have been sports stars to look up to, kids have played their heroes on the fields, courts, and sandlots. "I'm DiMaggio. I'm Elway. I'm LeBron." By pairing the superhuman Jordan with the Everyman Lee, the Nike commercials suggested that there was a way to bridge the gap—a hundred-dollar way, but a way nonetheless. It was a modern version of the old story: an ordinary kid could wear a pair of sneakers and jump like the Jumpman, just as a farm girl could put on a pair of red slippers to get home from the Land of Oz.

FOR A LONG TIME, SNEAKERS weren't something I thought about. When I was growing up, they were just shoes you wore every day until they wore out. The first sneakers I can remember treating with any reverence were a pair of Nike Air Flight Turbulence I wore when I played basketball freshman year of high school. I bought them partly because they'd been advertised in a campaign featuring Damon Stoudamire, a rookie point guard for the Toronto Raptors whom I knew from his time with the Arizona Wildcats, the most popular college team in my hometown. I also bought them because they were last year's model and retailed for $40 at the Nike outlet, a steal at a time when the latest Air Jordans sold for $150.

I loved them, with their wavy black-and-white lines and familiar swoosh. For the duration of my freshman season I wore them only for practice and games, after which they went right back into the box. They might not have helped a lanky, uncoordinated fourteen-year-old score a career high of five points, but I sure felt like they did. The one time I wore them off court was when friends who had moved away from my small town came to visit. They had new haircuts, new glasses, a binder full of new CDs. I had my new shoes.

It would be years before I again found that sneaker magic. Basketball had long since melted away and been replaced by distance running when I read Christopher McDougall's *Born to Run*, an ode to running that featured unforgiving 100-mile races, a colorful cast of "ultrarunners," punishing desert environments, and an indigenous Mexican tribe whose members seem to run forever in thin sandals. As a marathoner with recurring knee pain, I was interested in what McDougall had found to be a near constant among ultrarunners: minimalist footwear. The implicit promise of the book seemed to be that I could join their tribe and kiss knee pain good-bye by ditching my chunky Nikes. It had to be the shoes.

I zeroed in on the then-popular Vibram FiveFingers, which looked as ridiculous as their name—like gorilla feet, with a separate compartment for each toe. But I was suddenly a true believer; I wasn't looking for sneakers anymore, I was looking for a spiritual conduit to the natural world, a connection with some evolutionary past of perfect endurance and form. Shoes shaped like feet seemed about right. I walked into a specialty running store and told the clerk what I was looking for, how the FiveFingers would instantly cure me of pain and allow me to run forever.

The clerk broke the spell. He cautioned that plunging down from a big, chunky Nike to a barely there slip-on was a recipe for creating joint pain, not ending it. Instead I ended up walking out of the store with a pair of electric-blue Brooks PureConnect, an ultralight shoe that still had some cushioning—and, unlike the FiveFingers, still resembled a sneaker.

My new shoes made me feel different. Not just because of the way the Brooks sneakers were built (they gripped my midfoot in a way my previous Nikes hadn't) but also because they broke with my pattern of black, gray, or white shoes. For whatever reason, I realized, the all-blue shoes made me feel like a faster runner. Whether that was actually the case was beside the point.

NO SHOE IS MORE VARIABLE than the sneaker. Whether you know them as sneakers, trainers, gym shoes, tennis shoes, joggers, or runners, almost everyone has owned a pair. Sneakers can help us stand out or blend in. They can be the item we build our outfits up from or an afterthought we slip on before running out the door. And every sneaker we wear says something about us in both subtle and not-so-subtle ways.

I saw a glimpse of the many permutations of sneakers at the 2014 Boston Marathon. I had yet again missed out on qualifying for the race, but, being a marathon fan, I closely followed the broadcast on TV and online. One year after the terrorist bombing that had taken the lives of three people and injured hundreds of others, sneakers were the centerpiece of makeshift memorials at Copley Square near the site of the attack, draped over crowd barriers or carefully placed alongside more conventional offerings of flowers and handwritten notes. An exhibit in the nearby Boston Public Library artfully arranged running shoes collected from the previous year's memorial. Outside, high-tech racing flats were on the feet of tens of thousands of participants. Spectators lining the route wore a rainbow of basketball and tennis shoes. In addition with carbon-fiber prostheses, sophisticated engineering and innovative soles allowed amputee athletes to compete. Along the 26.2-mile course, old shoes hung from telephone wires overhead.

Athletic equipment, all-purpose fashion, memorial, artwork: in a century and a half of existence, sneakers have become one of our most quietly ubiquitous cultural objects. Sneakers were born at the meeting of the Industrial Revolution and its unlikely by-product, increased leisure time. They grew as sports began to organize. They helped US soldiers train for World War II. They evolved with fashion and consumer culture. They defined the image of both the suburban teenager and gang culture. They appeared in song lyrics at the birth of hip-hop, and they were part of the uniform of young punks and aging rock stars alike. They helped create the celebrity athlete and became a universal symbol of globalization. Presidents have worn them, and so has everyone else. In recent years, they have inspired a cottage industry of portraits, analysis, and scholarship, including the photo and interview collection *Sneakers*; the documentary *Sneakerheadz*, about the shoe's most ardent collectors; and *Out of the Box: The Rise of Sneaker Culture*, an illustrated history backed by strong academic research, to which this book owes a debt. The history of sneakers is, in a sense, the recent history of the United States.

So how did we get here?

1

THE FATHER OF INVENTION

The world was about to change when Charles Goodyear saw a life preserver in a New York City shop window in 1834. Goodyear was fresh off a stint in debtors' prison, having been forced to declare bankruptcy when his family hardware business failed. After a few long days in a squalid cell, he resolved on a bold new plan to bring his family back to prosperity. Instead of selling the products needed for modern life, he would invent new and better ones. His hardware business had, after all, manufactured its own scythes and forks, and his father had gotten his start by producing the buttons worn by American soldiers in the War of 1812. Looking into the shop window at the Roxbury India Rubber Company's life preserver, the thirty-three-year-old Goodyear decided it was time to start his plan.

Rubber products were relatively new to the United States, only becoming widespread in the 1820s. Investors flocked to this curious substance from the "weeping wood" trees of Central and South America. Rubber shoes were among the first rubber products sold to the new nation: overshoes, forerunners of modern-day galoshes, slipped over normal shoes to keep them safe and dry from rain and mud. The crude latex shoes were hailed as a triumph of design, providing protection that no leather or wooden shoe could. In 1826, 8 tons of overshoes were imported into New England from Brazil; four years later the figure was 161 tons. The rubber boom continued through the early 1830s, with rubber coats, hats, boats, and life preservers joining the expanding product line, buoyed by a fascination with the substance's waterproof properties.

Goodyear purchased the life preserver he saw in New York and took it back to his home in Philadelphia. It actually wasn't the "bag of wind" that had caught Goodyear's eye for improvement, just its valve, which had a leaky seal. He set about coming up with a better design. When he returned to the Roxbury store a few weeks later, the salesman was impressed with Goodyear's valve design, but there was a small problem. He took Goodyear to a nearby warehouse, where shelves and shelves were stacked with blobby masses that had once been life preservers. He explained that though the Roxbury company had been one of the most successful in the rubber trade, it was now on the verge of ruin. Rubber had the ability to resist water, but it also had a fatal flaw: it melted in the heat and turned brittle in the cold. The life preservers had been destroyed by the New York summer.

"Forget your valve," the salesman said. "The one invention that could save the rubber industry and earn a fortune for the inventor would be a method of preserving rubber from . . . this."

Goodyear's interest was piqued. It was the worst possible time to get into the business: the investors who had first flocked to rubber had backed out, and public interest was waning in products that could not hold their shape during the hot summer months. Nevertheless, the budding inventor set to work, purchasing the now-unwanted rubber for pennies on the pound. Goodyear used his wife's rolling pin to knead the raw bits of rubber into a pliable consistency before subjecting each batch to a battery of tests. He tried everything he could think of—dissolving bits of rubber in chemical solutions, sun curing, glazing—sure that if he could manage to achieve a temperature-resistant rubber, its potential was vast. With no scientific background to help him structure his experiments, his progress was slow and laborious.

The months of experiments turned into years, and Goodyear pawned his family's furniture for income. When he ended up back in debtors' prison (as he would a half-dozen or so times throughout his life), he continued his work there, much to the amusement of fellow inmates who watched him knead and roll his bits of rubber. He was dispirited each time he fell so low, calling his accommodations in one Boston prison "perhaps as good a resting place as a grave," but his creditors would always release him after a few weeks. (He might also have consoled himself that being jailed for owing too much money was not altogether uncommon, even for those not teetering on the brink of poverty—a signatory of the Declaration of Independence was imprisoned while serving as an associate justice of the Supreme Court.)

By the middle of the 1830s, Goodyear and his family had moved to a more affordable cottage in Connecticut that doubled as a laboratory. He had found an investor to fund his experiments, which had progressed to the point where he thought he had discovered the magic formula in a mixture of rubber, turpentine, and magnesia. Excited to impress his investor, he prepared hundreds of rubber shoes that winter.

When they turned gooey in the spring, Goodyear lost the interest of his only source of income as well as what remained of his reputation. To the world he was a man tinkering with an impossible substance rather than paying his bills. Three of his six children had died in infancy, two of them during a two-year span in the early 1830s, and the family had run out of furniture to pawn.

Still, when his brother-in-law paid Goodyear a visit in 1836 to discourage his experiments, Goodyear gestured to the room behind him, cluttered with kettles and chemicals. "Here is something that will pay all of our debts and make us comfortable," he said.

"The India rubber business is below par," the brother-in-law pressed.

"Well, I am the man to bring it back again," said Goodyear, smiling.

IN 1800, THE YEAR GOODYEAR was born, the world was in the midst of a dramatic transition. For most of human history, everything most people owned—clothes, tools, furniture, shoes—had been made nearby. The Industrial Revolution, catalyzed by the practical applications of coal in the eighteenth century and the invention of the steam engine, meant swift increases in the speed and efficiency of manufacturing. Textiles could be produced cheaply and en masse. Iron and steel became easier to forge into building materials and consumer goods. The nature of labor was changing as the workforce shifted from farms to factories, with workers flocking from rural agricultural areas to the cities and towns in which new economic opportunities clustered. From 1790 to 1820, New York City's population grew from 340,000 to 1.4 million, a change of more than 300 percent in just thirty years.

Advances in automation and the development of factories, warehouses, and a rail system to deliver new manufactured goods across the country would, along with stabilized rubber, soon make a product like the sneaker possible. But before the true birth of anything recognizable as the sneaker of today, demand for such a product needed to exist, and it would come from other changes wrought by the Industrial Revolution—changes outside the scope of industry itself. This was the development of sports and leisure.

Leisure time was a direct outgrowth of factory life. In England, where the Industrial Revolution first took hold, cotton mills and textile factories had to shut down once a year for repairs and maintenance. This led to a mandatory week off work, which, coupled with workers' disposable income and new access to rail travel, led to the popularity of seaside resorts. In the mid-1800s, tourism businesses started to spring up in coastal towns such as Blackpool and Brighton to serve the new demand for beachside holidays. Blackpool wasn't overrun with tourists arriving all at the same time; each town shut its mills down for "wakes weeks" during a different time period, ensuring a steady stream of vacationers. Once a luxury available only to the upper classes, leisure time was spreading down the social ladder to everyone else.

It wasn't long before fashions started to change in response. Alongside the overshoe, another early forerunner of the sneaker was the "sand shoe." These cheap, mass-produced beach shoes were available at seaside resorts in Great Britain as well as the United States and provided an alternative to getting sand in a worker's factory boots. They were usually canvas with a cork or sometimes rope sole—fine for the beach, though not so good when the shoes came into contact with the water. In 1832, Wait Webster of New York patented a way of affixing a rubber sole to shoes, and in the 1830s, the Liverpool Rubber Company was said to have tried rubber-soled sand shoes, but the soles would have melted as easily as those unfortunate life preservers.

Away from the beach, the new working class was inventing other ways to spend its free time: sports. In the early nineteenth century, the closest analogies to an athletic shoe—defined as specialized footwear required for a specific physical activity—were riding boots and ballet slippers. That was what recreation meant before the Industrial Revolution: pastimes for the elite patrons of the arts or followers of the hunt. But as leisure time and the income to do something with it became more commonplace, sports evolved as well.

One of the first competitive activities to rise up from the working classes didn't lend itself to special equipment. In 1861, Americans fell in love with a story of a man who, after losing a bet, walked from Boston to Washington, D.C., to witness the inauguration of President Abraham Lincoln. Watching people walk grabbed Americans in a way no other sport yet had. Rougher spectacles such as boxing and cockfighting existed on the fringes, and baseball, America's first real spectator sport, had yet to be popularized by Union troops across the country during the Civil War. With each town the Lincoln walker passed through, increasing crowds turned out to see him.

The best pedestrians gained a cultlike following, gossiped about and written up in the papers of towns and cities that, for the first time, set up large buildings for public events. Pedestrian competitors would face one another in matches that lasted up to six days (competition on Sunday being out of the question), sometimes walking from city to city, sometimes doing loops around an arena. People came either way: just as the new railroads in England helped beach culture thrive, in the United States they provided travel for athletes and fans to wherever a walking match was taking place.

Those early footraces incorporated something that would become inseparable from sport: money. In an early example of athlete endorsement, the man who walked to see Lincoln in 1861 handed out flyers along the way for the businesses that had sponsored his walk. "Pedestrian fever" also provided an opportunity for betting, an evergreen distraction from factory or farm life. And there was serious prize money, as in 1879, when people packed New York's Madison Square Garden to see two men compete over six days to be pedestrian champion of the world. The winner covered more than 230 miles and received $18,390, his share of the gate receipts.

Though walking had the higher profile, especially in the United States, it was runners who first got serious about shoes. By 1850, many British public houses and taverns began featuring dirt and cinder tracks, as much for the amusement of patrons as to make a quick shilling. In the United States, organizations such as the New York Athletic Club sprang up in the mid-1860s for amateur runners. As newspapers carried the exploits of racers, race promoters decided that distances and conditions ought to be standardized so that an effort made by a runner on one track could easily be compared with one made by another runner on a different one. By adding stopwatches to the mix, promoters could help build excitement by touting matchups between the fastest champions.

Special shoes could give a runner a slight edge on the new tracks, and with money often on the line and results becoming a matter of record, the demand grew. The earliest running shoes were made of leather, but with metal spikes driven into the soles to help dig into a track's surface. One from the early 1860s made by Thomas Dutton and Thorowgood looked like a men's dress shoe, complete with a heel, except for the metal spikes and a leather strap across the instep. Other shoes were made not for speed but for weight. Some runners used heavier shoes for training—a manual from 1866 advised sprinters to "wear heavy shoes for all exercises." Others used them to try to game the system. It was common to assign a handicap to slower runners to keep races competitive, so some faster runners would sandbag qualifying rounds by wearing shoes with heavy lead insoles.

With sports and recreation becoming a part of everyday life, conditions were right for the rise of the sneaker. But first an inventor had to make his rubber bounce back.

AFTER YEARS OF TOILING, GOODYEAR finally had a stroke of luck. In 1838, he visited a failing rubber factory in Woburn, Massachusetts, hoping to buy out the owner, Nathaniel Hayward, and use the place as a new staging ground for experiments. Hayward, like Goodyear, saw the potential of a stable rubber and had been conducting his own self-designed experiments. On a tour of the factory, Goodyear smelled sulfur in the air and deduced that this was the reason Hayward's rubber products, though not impervious to the heat, remained smooth on the surface even as they started to malform. Goodyear purchased the factory later that year, and Hayward stayed on as his foreman as the two worked with the sulfur technique. He was sure the mystery was all but unlocked.

Goodyear set out to persuade backers again and soon secured a contract to provide all-weather bags for the U.S. Post Office. In a familiar pattern, unfortunately, he was unable to deliver. While his solid rubber mailbags were sitting in the factory before delivery, their insides turned to goo.

His prospects, his money from previous patent sales, and now his new factory were soon gone. "He was not only reduced to extreme poverty, with a large family to provide for," Goodyear later wrote of the mailbag fiasco (in the third person), "but, if he continued his experiments, he could no longer expect the countenance or sympathy of his friends and acquaintances."

Yet he could not stop tinkering. In early 1839, he finally unlocked the secret to stable rubber by chance, when he dripped a mixture of rubber, sulfur, and white lead onto a hot stove and found that it not only didn't melt but held its shape. Hayward's sulfur additive was only a piece of the answer: the real breakthrough was adding heat to the mixture. Frustratingly, after he had made the initial discovery, Goodyear had difficulty replicating the results since the balance among the rubber, sulfur, and lead needed to be precise, as did the amount of heat applied to it. Goodyear was insistent on perfecting his process before filing a patent; he wouldn't jump the gun, this time. In 1842, he convinced a shoe manufacturer named Horace Cutler to go into business with him. But Goodyear's rubber was still as much art as science, and Cutler became fed up with the inconsistent results and persistently blistered shoes. Other entrepreneurs began to realize that Goodyear and Cutler's shoes—the unblistered ones—were something truly new, however, and they began to want in on the discovery.

In January 1844, Goodyear was finally confident enough (and could afford) to apply for a US patent, which was awarded a few months later. The process he had discovered came to be called vulcanization, named, by an acquaintance of Goodyear, after Vulcan, the Roman god of fire. Investors were hesitant to return after all but abandoning the rubber industry a decade earlier, but when it became clear that vulcanization was the game-changing discovery they had been waiting for, they flocked back. Goodyear's rubber would create entire industries and alter everyday life in ways neither he nor anyone else could imagine. By 1846, just two years after the British patent was awarded, Queen Victoria's carriage would boast solid rubber tires. Ten years after Goodyear's fateful encounter with the rubber life preserver in a New York City shop window, through much trial and much error, the secret of stable rubber was his.

But not his alone. Waiting so long to secure a patent had been a business blunder, as it turned out. Goodyear's miracle substance had already found its way into his rivals' hands.

IN MARCH 1852, everything was on the line for Charles Goodyear. The fifty-one-year-old's future as an inventor, his path out of poverty, and his chance of owning one of the greatest technological discoveries of the century were now to be decided in a US Circuit Court in Trenton, New Jersey. Goodyear and his licensees had spared no expense in trying to win the fight. It was about shoes.

The rubber shoe industry had grown substantially since the rubber boom of the 1830s. At that time, the world market had been barely half a million pairs. By the early 1850s, licensees of Goodyear's patents alone were producing 5 million pairs a year. The way for the inventor to make money wasn't as the producer of rubber goods per se but through the royalties paid to him for the use of the vulcanization process. Early shoe manufacturers that licensed the vulcanization method formed one of the first trade associations in the United States to protect their mutual interests.

In 1843, a year before Goodyear secured his patent, a rival rubber manufacturer named Horace Day had persuaded Goodyear's frustrated business partner, Horace Cutler, to travel from Massachusetts down to New Jersey to meet with him and spill the secrets of Goodyear's process. Day had been a thorn in Goodyear's side ever since. Besides flooding the market with inferior, competing goods, Day went so far as to claim that he was the rightful inventor of vulcanization and that Goodyear's patent was "a fraud and a swindle." Goodyear had taken Day to court in the past, but in 1851, he and his licensees banded together to challenge the misuse of Goodyear's patent once and for all.

Patent infringement cases were nothing new in the mid–nineteenth century, as opportunists looked for ways to use the many new technologies of the Industrial Revolution without paying royalties. In *Goodyear v. Day*, Goodyear and the licensees were not just going after Horace Day but also seeking a perpetual injunction against other interlopers who had used the vulcanization method without paying for it. Goodyear's discovery had made him comfortable but not vastly wealthy, and any future wealth was threatened unless he could secure what was his. Legal fees had eaten up most of the money Eli Whitney had received on his cotton gin patent, after all. But a victory would solidify the rights of both inventors and licensees.

Goodyear persuaded Daniel Webster, the sitting secretary of state and one of America's greatest orators, to represent him. Webster was reluctant—until Goodyear and his licensees offered him $10,000 for just showing up and another $5,000 if he won. At a time when an unskilled laborer could expect to make 75 cents for a day's work, the sum was greater than any previously offered to an American lawyer and enough to pay off the massive debts from Webster's high-roller lifestyle. He agreed.

Day brought his own legal champion to face off against Webster. Nicknamed the "Wizard of the Law," attorney Rufus Choate was skilled at winning cases that seemed to have little chance, including successfully establishing the "sleepwalking defense" in a murder trial. Suddenly Goodyear's case was a sensation: Webster was a living legend, this might be the last time the public could witness him in action, and to top it off he was facing another legal titan. So many people flocked to the courthouse that the venue had to be changed, and even then, some newspaper reporters had to rely on accounts from the seven hundred or so spectators who managed to get a seat.

For two days in March 1852, Daniel Webster worked his

magic on the packed courthouse. Goodyear sat to the left of his lawyer, who stood while giving his lengthy, eloquent remarks that painted a picture of the inventor's hard-luck story.

"It would be painful to speak of his extreme want," Webster said, outlining Goodyear's hardships, which the inventor seemed to wear on his sallow face. "The destitution of his family, half clad, he picking up with his own hands, little billets of wood from the wayside to warm the household—suffering reproach—not harsh reproach, for no one could bestow that upon him—receiving ridicule and indignation from his friends."

In the short story "The Devil and Daniel Webster," a fictionalized Webster successfully argues a case for a farmer who has sold his soul to the Devil. In this case, instead of advocating against the demonic Mr. Scratch, the real Webster was after Goodyear's "patent pirates." He explained his scientific arguments in plain terms ("All know that the general effect of heat upon natural substances is to make them expand; and the general effect of cold upon natural substances is to make them contract") and used humor to illustrate pre–vulcanized rubber's problems ("I took the [rubber] cloak one day and set it out in the cold. It stood very well by itself. I surmounted it with the hat, and many persons passing by supposed they saw standing by the porch, the Farmer of Marshfield"). But Webster saved his highest rhetoric for Goodyear's noble suffering: "He had but two objects, his family and his discovery. . . . Notwithstanding all the difficulties he encountered he went on. If there was reproach, he bore it. If poverty, he suffered under it; but he went on."

It would be Webster's last great speech. A few months later he would be dead as a result of falling from his horse. Having won the court's sympathy, Goodyear won his injunction against any future patent infringements. It looked as though he would be the man to bring the rubber trade back after all.

———

THE FIRST SNEAKER WAS MADE for an unlikely game: croquet. Whereas footraces and other newly popular sporting events attracted gamblers, the game of croquet emerged as a moral and social alternative among the middle classes. Mass production of equipment and the proliferation of parks helped the game gain widespread popularity in the 1850s and '60s. As men and women were allowed to play at the same time, one of the first mixed-gender activities, the croquet field also became a popular and socially acceptable meeting ground for young people. The risqué practice of women lifting their hoop skirts to hit the croquet ball was much discussed; for the first time in generations, a woman's foot and ankle were visible to the opposite sex in public. Women's magazines noted the importance of having the right footwear.

The potential to pick up grass stains made white shoes impractical. A solution came in the 1860s in the form of an American-made "croquet sandal," a type of shoe that took several forms, from a rubber overshoe to a lace-up canvas upper with a rubber sole. By featuring a rubber sole, the shoe also protected the croquet lawn, minimizing the indentations caused by a shoe with a stiff, cornered edge. The sole is also what gives the croquet sandal an argument for being the first sneaker, using the sneaker's most prosaic definition as a mass-produced, rubber-soled athletic shoe. Some croquet shoes stretched that definition farther than others—in 1886, Bloomingdale's department store advertised the "Ladies' Croquet" slip-on pump, which came in a lightweight, all-rubber variation.

Croquet mania would last only a few decades as the sports-hungry public moved on to other games. A relic from croquet's glory days is its mention in *Alice's Adventures in Wonderland*, published in 1865. Had Lewis Carroll's book come out a few decades later, Alice might have instead been invited by the Queen of Hearts to play tennis.

Canvas-and-rubber shoes were here to stay, though. Eventually they developed a nickname: "plimsolls." In the 1870s, a British MP named Samuel Plimsoll devised a method for gauging whether overloaded cargo ships were seaworthy by painting a series of horizontal lines on their hulls. A boat sitting high enough in the water would clearly display the Plimsoll line. The mark resembled the horizontal line separating the shoe's canvas upper from the rubber sole, which also served an aquatic purpose: if water was kept below the line, your foot would stay dry. The nickname began in England but, as with so much else, soon hopped the pond.

GOODYEAR NEVER STOPPED DREAMING UP new uses for his miracle rubber. He published a book that listed every product he could think of: desks made of rubber, books with rubber pages, "sportsmen's boots." Unfortunately, he never lived to see the success of any of them.

The inventor's bad luck and poor business sense continued to make him his own worst enemy, and his victory in *Goodyear v. Day* was not the end of his patent troubles. For one, it was a moot point in Great Britain. Two years before he was awarded the US patent, he had sent samples of his vulcanized rubber to British rubber companies in the hope of attracting investment, and one of those companies had been able to reverse engineer the samples and patent the product in the United Kingdom before Goodyear could. Goodyear also lost out on a French vulcanization patent on a technicality, and even in the United States he still had to spend time and money fighting patent infringement cases in court. When he died at age fifty-nine in 1860, only eight years after his victorious case against Horace Day, he was hundreds of thousands of dollars in debt.

After Goodyear was gone, his widow and children did begin to see significant income from the inventor's royalties, and Charles Goodyear, Jr., decided to follow in the family business. His most famous invention was also a contribution to the shoe industry. In 1875, with the help of two inventors, he patented an improved welting machine to attach the heel of a shoe to a rubber or leather sole without adhesives or meticulous stitching. Though more expensive, shoes constructed with a Goodyear welt were more waterproof and lasted longer. This method, though not the machine itself, is still used today.

Ironically, Goodyear's name managed to achieve the worldwide fame and fortune that had eluded him. Forty years after his death, the entrepreneur Frank Seiberling was looking for a name for his new rubber factory. Rubber was already a fixture in Akron thanks to the Goodrich plant across town, and Sieberling reflected that "Goodrich" was a synonym for what he wanted his company to be: "good" and "rich." He settled on a similar name that already had a built-in history in the industry. When his company started churning out bicycle tires, horseshoe pads, and later rubber-soled canvas sneakers, it did so under the name Goodyear.

2

PEACH BASKETS AND TENNIS SETS

I f Springfield, Massachusetts, had enjoyed a milder winter in 1891, there's a chance that no one would ever have heard the word "basketball." Fortunately, that December brought a harsh New England blizzard to Springfield and the International Young Men's Christian Association Training School, where the thirty-year-old Canadian James Naismith was a PE teacher.

Naismith, an ordained Presbyterian minister, had been tasked by the school's president to come up with a game to distract from the terrible weather outside. Football season had ended, and baseball season was months away; all there was to do during the winter months was gymnasium exercises of tumbling, push-ups, and other rote calisthenics. "This new generation of young men wants the pleasure and thrills of games rather than the body-building benefits of exercise," Naismith's superior told him.

Naismith recalled a game from his childhood that had involved throwing a rock at a target. The school gym had an elevated running track circling ten feet above the floor. He nailed two peach baskets to the edge of the running track on either end of the gym and told his students to throw a soccer ball into the basket. The first game of "basket ball," between two teams of nine students, was more of a brawl. "The boys began tackling, kicking and punching, and punching in the clinches," he said. Despite black eyes, a dislocated shoulder, and one student being knocked unconscious, the participants begged Naismith to play again.

First, there would have to be new rules. Some sports, such as soccer, can point to a definitive time when the rules were first agreed upon and laid down, but that has usually been after many years of "unofficial" practice. Not so with basketball. On January 15, 1892, Naismith published the first rules of the game in the school's newspaper; some of them are no longer used (three consecutive fouls result in a goal for the other team), but many of them still exist today (a player may not run with the ball).

Naismith's school offered a training program for YMCA administrators, and his new game spread quickly through the national YMCA network. Being an academic, Naismith also published his new rules in the *Journal of Physical Education*. A year after the game was invented, an instructor at Smith College, just a few miles north of Springfield, read Naismith's published rules and adapted them for women, in turn publishing her own rules. Within just four years of its invention, basketball was played at most schools that had women students and reached the West Coast as a women's sport before it caught on with men's teams.

As basketball spread, the ten-foot height of the basket remained the same as it had when Naismith had first nailed it to the running track above the gym floor, which would prove a serendipitous sweet spot. Had it been placed lower, basketball might have evolved into a more dunk-friendly game; placed higher, and shooting would have become even more critical, as even the tallest players would be unable to touch the basket. Ten feet, in other words, allowed the game as we know it today to evolve.

The early game was less fast paced than modern basketball (among the first innovations was cutting a hole in the peach basket so the ball didn't have to be fished out by someone on a ladder). Part of its initial popularity had a lot to do with the ease of play—so little equipment was needed that the game could be played almost anywhere. During his later travels, Naismith recorded an old barrel hoop attached to a tree in Wisconsin and a rusty iron hoop nailed to a weather-beaten shed near the Mexican border. US soldiers took the game overseas with them during World War I.

Basketball is just one example of how the spread of organized sports during the early part of the twentieth century not only gave athletic sneakers a reason to exist but also created a mass market to buy them. Things had come a long way since the croquet boom a few decades prior, as gymnasiums and public parks provided locations for new sports and games to flourish in.

Another sports innovator of the day was a five-foot, three-inch, handlebar-mustachioed French education reformer named Pierre de Coubertin. He wasn't especially athletic, and his interests lay more in implementing the English-style school system in France, but in 1883, the twenty-year-old, aristocratic Coubertin traveled to England's Rugby School to see how athletics were being incorporated into education. (The Rugby School had already marked its place in sports history: in 1845, three students had written the rules of the game that would bear the school's name.) Coubertin was so impressed at how sport could create a "moral and social strength" that he set about replicating the Rugby School model in his own country, helping school sports spread throughout France in the 1880s.

Yet Coubertin had even bigger things in mind to promote his sports, culture, and education philosophy. Well-publicized archaeological expeditions to Olympia in 1875 and 1881 stirred the young Coubertin to turn his attention to ancient Greece for the inspiration that would become his legacy. In 1894, he created the International Olympic Committee, originally made up of delegates from thirteen nations and dedicated to reviving the ancient Olympic Games. The committee persuaded the Greek government and wealthy benefactors to reconstruct a stadium in Athens where the first competition could be held.

Coubertin believed that amateur athletes, not professionals, would make the purest modern Olympians, a distinction that would have deep implications for the next century. By modern standards, the equipment used in the early modern Olympics might have well been used in ancient times. Races were held on a dirt track, the high jump consisted of a bar and a pile of sawdust for cushioning, and shoes resembled little more than oxfords made of soft leather with spikes driven through the soles. Yet the first modern Olympic Games in Greece in 1896 were such a success, not just for international competition itself but for Greece's image, that the country volunteered to host them every time. Coubertin insisted that the Olympic spirit should move from country to country; subsequent Games were held in Paris, St. Louis, London, and Stockholm.

Other sports in the nineteenth century were beginning to standardize their rules, which would have their own effect on footwear. Up until the 1800s, soccer was more "survival of the fittest" than "the beautiful game." The game was even banned by seven monarchs in the fourteenth century because it was too dangerous and therefore a threat to civilized society. In Great Britain, schools began fielding their own soccer teams, each with its own set of rules. If schools wanted to play each other, they had to first agree on the rules. In December 1863, a rule dispute over whether kicking an opponent, or "hacking," was allowed essentially created two new sports; those who were against the practice went on to lay down the rules of association football (from which the word "soccer" is derived), while those who were prohacking split off to form rugby.

Shoes designed for soccer began to appear in the 1880s, as manufacturers took an interest in the game's growing popularity. The way the early game was played influenced the shoes' design. Kicking was done primarily with the toe of the shoe, not the sides or the top of the foot, as today, and therefore early soccer boots all featured a reinforced leather toe. Besides protecting the foot, the shoes could disable an opponent via a sharp kick to the shin, as early canvas or leather shin guards didn't do much to blunt the force of the tough toe cap. The British practice of calling soccer cleats "boots" derived from their original appearance; they were really little more than boots with studs in the sole—tough for elegant ball handling but perfect for "hacking," legal or not.

BASKETBALL SHOES DID NOT, of course, exist before 1891, when the game was invented. All-purpose gym shoes, on the other hand, were widely available, due to the simple fact that millions of schoolchildren needed cheap shoes for PE class.

Sneakers got their name from the wearer's ability to walk silently. One of the earliest references comes from an 1873 account of London life called *In Strange Company* in which a jailer is quoted as saying "sneaks . . . are shoes with canvas tops and india-rubber soles." In the first American reference, the 1893–95 *Standard Dictionary of the English Language* cited them as "[Thieves' Jargon.] A soft-soled, noiseless shoe." A tiny 1895 ad for Boston's Guyer's Shoe Store said, "A man is not necessarily a sneak because he wears sneakers. That is the name applied to rubber sole tennis shoes." "Tennis shoe" had itself appeared in a dictionary three years earlier. According to an early-twentieth-century article in *Baseball Magazine,* one particular player "dressed his feet in a pair of rubber-soled canvas shoes—call 'em 'sneakers' now,—and journeyed to Fall River." This suggests that the term "sneakers" had become commonplace by 1909. Though the two most common terms were interchangeable, they were also regionalized: "sneaker" was more common in the Northeast, "tennis shoes" everywhere else. Calling them "gym shoes" was significantly less common, and the British term "plimsolls" was becoming more rare.

By the turn of the century, sports enthusiasts had their choice of gear. In the United States, shoes were made specifically for basketball beginning around 1894 and mostly resembled other above-the-ankle lace-ups of the time. One English catalog from 1897 featured four different soccer boots, two kinds of spiked running shoe, and a cross-country running shoe featuring a corrugated sole. Along with their cleated athletic cousins, rubber-soled sneakers were now a part of the budding athletic shoe landscape and it wasn't long before their makers got creative. That same year in the United States, "strong canvas rubber sole shoes" were marketed as part of a sports outfit package. "The first suction-sole basketball shoes were advertised by the Spaulding Company in 1903," Naismith wrote in his book *Basketball: Its Origins and Development.* "There was also a statement in the advertisement that the team equipped with these suction soled shoes possessed a decided advantage over the team that did not have them." The ad was one of the earliest instances of a sneaker's design gimmick promising a performance boost—and certainly not the last.

Companies such as Spaulding were also making rubber-soled tennis shoes, an update to the "croquet sandal" of three decades earlier. For these they had a women's audience in mind. The American women's magazine *The Delineator* made detailed note of the latest styles of the summer of 1892: "Tennis shoes are preferred low-cut and can be had in white canvas trimmed with white kid, and in russet and tan leather, the soles being always rubber. Low shoes of black and tan ooze-leather [suede], with patent-leather tips, are also well liked for tennis. . . . The hosiery invariably matches the shoes."

TWENTY-ONE-YEAR-OLD Mary Ewing Outerbridge didn't know what she was seeing when she watched two British Army officers hit a small ball back and forth over a net while her family vacationed in Bermuda during the winter of 1873–74, but she became fascinated with it. When the SS *Canima* sailed back from Bermuda to New York in February 1874, it was carrying Outerbridge and her family as well as a set of racquets, balls, and a net.

Back in England, tennis was on its way to supplanting croquet as the outdoor sport of taste. It had been played in some form since the Middle Ages, first in a walled court. Simple racquets had replaced bare hands in the sixteenth century, and in the nineteenth century the sport had found its way into upper-class clubs. Tennis had come to Bermuda thanks to a shipment of several kits from Major Walter Clopton Wingfield, who had recently popularized and commercialized the game as "Sphairistike," though nearly everyone else called it lawn tennis. Major Wingfield's equipment sets and eight-page rule book made it easy for the game to spread in England, and the kits were often sent to soldiers stationed in far-off lands. When Mary Outerbridge arrived in New York with the set the soldiers had given her, it was so novel that the customs agent didn't know how much to charge.

In the summer of 1874, Outerbridge and her brother set up the game in the Staten Island Cricket and Baseball Club, and tennis officially became part of the American sports landscape. Most larger US cities featured an "athletic club"—an exclusive social venue along with private sporting facilities—and in this setting tennis grew quickly as a sport for the moneyed class. By the end of the summer, other clubs in the Northeast had begun featuring the game. The sport's soaring profile in England helped—the All-England Croquet Club added "Lawn Tennis" to its name in 1877, the same year it held its first Wimbledon tournament, and dropped croquet altogether five years later (though it was later added back to the name).

In the private club setting, women played tennis just as men did, in contrast to almost every other sport of the day. Women first competed in the 1900 Paris Olympics but made up only about 2 percent of the athletes, taking part in five sports: croquet, tennis, sailing, equestrianism, and golf. For all of Pierre de Coubertin's ideas about the unifying power of sport, he was still a product of nineteenth-century thinking about gender equality. "As for the participation of women in the Games, I continue to oppose such a move," he wrote in a 1928 International Olympic Committee bulletin. "It is against my wishes that they have been admitted to an increasing number of events."

Women's sports were growing, though haltingly. Mary Outerbridge died in 1886 at the age of thirty-four and would never see the game she had imported to the United States break out of athletic clubs and into public parks, played by both men and women. By World War I, women's collegiate sports programs had become more widespread, and by 1932 the United States had true female sports celebrities in figures such as tennis player Helen Wills, swimmer Gertrude Ederle, and the former Olympic champion Babe Didrikson, who excelled at golf, track and field, baseball, and basketball.

Attitudes toward women's sports fashion remained largely

stuck in the past. Though croquet had introduced the titillating concept of bared ankles, the swishing skirts and clothing that accompanied the tennis of the early 1900s was sometimes too much for prudish Victorian attitudes. An outfit "appropriate for tennis" in the 1880s had included tight-fitting corsets and a flowing bustle, topped with a hat and gloves (one to hold the racquet, the other to hold the train of the gown), and footwear had meant heels. After the turn of the century women playing tennis wore floor-length skirts and high-necked, long-sleeved blouses, no matter the temperature. White was the preferred color, shoes included, in accord with the upper-class roots of the game; those who were able to keep white clothing clean proved that they had the means to do so.

In 1905, an eighteen-year-old American named May Sutton traveled to England to compete in her first Wimbledon tournament. A year earlier, she had won the U.S. Open. Sutton not only rolled up her sleeves but wore a shorter-than-average skirt that flashed her ankles when she made a strenuous shot. Her "revealing" outfit shocked the British spectators and her opponent, who insisted that the match be halted until Sutton agreed to lengthen her skirt. The change in dress didn't hurt Sutton's playing—she ended up becoming the first American player, man or woman, to win Wimbledon.

In northeastern women's colleges at the turn of the twentieth century, exercise outfits were never meant to be seen in public. The only men permitted at sporting events were relatives of the students. This allowed for more practical options: along with the trousered dress and the skirtless basketball outfit, college women could be forgiven for wearing flat-soled rubber gym shoes. Those innovations sometimes foreshadowed later women's fashion. The 1910 Mount Holyoke College basketball team, for example, sported knee-high skirts before they would become accepted by tastemakers a decade later. Their shoes, on the other hand, were typical low-top plimsolls; high-top basketball shoes were a few years away.

Collegiate women's sport was conducted behind closed doors as much because of the rough-and-tumble that came with competitive athletic competition as because of the "revealing" outfits. As the Smith College educator Senda Berenson wrote, "Unless a game as exciting as basketball is carefully guided by such rules as will eliminate roughness, the great desire to win and the excitement of the game will make our women do sadly unwomenly things." Berenson's solution was a set of rules that banned physical contact and confined teams to separate areas of the court. These "Smith Rules" were readily adopted, especially in high schools, and neatly conformed to the view of women in sports at the time. A 1911 article in *Lippincott's Monthly Magazine* titled "The Masculinization of Girls" stated that although the new trend of the "athletic girl" was ultimately good, as women loved to do many of the same physical activities men did, there was a worry that through sports girls could lose their femininity. A year later, in an article titled "Are Athletics Making Girls Masculine?" a physician named Dudley A. Sargent wrote in the *Ladies' Home Journal* that girls' basketball should be limited in high school because of the "well founded" danger of "nervous collapse."

The popularity of the watered-down "Smith Rules" wasn't the only result of this line of thinking. Following World War I, out of a fear of the corrupting "win at any cost" mentality of men's college sports, athletics programs for collegiate and high school girls began to disappear.

BY THE 1920S, VICTORIAN-ERA PRUDISHNESS had finally relaxed, helped along by a distinctly twentieth-century phenomenon:

mass media. Film production began to coalesce in California in the 1910s, which translated into the early development of a celebrity culture as savvy Hollywood marketers realized that the way to sell a movie was to sell its stars. Newsreels and film magazines presented actresses such as Greta Garbo, Mary Pickford, and Clara Bow to be emulated and admired—along with their lower necklines, bare shoulders, and other clothing befitting California's warm climate.

Along with the new Hollywood class, the upper class set fashion trends, themselves emulating influences from Europe. Images of the elite at work and play were available to the masses via radio, newspapers, and newsreels, which helped make fashion something for everyone. The power of celebrity grew quickly: police were called out to manage the 100,000 people lining New York City streets in 1926 to pay their respects to Rudolph Valentino, the movie star heartthrob, who had died at age thirty-one.

The post–Industrial Revolution economy gave the working classes the means to enjoy their new free time, even if just via a trip to the movies or a ball game. People like James Naismith and Mary Outerbridge, meanwhile, introduced new sports to the broader public, while figures like Pierre de Coubertin lifted athletic competition from a pastime for gambling to lofty new heights. The percolating of leisure down the social ladder, combined with the development of organized sport and the wide availability of consumer goods, set the stage for the early-twentieth-century sneaker to become what we recognize today: a product with a purpose and a celebrity to sell it.

3

JOHNNY BASKETBALLSEED

I n 1937, a Notre Dame junior named Ray Meyer was picked out of the stands. A traveling salesman named Chuck Taylor was conducting a basketball clinic, and he wanted someone from the audience to try to stop his passes. Taylor chose well. The year before, Meyer had been part of a national championship team that the *Chicago Tribune* had called the most "feared in basketball." Taylor issued a simple challenge, one that regularly featured in his clinics: try to stop the ball. He was in his mid-thirties and slightly pudgy, with a high, receding hairline; Meyer was fighting fit and a decade younger. How hard could it be?

"I couldn't stop his passes," Meyer recalled years later. "He was a great ball handler."

Taylor's "invisible pass" technique, which centered around passing without looking at the recipient to confuse his opponents, was just a part of his repertoire. Once a basketball journeyman in his own right, Taylor had a pedigree, as he called it, that included stints on pro teams such as the "world champion" Original Celtics and "Olympic champion" Buffalo Germans. Local newspapers featured interviews with him in advance of his free clinics, which packed gymnasiums with people eager to see a professional athlete demonstrate the game's fundamentals. But Taylor hadn't come to Notre Dame just to share his skills. When he called for a volunteer to try to stop him from dribbling past, he had his spiel ready.

"That's what the problem is," he would say as he walked back to the embarrassed volunteer, looking down at his shoes. "He doesn't have Converse All Stars on."

Since the turn of the twentieth century, with sports becoming more and more popular and manufacturing techniques improving, two iconic sneaker brands had gotten their start: Converse and Keds. They had a lot in common, but they had different strategies to reach the nascent sneaker consumer. Converse, in the person of Chuck Taylor, relied on the new concept of the celebrity endorsement. Keds chose a more conventional route, appealing to the consumer's desire for a well-made product. Those two approaches set the stage for the modern concepts of brand identity and brand loyalty.

THE VULCANIZED RUBBER REVOLUTION WAS in full swing. Inflatable rubber tires had transformed the transportation industry by giving rise to the bicycle craze. Rubber hoses, gaskets, and belts had made the mass production of automobiles possible. Companies were springing up everywhere, often with rubber shoes as a staple product, cheap to make and dependably in demand. In 1892, nine rubber companies in Naugatuck, Connecticut, once home to the manufacturing business of Charles Goodyear's father, consolidated to form the United States Rubber Company. The new conglomerate owned half of the rubber shoe market, selling shoes under thirty different brand names.

In 1916, U.S. Rubber consolidated the companies under a single brand name: "Peds," after the Latin word for feet. The name, though, was already trademarked, so the company changed the *P* to a *K*. Keds shoes had an immediate advantage over the competition. In place of the confusion of differing but co-owned brands, the subsidiaries now all made Keds and knew they no longer had to compete with one another. Marketing the product became much cheaper, with each company working for the same name recognition. That same year Keds released its first shoe, the Champion, a classic plimsoll with a white canvas upper and rubber sole. Fashion-wise the sneaker was particularly suited for the tennis courts, but advertisements for the Champion highlighted the shoe's versatility. That versatility extended not just to sports, but to consumers themselves: the sneaker was popular with both men and women.

The Converse Rubber Shoe Company was founded in 1908 by Marquis Mills Converse, a department store manager. The Malden, Massachusetts–based company began with fifteen employees and originally produced galoshes. In 1915, Converse added canvas shoes, and two years later, the All Star made its debut. The all-purpose gym shoe came in a light brown canvas with leather for reinforcement where the laces were inserted. The rubber toe cap found in later versions is in the 1917 original but was a dullish brown instead of white. The ankle patch, a feature that would remain with the shoe for the next hundred years, was not so much a design choice as a practical one: it lessened the pain of knocking your ankles together.

The All Star, and similar sneakers, was the solution to a problem for Converse. The demand for galoshes was seasonal; by Christmastime, workers were sent home for the winter until demand crept back up again in the spring. Canvas-topped sports shoes helped smooth seasonal employment since the sneakers could be marketed during basketball's winter season. Marquis Converse was reluctant to sell his shoes to wholesalers, as companies like U.S. Rubber did, and instead employed a sales team that marketed directly to stores, bypassing middlemen who did not deal with the public. In 1922, Chuck Taylor became one such salesman.

BY THE ROARING TWENTIES, the world of national celebrities had expanded to include sports stars. Professional baseball was in its golden age, with names such as Babe Ruth, Lou Gehrig, and Ty Cobb gracing newspapers and radios. Ruth owed his fame as much to his press agent as to his massive home runs. The boxer Jack Dempsey held the heavyweight title through most of the 1920s, and his popularity grew even greater after he had lost his championship title in 1926. Stars such as running back Red Grange, tennis star "Big Bill" Tilden, and golfer Bobby Jones filled out the landscape. New cathedrals were built to house those athletic saints: Yankee Stadium opened in the Bronx in 1923, and a third iteration of Madison Square Garden hosted its first of many boxing matches in 1925.

The celebrity surrounding such athletes helped fuel an appeal much broader than sports. Olympic athletes were bound by strict amateur rules that prohibited them from making endorsements or receiving a paycheck, but not so with major American sports. Baseball players were free to make money off of their fame itself, and some of them did. Trademarked merchandising surrounded Babe Ruth, especially: fans of the slugger could buy his own line of dress shoes, cars, and fishing poles.

Basketball, meanwhile, was still a young sport. Its popularity had spread to the point that the game was a fixture of high schools and colleges, but professional basketball was little more than a collection of no-names playing in regional leagues across the country. Even the rules were negotiable and still evolving from the original set of thirteen James Naismith had published in 1892. Professional ball allowed the double dribble and an unlimited number of fouls, while the college game did not; some exhibition games would even mix the rules, playing the first half with collegiate regulations and the second half with pro rules. If you were an organizer with at least five good players, you often played exhibition matches and made money on the gate receipts or barnstormed your team around the area, taking on any comers.

Chuck Taylor's professional debut was for one such team, and amounted to little more than a line in the local newspaper the next day. The Columbus Commercials were sponsored by a businessmen's group and would be considered a semipro team by today's standards. The Commercials played other regional teams or the occasional traveling squad that happened through southern Indiana. They played their games in City Hall, the only venue available, and lasted only one more season after the seventeen-year-old Taylor joined the roster.

His next team was better known. The nineteen-year-old Taylor joined the roster of the Akron Firestone Non-Skids and earned his spot on the starting lineup thanks to a game-winning shot in the final seconds of a match against their cross-town archrival, the Akron Wingfoots. Backed by corporations (partly as a marketing tool), those industrial teams had staying power: in 1937 the Non-Skids and the Wingfoots were some of the founding teams of the National Basketball League, which after World War II merged with the Basketball Association of America to form the National Basketball Association. The 1921 Non-Skid team Taylor played on was good enough to earn a berth in the American Industrial Athletic Association's national championship tournament that year. Though Taylor's quick passing and reliable scoring helped the Non-Skids to a victory against General Electric, the success was short-lived. They lost the tournament, and Taylor left the team to move to Detroit.

Though the Midwest was the cradle of basketball, the game flourished in other places, too. One particularly successful team of the 1920s and '30s was the New York Renaissance, an all-black pro team that played on a converted dance floor at Harlem's Renaissance Casino and Ballroom. The "Rens" drew packed crowds, which not only helped solidify the sport's popularity in Harlem but also made the case for the profitability of professional basketball—even if that case included a distinct racial element. Organizers found that games pitting a top black team such as the Rens against a top white team such as the Original Celtics (which Taylor claimed to have once played for) sold significantly more tickets than a white-versus-white or a black-versus-black game, a harbinger of controversies in the sport's future.

Basketball shoes didn't exactly sell themselves, something that Chuck Taylor discovered when he started working for Converse.

"Who needs the shoes?" his mother asked him at the beginning of his sales career.

"Basketball players," he replied.

"Who buys them for the players?"

"The coach and high school officials."

"I think you've been going to the wrong people," his mother replied. "Why don't you go to the coaches and show them your shoes?"

Taylor and other salesmen in the 1920s were just discovering this bit of insight about their customers. Who was the shoe for, the wearer or the buyer? If you wanted to buy a basketball shoe in the early part of the twentieth century, you couldn't just wander down to the nearest Foot Locker, which wouldn't exist for another sixty years. Ordering a pair via mail was also tricky. If you wanted a canvas-and-rubber plimsoll-style shoe for shooting hoops, your coach was often the best person to get you a pair.

Taylor realized that his time as a professional basketball player might come in handy. He had newspaper clippings and a photo of himself from his days playing for the Akron Firestone Non-Skids; why not parlay that experience for his salesmanship? Taylor embarked on a one-man barnstorming tour of his own, one that would spread the game not through pro matchups but through seminars with impressionable teenagers. The high school basketball coaches themselves were not specialists; often a football or baseball coach was put in charge of a team and had few opinions on strategy, much less which shoes his team should wear. Enter Taylor, who could offer much-needed instruction, a chance to meet a real professional athlete, and a gentle nudge to the nearest sporting goods store that stocked the Converse All Star.

Besides playing Johnny Basketballseed at every school and company he visited, Taylor's great contribution to the game, and the brand, was the Converse Basketball Yearbook. Beginning in 1922, the yearbook featured articles on strategy from leading coaches and, of course, team photos. The only catch: to have your team's photograph published alongside basketball greats, most of you had to wear Converse shoes. It was a brilliant piece of marketing, but the yearbook also became a kind of bible of the game. The team photos appeared along with rosters and season reports, and the articles on playing techniques and tips made it useful to players beyond as a keepsake. And most important of all, there were Taylor's All-Americans.

Taylor's annual picks for the top All-American players were the centerpiece of the yearbook. His extensive interaction with coaches, players, and fans gave him an unrivaled exposure to the game and helped him develop an eye for talent. At first, he included only athletes he had personally seen play, though he always consulted with the top coaches before his final selections were published. What made his picks notable was they included athletes outside the New York sportswriter bubble. If you were a player from, say, a high school in Nebraska, the yearbook might be your one shot at nationwide recognition, appearing in the tens of thousands of copies mailed out each fall.

By 1934, Converse knew how much Taylor's salesmanship and showmanship were adding to the brand. Even though he had been there for only a decade, the company decided to do something unique: it added Taylor's signature to the ankle patch, essentially rebranding the shoe as the Chuck Taylor All Star. Taylor offered Converse suggestions on improving the shoe from his interactions with players. The cult of Chuck only grew: the All Star would later be known by nicknames including "Chucks," "Chuck Ts," and "Chucker Boots" (the last likely a bastardization of "chukka boot").

Other companies saw the benefit of having a name connected to their shoe. In 1934, B. F. Goodrich, looking to branch out from selling automobile tires and into the sneaker market, started selling the Jack Purcell shoe. B. F. Goodrich had signed Purcell, a Canadian badminton player who had been declared the world champion the year prior. Normally there would've been tough restrictions against "amateur" athletes endorsing products, but Purcell had lost his amateur status and with it the chance to compete in as many tournaments as possible, after being paid for writing a newspaper badminton column. For B. F. Goodrich, the timing couldn't have been better: it was getting an athlete who not only was the best at his sport but could put his name on the shoe. The shoe was in the plimsoll style with a rubber toe cap and a thin color line (usually blue) along the front, resembling a smile. Purcell helped design the instep of the "smileys" to give the shoe more support, which he said was needed in badminton. Long after it became obsolete as an athletic shoe, the Purcell would achieve cultural cachet when the likes of James Dean and Steve McQueen were seen in them.

While the Purcell shoe sported a bona fide professional athlete's name, Taylor continued to do his thing traveling from city to city. His showmanship during clinics, especially his passing, sometimes worked against him; University of Kansas basketball coach Forrest "Phog" Allen switched his team's shoes from Converse to Keds for the 1951–52 season because he felt upstaged in front of his players by one of Taylor's demonstrations. Kansas went on to become the 1952 NCAA champion. In general, though, Taylor knew how to stay in his clients' good graces. For years he made payments, sometimes as much as $50,000, to a group founded by Allen, the National Association of Basketball Coaches, which would be responsible for keeping dribbling in the game, founding the National Basketball Hall of Fame, and establishing the NCAA tournament format. Taylor's reputation as a coach's coach ensured decades' worth of Converse brand loyalty.

Teams that switched from Converse did so at their own risk. In the 1930s, years before John Wooden made his name as UCLA's longtime coach, he headed a high school team in South Bend, Indiana. As a high school, college, and then professional player, he had worn All Stars and liked them enough to have his South Bend team wear them, too. One year, the team switched to a similar-looking Ball-Band shoe at the request of a school board member. "In one of the games we were playing one of the players came down on the floor and made a quick stop and turn and the whole sole of one shoe practically came off," Wooden recalled years later. "It was just hanging from the back. Just his sock foot was on the floor. I went back to the Converse."

U.S. RUBBER AND ITS KEDS took a seemingly more conventional approach to creating a brand. In advertisements Keds relied on highlighting the shoe's quality, filling full-page magazine ads with positive copy. A 1924 issue of *Boys' Life*, the magazine of the Boy Scouts of America, featured a parable about boys in a New England village who wear a Keds sneaker on one foot and a non-Keds brand on the other. After playing baseball, climbing trees, and doing whatever else boys in a New England village do, they report to the local Keds factory, where both shoes are tested for wear and durability. Told through the lens of product testing, the ad hit a classic marketing theme: getting the best for your money. An ad in *Popular Mechanics* stated, "The more you pay, the more you get—but full value whatever you spend." When the ad ran in April 1929, a pair of Keds ranged from $1 to $4, or about $60 in 2017 dollars. A few years earlier, a men's Converse All Star retailed for $2.85.

What was innovative about Keds' branding was how equal opportunity it was, particularly toward gender. In a 1928 issue of *Everygirl's Magazine*, the magazine of the Camp Fire Girls, Keds were praised for much the same qualities as in *Boys' Life*: the traction they provided when climbing, the speed they provided on the sports field, and the silence the rubber sole afforded bird-watchers when trying to approach a feathered specimen. The implicit message seemed to be that such activities were for everyone, and so, too, were Keds. The message worked, especially at a time when few other sneakers were being marketed to women.

Keds, like Converse, could have pursued the endorsement track if it had wanted to: in the 1920s, the shoes were popular among tennis players, especially women. One might-have-been was Helen Wills, an international tennis star who would go on to win nineteen Grand Slam singles championships, a feat only recently surpassed by Serena Williams. In 1924, Wills won her first Wimbledon and gold medals in the Paris Olympics in both singles and doubles play. That year the Games saw the Americans win all five Olympic tennis medals, every one of the players wearing Keds—a point that some enterprising shoe stores made sure to highlight, even if the brand itself didn't.

Another feature of Keds' advertising at the time, whether it was for the tennis-playing adult or the boulder-scrambling boy or girl, was the insistence that only a Keds shoe had "Keds" written on the side. This focus on authenticity, on not being confused with imitations, was something Keds had in common with Converse, and it would be critical for both companies in the coming years. Companies that were able to weather the double whammy of the Great Depression and World War II would come out on the other side as household names, and Keds and Converse would be among the survivors. But they would need all the power of their branding to defend against overseas competitors, who were about to enter the fight for sneaker supremacy.

4

WAR AND BROTHERS

On August 5, 1936, twenty-two-year-old Jesse Owens crouched into starting position on the back curve of Berlin's Olympic Stadium. The runner from Ohio and five other sprinters waited for the race official to raise his arm and fire the starting pistol that would send them off in the 200-meter dash final.

The track was a far cry from the polyurethane all-weather surfaces ubiquitous today. Prior to the sprint races at the Berlin Games, coaches and trainers would use spades to carve notches in the dirt track so runners could get a better grip when starting. Metal starting blocks were not used then, so athletes had to literally "dig in" to get a proper push-off.

Sprint shoes, too, were different. On Owens's feet, as the story goes, was a pair of shoes handed to him at the Olympic training grounds by a short, unassuming German, who had made them himself. The German wanted as many people as he could find to wear the shoes he had assembled in his native Herzogenaurach, a small town in the southern province of Bavaria. When Adolf

Dassler, "Adi" to his friends, drove up the Autobahn to Berlin with his bag of shoes, he did so in the hope that at least one Olympic champion would be wearing a pair from the Gebrüder Dassler Schuhfabrik.

Dassler was friends with the German track and field coach, so it was easy to get the Nazi track team outfitted with his creations. To increase his chances of shoeing a winner, though, he approached foreign athletes as well. At the top of his list was a talented young American runner whose name was already making news prior to the Olympics, for more than one reason.

The year before, Owens had set three world records and tied for a fourth, all within less than an hour. Despite that astonishing success, Owens, with the other Ohio State University black students, had to live off campus at school and had to eat at separate restaurants and stay at separate hotels from his white teammates. Racist comments and antiblack propaganda in the German press marked Owens's time at the "Nazi Olympics," and there was much talk about both his talent and his skin color. Curious crowds gathered to catch a glimpse of him when his boat arrived in the country.

After being let in to the Olympic Village by the German coach, Dassler, speaking little English, gestured for Owens to try on his shoes. The black track spikes Owens chose were tanned calf leather and featured hand-wrought metal spikes that measured 17 millimeters at the toe, gradually decreasing to 15 millimeters at the ball of the foot. The spikes splayed outward to claw more of the track. Along the side of each shoe ran two dark leather stripes.

Owens cruised to a world record 20.7-second victory in the 200 meters, several lengths ahead of the second-place finisher, teammate Mack Robinson (an older brother of Jackie Robinson). Four days later, as the lead-off in the 4×100-meter relay, Owens again won gold and again set a world record.

The Nazi elite managed everything about the presentation of the 1936 Games. The torch relay, synonymous with the run-up to the Olympics today, was dreamed up for those Games by a German sports official. Every detail was choreographed to portray Adolf Hitler's Germany in a positive light, which also meant subordinating anything that didn't fit in with Hitler's vision of the *Übermensch*. German Jews had been banned from sports facilities and playgrounds in the years leading up to the Olympics, and Jewish athletes, including those who had competed for Germany in the past, were barred from competing or even practicing. To appease the international community, some Jewish athletes, such as the high jumper Gretel Bergmann, had been permitted to train with their Nazi teammates but were unceremoniously cut from the team at the last moment. Similar measures to "dress up" the regime for the foreign visitors included the temporary removal of anti-Semitic signs in public and the toning down of the worst of the racial references in the Nazi press. In the same out-of-sight, out-of-politics spirit, hundreds of Gypsies were removed from Berlin to a camp just outside the city.

Hitler's favorite director, Leni Riefenstahl, who had recently completed the Nazi propaganda documentary *Triumph of the Will*, was on hand to film *Olympia*, the first feature-length documentary about the Games. Riefenstahl trained her camera on Owens in his 4×100 performance—and undermined everything the Nazis wanted to convey. She had "painted Adolf Hitler as a Wagnerian deity come to earth ... [and] gave the same heroic treatment to Jesse Owens," the film critic Richard Corliss wrote decades later. It would prove to be the most lasting image from the 1936 Games: a black sprinter defying the Nazi Aryan ideal by winning a record four gold medals at Hitler's Olympics.

Dassler and his brother Rudolf ("Rudi" to his friends), who co-ran the Gebrüder Dassler Schuhfabrik, couldn't have been more pleased at the American sprinter's performance. In Europe, more than in the United States, the early days of the athletic shoe market were not dominated by expensive, athlete-driven ad campaigns as they are today; word of mouth, whether from a coach, trainer, or fellow sports club member, drove sales. In the burgeoning German athletic industry of 1936, there could be no bigger mark of success than getting a four-time gold medalist to wear your shoes. Of course, it also helped that the German team collected sixteen track and field medals, second only to the Americans.

The Berlin Olympics were the high point of Owens's career. His amateur athletic status was revoked not long after the Games. But for the Dassler brothers, the 1936 Olympics were only the first instance of how they would reshape sports and shoes.

IN 1920, ADI DASSLER SCROUNGED the fields and forests surrounding Herzogenaurach looking for cast-off scraps of leather, bread pouches, torn parachutes, and anything else left over from the First World War. As a child he had collected sticks and stones from the same places to invent games for himself. Now he took the soldiers' castoffs back to the makeshift workshop in his mother's washroom to assemble the pieces into shoes.

Before the war, Adi and his two older brothers, Fritz and Rudolf, had been known as the town's "laundry boys," running deliveries from their mother's washing business around tiny "Herzo." Cloth manufacturing had driven the town's fortunes since the Middle Ages, but the Industrial Revolution had put the town's dyers and weavers out of work, and their father's modest slipper-making business was failing as well. When the brothers returned home after serving in the war, both their father's and mother's businesses had shuttered. Adi decided to pick up where his father had left off.

In 1923, Adi enlisted the help of Rudolf, two years his elder, to help run the shoe business. Alongside making practical, everyday shoes and slippers, the outdoorsy Adi amused himself by thinking up sports shoe designs. He enlisted the help of his best friend, the son of the town's blacksmith, who had accompanied Adi on many long forest runs, to fashion thin metal spikes for sprint shoes. Each brother's role in the Gebrüder Dassler Schuhfabrik played to his strengths: Adi, the soft-spoken tinkerer, preferred the quiet solitude of the workshop, while the extroverted, social Rudolf made a natural salesman. (Fritz, the eldest brother, was occupied with his own lederhosen business.)

The following year Adi and Rudolf turned their attention to sports shoes almost entirely. The shaky postwar economy of the Weimar Republic wasn't the best time to start such a specialized venture, but the Dasslers saw an opportunity in the organized sports clubs that were beginning to pop up around Germany. Outdoor activities such as soccer and running dominated—gymnasium-based sports, and the rubber-soled sneakers that went with them, were less popular—and they tailored their business accordingly. Aided by Adi's designs and Rudolf's business acumen, the Gebrüder Dassler Schuhfabrik was soon struggling to keep up with the skyrocketing demand for its soccer boots and track spikes. The brothers cut a dashing figure in their tailored suits and new cars. The reputation of the Dassler shoes caught the attention of a German national track and field coach, who made a special trip down to Herzo to check out the shoes and then befriended Adi.

The business was going strong for the Dasslers, and an even bigger boost awaited them in the 1930s, but it came with a Faustian bargain. As Hitler's National Socialist German Workers' Party swept into power, changes were swift: political opponents were jailed or murdered, labor unions were abolished, the persecution of German Jews began. Physical education was a seemingly benign party preoccupation, but with dark undertones. The Party's twenty-five-point program highlighted the "encouragement of physical fitness, by means of the legal establishment of a gymnastic and sport obligation, by the utmost support of all organizations concerned with the physical instruction of the young." According to Adolf Hitler, writing in *Mein Kampf*, the "impeccably trained bodies" of the German populace could be made into an army in as little as two years. The 1936 Berlin Olympics provided the perfect opportunity for the Nazis to demonstrate to the world their ideal *Übermensch*.

Nevertheless, businesses that curried favor with the new totalitarian rulers, especially those making athletic gear, stood to gain considerably. The Dasslers did not fully buy into Hitler's monstrous ideology, but they had no qualms about making a deutsche mark or two off it, as long as they kept their heads down. Rudolf was said to have received the movement more warmly, often expressing his support for the Party; to Adi politics was politics, but sport was something more. On May 1, 1933, only a few months after Hitler was appointed chancellor of Germany, Adi and Rudolf Dassler registered for membership in the Nazi Party.

BUSINESS WAS GOOD FOR THE DASSLERS following the Olympics. Adi's Jesse Owens strategy had paid off—as had his friendship with the Nazi track and field coach, which had put the German team into Dassler Brother shoes as well. No one in the Party seemed to notice that one of their own had possibly helped a black American sprinter, and meanwhile Adi continued to view his association with the Nazis as a business opportunity, joining the Hitler Youth as a coach and a supplier to boost his contacts for the group's athletic activities. Adi did, however, more than once ignore a Nazi order to fire someone. Such incidents caused friction between the brothers over who, exactly, was in charge.

Despite the growing success of the Gebrüder Dassler Schuh-fabrik, long-simmering tensions were starting to create a rift be-tween the brothers. The three-floor mansion they had built for themselves near the factory in the late 1920s was proving to be a mistake. In those close quarters—Adi's family on the ground floor, Rudolf's above him, and their parents on the top floor—Rudolf's temperament often caused him to butt heads with those around him, especially with Adi's outspoken wife, who herself feuded with Rudolf's spouse. Adi and Rudi's bickering and one-upmanship became the norm, each brother unyielding in how he thought the company should be run.

The war would deepen the fissure between the families. Adi, after a brief stint as a soldier, received an exemption from mili-tary service on grounds of being indispensable to his shoe factory, which was doing everything it could to stay open. (In a bid for government sympathy, he named new soccer shoes "Blitz" and "Kampf.") Rudolf, taking Adi's return as a hint that he was not the most important brother, began to believe that his brother would try to oust him from the business once he got the chance. One night during an Allied air raid, Adi and his wife climbed down into the cellar the family used as a bomb shelter.

"Here are the *Schweinehunde* again," Adi said.

Rudolf, already in the cellar with his family, angrily jumped up, thinking for sure that the "pig-dog" insult was aimed not at the British bombers pummeling the area but at himself.

"It was impossible to persuade Rudolf that the comment was not [directed at] him," Rudolf's sister-in-law, who was also in the bunker, recalled years later.

The bunker incident is commonly cited as the point of falling out between the two sides of the family, but more strife awaited the Dasslers. In early 1943, more of Germany was being mobilized for the war effort. Rudolf was assigned to a customs office in Poland and blamed his army post on Adi's machinations to get rid of him. As the war went on, he tried to exact revenge on his brother by having some of his high-ranking friends in the regional authority offices disrupt production or switch the factory's wartime production assignments so that he might be called back to run operations.

"I will not hesitate to seek the closure of the factory," Rudolf angrily wrote to his brother, "so that you will be forced to take up an occupation that will allow you to play the leader and, as a first-class sportsman, to carry a gun."

The factory did, in fact, close but was soon pressed into the failing German war effort to make spare tank parts and bazookas, keeping Adi employed. Rudolf didn't fare as well. As the Red Army closed in, Rudolf's unit was folded into the SS, bringing him to a breaking point. He was soon transferred into the SD, the Nazis' notorious intelligence branch, and when he refused to report for duty, the Gestapo arrested him and detained him for two weeks.

When Allied troops liberated Herzogenaurach, it was Adi's wife, Käthe, who persuaded them not to destroy the factory, saying they only wanted to make sport shoes. Both brothers, though, had to answer for their involvement with the Nazis. During Adi's denazification hearing, several witnesses, including Herzogenaurach's former mayor, stepped forward to insist that Adi was concerned only about sports, not politics. In 1946, Adi was labeled a *Mitläufer*, or follower, a less serious denazification classification reserved for Germans who had been Party members but did not contribute to the regime. Rudolf was arrested again, this time by the Allies. They kept him in custody for nearly a full year after the war ended, convinced that he was involved with the Gestapo. In typical Rudolf fashion, he was sure his brother had ratted him out to the Allies.

Putting the pieces of their shoe company back together was impossible. The brothers meticulously divided the assets and patents. In 1948, with the rest of the Dassler family already having chosen sides, there was one more thing to do before their split became final. The brothers assembled all of the Gebrüder Dassler Schuhfabrik's workers and gave them a choice: follow Adi, or follow Rudolf. Most of the shoe builders and designers, two-thirds of the company, chose to go with Adi, while Rudolf attracted most of the sales staff.

Rudolf originally wanted to call his new company "Ruda" but was persuaded to use a more agile-sounding alternative: "Puma." Adi Dassler combined his first and last names to form "Adidas." The brands were quick to visually set themselves apart. Gebrüder Dassler shoes like the ones Jesse Owens wore had had two stripes running down each side, not so much for branding purposes as to add support to the shoe leather, which was so soft it often held its shape about as well as a sock. When registering the name Adidas, Adi also trademarked three parallel white stripes (four, he felt, would be too busy). Puma, at first, used a thick white stripe up the side of the foot before later settling on a curved horizontal design the company called the "Formstripe." As Converse had when it had formalized the circular ankle patch with a star on its All Star sneaker, Adidas and Puma understood the importance of a distinctive look. They made sure it was always clear which Dassler you were wearing.

SINCE THE SPLIT, the Aurach River—a tributary of the Regnitz, which flows into the Main, which flows into the Rhine, which flows into the North Sea—has formed a physical barrier dividing

Adi and Rudolf, Adidas and Puma, and the northern Bavarian town of Herzogenaurach, near Nuremburg. In Herzo, your shoe affiliation determined where you went to school, in which bar you drank, in which bakery you bought bread, even who cut your gravestone. Shortly after each brother packed up to his respective side of the river, Herzo became known as the "town of bent necks" because people were always looking down at your shoes, trying to size up which half of the town's main industry you or your family worked for. It's unclear whether either Dassler brother had seen the 1932 movie *The Western Code*, but they lived the movie's famous line: "This town ain't big enough for the both of us."

Puma had the strength of the sales force Rudolf had brought with him, but Adidas was better at forming strong relationships with athletes and coaches and in a better position to give them the shoes they wanted, most of the designers having followed Adi. Both companies were producing high-quality running and soccer shoes, though, and neither Adidas nor Puma had any intention of ceasing efforts to outdo the other.

Up until the 1950s, the companies were more or less on an equal footing, but in 1954, Rudolf thought he was on the cusp of finally besting his brother. The Swiss-hosted soccer World Cup was just around the corner, and the West German team sported a light, low-cut leather Puma soccer cleat. It was the first tournament since the war that West Germany was allowed to compete in, and the cleat was truly innovative—less of a boot, more of a shoe—at a time when the English national football team was still wearing the clunky workboot-esque soccer shoe. It was the perfect opportunity for Puma to pull ahead of its crosstown rival— until, that is, the elder Dassler's boastfulness got the better of him.

Rudolf, the German national team coach, Josef "Sepp" Herberger, and another coach were talking shop about the new soccer boot. The subject turned to Herberger's career. It was mentioned that Herberger had gotten his job when his predecessor had been fired by Adolf Hitler, who hated soccer, after he had witnessed an embarrassing 0–2 loss to Norway in the 1936 Olympics.

Rudolf was in the mood to flex his own muscles. "You are only a small king," he told the German national coach, comparing him to the previous coach. "If you do not suit us, we will choose another national trainer."

Herberger's West German team would indeed wear Dassler shoes in the World Cup—they would just be made by the younger brother. Following Rudolf's bullying comment, Herberger dumped Puma in favor of Adidas. Herberger took a liking to Adi, and the shoemaker began to appear constantly at Herberger's side, whether on the field or the team bus, a detail that annoyed his older brother.

"First comes Herberger, then the Lord God!" Rudolf said with a grimace, mocking the way Adi seemed to relish his new position as the coach's right hand.

The West German team made it all the way to the 1954 World Cup final, where they faced off with a heavily favored Hungarian team. Dubbed "The Magnificent Magyars" and "The Golden Team" by the press, going into the tournament the Hungarians held the highest ever Elo rating, the metric used to compare teams in international play, and would in fact hold the record for sixty more years. They played an early version of what would later be called "total football," in which players could swap positions on the fly, overwhelming the other team. West Germany had already faced the Hungarians in its second match and was soundly routed 8–3.

The day of the final was cursed with heavy rain, a nuisance for everyone. Yet the Germans, or simply *die Mannschaft* (the Team), had something that might help: brand-new screw-in studs on their Adidas soccer shoes, which could be swapped out to match the conditions. The field turned soggy by the second half, and the West Germans employed their secret weapon.

"Adi, screw them on!" Herberger told the Adidas boss. Adi went to work taking out the normal studs and replacing them with longer ones that provided a much better grip on the muddy field.

Heading into the second half, the Germans managed to remain level with the Hungarians at two goals apiece. Six minutes from the end of the match, twenty-four-year-old striker Helmut Rahn recovered an errant header at the top of the penalty area, dribbled just inside, and shot the World Cup–winning goal. The match earned the nickname "The Miracle in Bern," and Herberger, recognizing the shoes' contribution, pulled Adi into the victory snapshot.

Orders for Adidas shoes like the ones Rahn had worn flooded in, launching Adi's company past Puma and into global prominence. Of course, each company insisted that it had been the one to invent the screwable cleats. And the shoe coup at the 1954 World Cup was hardly the last shot in the war between brands and brothers.

Another memorable battle played out in the 1960 Rome Olympics. As in every Olympics, Adidas, Puma, and others raced to make sure that their shoes were on the feet of as many runners as possible. As with Jesse Owens in the 1936 Olympics, the company that provided the shoes to the "World's Fastest Man" would earn a special kind of clout, and in 1960 the favorite was a German sprinter named Armin Hary.

Hary was a talented runner, but he also bent the rules as far as they would go. His go-to move was to rise into the "set" position last of all the racers, thereby anticipating the firing of the starter's pistol. Sometimes that would earn him a false start, but most times he would gain a crucial fraction of a second. In 1958, he became the first person to run the 100 meters in 10.0 seconds, though the effort was not recognized as a world record because the track pitched downward too much. Two years later, he briefly held the "World's Fastest Man" title outright, until another runner equaled it a few weeks later. The sprinter ran in Adidas shoes but had asked the company to pay for him to continue to wear them, a request Adidas reportedly refused.

Heading into the Olympics, Hary was the favorite. Throughout the qualifying heats of the 100-meter dash he breezed to the finish line wearing a pair of Adidas spikes. Adi Dassler's company seemed poised to have another winner on its hands; Hary had even set an Olympic record in the quarterfinals. Yet when the sprinter lined up for the 100-meter final, it became clear that he was wearing Puma spikes. After being rebuffed by Adidas for his payment request, Hary had crossed the river to its rival—for a price, as a Puma sales rep later admitted. It wouldn't be the last surprise of the day. When he mounted the winners' podium to collect his gold medal, the pair of Adidas was back on his feet, an attempt to play both Dassler brothers against the middle.

As the 1960s proceeded, Adidas continued edging out its rival at the top of the international sports shoe game. The three stripes were on World Cup winners and Olympic gold medalists. Even as far away as Japan, which had a growing running culture, the Adidas brand was emulated, copied, and sought after. But Puma was following; the fierce competition had pushed both companies out of provincial Bavaria and onto the global stage.

Adi and Rudolf's focus on beating each other would bring more success but also create a few blind spots. For all their dominance in high-profile sports such as sprinting and soccer, both Adidas and

Puma remained relatively weak in sports not as popular in Germany, such as basketball and tennis. Another layperson sneaker sport was about to join this mix: unbeknownst to Adi, a track coach a thousand miles away, in small-town Oregon, had taken note of Adidas' success and had the German titan in his sights.

5

BUILDERMAN

I n the spring of 1964, twenty-year-old Kenny Moore stood on the infield of the University of Oregon track with a pair of hands around his throat. The hands belonged to Bill Bowerman, his track coach. Moore had just finished running "an easy twelve miles" and was discussing his progress after coming off a bout of the flu. Bowerman, bear of a man that he was, had been taking Moore's pulse moments before, when he slipped his callused hands around the middle-distance runner's neck with an ultimatum.

"Mr. Moore, I'm going to ask you to take part in an experiment." The coach began lifting most of the runner's weight off his feet. Moore was not to run, jog, or otherwise move a single step faster than a walk for three weeks unless the Oregon coach himself was watching him in practice. If any of his teammates saw him putting in extra mileage, Moore would be off the team. Three weeks later, after following Bowerman's "experiment," Moore ran the 2 mile against Oregon State in 8:48, winning the race and clocking 27 seconds faster than he ever had before.

At the beginning of every track season, Bowerman would invite his athletes up to his ranch overlooking the McKenzie River. The meetings would always start the same way, with a parable about a motivational mule driver (or "skinner") that summed up the track coach's philosophy.

"Farmer can't get his mule to plow," Bowerman would say. "Can't even get him to eat or drink. Finally calls in a mule skinner. Guy comes out, doesn't even look at the mule. Goes in the barn, gets a two-by-four, and hits the mule as hard as he can between the ears. Mule goes to his knees. Mule skinner hits him again, between the eyes. Farmer drags the mule off. 'That's supposed to get him to plow? That's supposed to get him to drink?' the farmer asks. 'I can see you don't know a damn thing about mules,' says the skinner. 'First you have to get their attention.'"

For many University of Oregon athletes, getting that attention wasn't as extreme as holding Kenny Moore nearly off the ground by the throat, but the message was the same: you changed your bad habits, or else you were off the team. "Fundamentally, that was the proof, that was my two-by-four, that I had to take those easy days." Moore said. "That I'd just been wasting all that effort and not been getting any improvement for it."

Coaching track involves more than telling athletes to run more quickly. Bowerman would look for any advantage to shave off precious seconds at the finish line. In addition to his unorthodox way of telling Moore he needed more rest after having had the flu, the coach had a lot of feelings about shoes.

In 1965, Moore was called in to Bowerman's office. The runner had split his foot open during a track meet and the long run afterward (a quarter mile farther than Bowerman had prescribed) caused a stress fracture in his foot. "You will lay before me the shoes you wore," Bowerman ordered Moore, who placed the blue-and-white flats on his coach's desk. When not racing in spikes, runners often wear a different type of shoe called a flat, which, as the name suggests, has a thin, flat rubber sole. Bowerman ripped Moore's shoe apart in front of him, revealing only a small amount of padding and no arch support. "If you set out to engineer a shoe to bend metatarsals until they snap you couldn't do much better than this," he said. "Not only that, the outer sole rubber wears away like cornbread. This is not a shit shoe, it's a double-shit shoe."

Six weeks later, Bowerman gave Moore a pair with the proper cushioning and arch support. He had made them himself.

WILLIAM JAY BOWERMAN WAS BORN in Portland, Oregon, on February 19, 1911. His father had been the thirteenth governor of Oregon but had held the post for only six months (voted out of office for, among other things, having an affair with his secretary). Bowerman had an older brother and sister, as well as a twin named Tommy, whom he watched die in a grisly elevator accident when he was two years old. His parents' marriage dissolved after the scandal and Tommy's death, and afterward his distraught mother moved what remained of the family to her childhood home of Fossil, a rural northern town with a population just shy of 500. Bowerman, estranged from his father most of his life, identified with his mother's "pioneer stock" side of the family; his maternal great-grandfather had come to the state along the Oregon Trail in 1845.

Bowerman went to the University of Oregon in Eugene in 1929 to play football, though with his eye on becoming a doctor. The football he played was more physical than today's game, as players in leather helmets and thick, hand-sewn uniforms plowed into one another, preferring running plays to forward passes. Bowerman, a particularly good blocker, turned heads from the get-go and was a starter by his sophomore year. Watching him play against the University of Washington was Oregon's track coach, Bill Hayward. When Bowerman, still riding high off a 90-yard touchdown run, was on his way to a postgame dinner with his teammates, Hayward approached the young player and asked, "Did you hear me? I was trotting with you down the sideline yelling, 'Lift your knees! Lift your knees!'"

"My running was just bad," Bowerman said. "And I didn't know it. If Bill Hayward had not tidied up my running technique, I would've never made the track team at the University of Oregon."

Hayward didn't just get Bowerman's running form into shape; he planted the seed of an idea that would inform Bowerman's coaching for decades to come: that tiny changes can yield big results. After graduating, Bowerman was accepted to medical school but lacked the money for tuition. To save up money, he decided to work at his old high school as a biology teacher and as the football and track coach. Just after the United States entered World War II, Bowerman joined the army and was deployed to Italy with the 10th Mountain Division, where he was in charge of supplies, including a team of mules. After the war, Major Bowerman, who had earned a Silver Star and four Bronze Stars, returned to his teaching position until Hayward, his mentor, retired from the University of Oregon and offered him his old job.

He wasn't "Coach" or Mr. Bowerman to his athletes, just Bill. Perhaps because he was also a professor of physical education at the university, Bowerman saw himself as a teacher, someone who educated the "whole self," not just the athletes. He would handwrite individualized workouts for each runner, including instructions such as to finish the exercise "exhilarated, not exhausted." He cautioned against overtraining, employing what he called the hard-easy principle. "If you work hard, you have to rest. You have to recover," he said. That ran against "the more you put in, the more you get out" approach to training that most US coaches swore by at the time.

Often seen at practice in a jacket, tie, and Bavarian hat just covering his short-cropped hair, Bowerman appreciated it when an athlete knew his Shakespeare, often quoting the Bard or scripture during impromptu lectures. At the same time, he loved a locker room prank. He often joined the team in the community shower after practice, and more than once he singled out an unsuspecting freshman runner. Sometimes the incident would begin with a conversation about race strategy; middle distance runner Geoff Hollister remembered a more abbreviated encounter in the cold shower. "Then inexplicably warm water lands on my calf and runs down my ankle," he wrote in his 2008 memior. "How can there be warm water when I have none? I turn around straight into the stare of Bowerman who is smiling as a stream of pee continues to land on my lower leg." Upperclassmen who hadn't fled the shower by then said, "Today is your day, Geoff." Hollster speculated that the reason Bowerman "marked" his runners was a way to learn something about their character. "Is this young man going to attack me, run, or simply return the favor and pee back?" Other times the track coach would heat up his set of keys and sneak up beside unsuspecting students in the sauna to brand them. The keys never left a lasting mark, but once he pulled the prank on a runner, he was in the club, part of Bowerman's chosen. No longer mere undergraduates, they were the Men of Oregon.

Bowerman was unconventional, but he knew how to squeeze every drop of effort out of his athletes. At the time when Kenny Moore was at Oregon, the four-minute mile, first broken by the British runner Roger Bannister in 1954, was still considered the sound barrier of running. Bowerman had coached nine sub-four-minute milers; the most any other coach in America could claim at the time was two. Runners came to Oregon to run specifically for him, sometimes turning down better scholarship offers. He was the king, and the university's Hayward Field track was his kingdom. He had four NCAA championships to prove it.

When he wasn't at the track or in the gym, locker room, or classroom, Bowerman would spend hours in his ranch fiddling with designs and materials—all the variables outside his runners' control. To him, the enemy was weight; everything could benefit by being made lighter. He experimented with making running shorts out of superlight nylon parachute cloth. He deemed the stitched-on "O" of the team's running singlet to be too heavy, so subsequent uniforms had the letter screened on. And every ounce shaved off a pair of shoes, he calculated, would save a runner from lifting fifty-five pounds over the course of a mile.

IN THE DAYS OF MAIL ORDER, customers wanting a specialty shoe such as a track spike needed a hookup. The market was small, scattered, and difficult to target; manufacturers needed middlemen who knew where competitive runners were and what they needed, and runners needed their shoes. As Chuck Taylor had discovered with the All Star, coaches proved to be the ideal conduits for this business. Make a track shoe that impressed a coach, and you might sell several dozen pairs a season, more still if he told his coaching friends. High school coaches needed only to reach out to their nearby college counterparts to find out what shoes were being worn and how to get them. No one had a better bead on the market than Bowerman, who would get letters from people asking which foreign shoe performed the best and whether a four- or six-spike pattern was ideal. High school coaches would sometimes write asking for an order for their star athlete from some small shoemaker in England, West Germany, or wherever Bowerman happened to be ordering from that year.

In the mid-1950s, the track spike that ruled the professional and collegiate market was the Adidas Olympia, which retailed for $12.50 at a time when a saddle shoe cost about $5. Most of the athletic shoes suitable for running were in the style of either canvas high-tops similar to the Converse All Star or leather racing spikes like the Olympia. Bowerman ordered a sample of the shoe directly from Adidas in 1954. A written response from Adi Dassler's office contained a proposition: the German company wanted Bowerman to use his connections to sell Adidas shoes on the West Coast. The company was unknown in the United States outside elite circles, and Adidas knew that people such as Bowerman were necessary to make inroads with the American public.

"I am quite certain," Bowerman replied the following week, "that we would have a good market for your product." He promised to get back to Dassler after his athletes gave the Adidas Olympia a "good workout."

After months of back-and-forth, Bowerman turned down Dassler's offer to sell Adidas, citing university rules that prevented him from such an arrangement. He had other irons in the fire, in any case. Though he mentioned to Dassler that his team wore primarily Adidas, he was hard at work throughout 1955 testing half a dozen different brands of shoes and sending recommendations back to their makers. A letter to the Brooks Shoe Manufacturing Company in Philadelphia suggested that the company use a rubber or Neolite sole on its #3-S track shoe to accommodate rainier climates such as Oregon's and perhaps they could add a light rubber insole for comfort and more room for the toe, as seen in the Olympia. He sent along a pair of old Adidas with the letter.

The shoe companies responded with mostly a lack of interest, which began to wear on Bowerman. It was one thing to offer suggestions on how to improve an existing product, quite another to tell a company to produce an entirely new shoe. One company said a new model would be too risky; another commented that the design would be too expensive to produce. One company wrote that it wasn't telling him how to coach, so he shouldn't be telling it how to make shoes. That last rejection discouraged Bowerman, but a few days later he found new inspiration.

"I was giving some new team members a pep talk and quoting, as I often did, the apostle Paul," he wrote of the incident. "On this day to my own charges I was quoting Paul's familiar '. . . they which run in a race run all, but one receiveth the prize' and explaining that although winning is important, it is not the only goal.

"If it were, then there will be a lot of disappointed runners. So I want you to do your very best, not just for the prize, but also for what the *very trying* will do for you."

Bowerman was hardly religious, but he realized that there was advice in that speech for himself as well as his runners. On the drive home from practice later that night, the lesson became clear to him: he'd have to keep on trying to get the shoes made, even if he had to make them himself.

Bowerman visited a shoe repair shop in town to find out how he might go about constructing his own. He attributed his athletes' shin splints to poor footwear and was after a new kind of shoe, one with a heel wedge for support and a lighter sole for stability and traction. Night after night he sketched out designs at his kitchen table while his three sons did their homework. An all-purpose running shoe began to take shape, one that was usable on grass, mud, or pavement, not just for track and field training, but for cross-country racing and jogging as well. From his days as a high school coach, he knew the shoe had to be cheap; most schools didn't have money to buy multiple pairs of expensive shoes for each student.

At first the shoe repairman tried to convince Bowerman that he would need a factory to produce shoes. After some pressing, however, he began to explain the fundamentals to Bowerman. First, he would need a wooden last, a kind of model foot he could use to make patterns, similar to using a mannequin to pin patterns on when designing a shirt. Automated shoe production might have sped the process along, but shoes made by hand still followed the same process they had for hundreds of years.

"You can make the patterns from old brown-paper grocery bags," the repairman offered.

The patterns would be cut out and either sewed or glued together to form the upper, the top part. A sole would then be attached the same way, and he would have his shoe. Attaching spikes was another issue. Bowerman quickly discovered that without a metal or plastic sheet, or spike plate, to hold them in place under the ball of the foot, the force of a runner's foot strike would tear the shoe apart. But that addition would add weight. Bowerman dissected shoes with his band saw so he could mix and match different materials for the sole, upper, and spike plate.

While Bowerman was ripping shoes apart, he was also occupied with another material problem: running surfaces. Tracks at the time were still little more than dirt pathways encircling football fields. A "high-tech" midcentury running track might have a top layer of crushed cinder lined with white chalk to separate the lanes. A flat-soled tennis shoe would dissipate much of the propelling force coming from a runner's legs in the scramble for traction. Spiked shoes clawed the track, but even from a spectator's vantage point in the stands it was hard to miss the clumps of cinder runners kicked up and the footprints in the dirt their feet left behind.

In the world of American running, the University of Oregon's Hayward Field track inspires as much reverence today as Wrigley Field and Fenway Park do for baseball fans. Runners make pilgrimages to the "mecca" just to put in a few laps, and the facility often hosts national and international meets in addition to its collegiate schedule. The track at Hayward was resurfaced several times over the course of Bowerman's twenty-four-year tenure as coach. The track he inherited was made of volcanic ash, later replaced by crushed cinder, later replaced by a polyurethane rubber composite, the forerunner of the modern all-weather tracks made of layers of synthetic rubber. The ash and cinder tracks were anything but "all weather," turning muddy in the rain and rock hard in the sun. Therefore different shoes were used for different conditions, but even the right spikes could take you only so far when it came to running on a soggy track. Spring and fall in Eugene feature long periods of light rain; it was not uncommon for the first three lanes of Hayward Field's track to flood completely. That required a time-consuming process of draining, drying, raking, and relining the track with lime to get it race ready.

Like other inventors before him, Bowerman decided that rubber might be the answer. He wrote to rubber companies, requesting samples of roof coating for his tests. The companies sent him back catalogs and brochures while at the same time expressing skepticism that their product could be used for foot traffic. Over several days in mid-August 1958, Bowerman mixed up buckets of rubber and urethane at his ranch outside Eugene, laying out paths of prototype track in his yard to test how well they stood up to the rain. In a notebook he recorded more than two dozen different chemical tests, with results such as "sticky mess . . . did not set . . . probably too hot" and "possibly too fluffy." He once delivered samples to his next-door neighbor who owned cows, asking him to put the rubber mats in the feed area to see how long they'd last amid the constant stamping of hooves. In the end, he found a blend that worked well enough to resurface the long jump runway at Hayward Field.

BY 1958, BOWERMAN WAS READY to test his shoes. Phil Knight, a miler, and Otis Davis, a promising sprinter, were the first Men of Oregon to wear the premiere Bowerman track spike one evening at practice. Knight, a quiet blond-headed journalism student more often known as "Buck," was a capable enough runner, at least when the team's big guns weren't around. He had been a top half-miler in Portland in high school, and though he was still adjusting to being middle of the pack on a team of top collegiate talent, he impressed Bowerman with his work ethic. "All will not be fun and frolic," Bowerman wrote to Knight's parents before he joined the team. "It takes hard work for success in anything."

Davis, on the other hand, excelled no matter what the company. He had served in the air force during the Korean War before coming to Oregon on a basketball scholarship, a long way from his native Tuscaloosa, where attending the pre-integrated University of Alabama was out of the question. Davis switched sports after spying a track workout from his dorm room across the street from Hayward Field. He walked up to Bowerman, asking to be on the team. The lean twenty-six-year-old was placed in the high jump and long jump before Bowerman decided he would fit best as a sprinter.

The shoes Bowerman brought to practice that night were made from a thin, rubber-coated fabric similar to a picnic tarp. Knight jogged for a bit in them and seemed to like their fit. Davis was skeptical at first but somehow snagged them away from Knight to try for himself.

"All you could see of [Davis] was these white, white, shoes, taking long, long steps," Bowerman recalled decades later. "You could hear him yelling that he liked them and he'd keep them and be grateful forever."

That was the proof Bowerman needed. He returned to his workshop. He made uppers out of leather, canvas, and even rattlesnake skin (most likely from his own backyard) and then weighed each creation on a scale. Stitching added too much weight, so he fixed the upper to the sole with glue. He would trace each of his runners' feet on paper, believing, as with his individualized workouts, that an athlete would perform best in shoes made for him. Bowerman's team (and his high school–aged son) provided the perfect feedback for trial-and-error tests. By 1959, his runners, or "test pilots," were winning races in his creations. As long as his runners turned in a good time, it didn't matter that the some of the shoes fell apart after only one race.

As his craftmanship improved, he sought better materials. He wrote to companies such as Mizuno, Converse, and Adidas to tell them of his Frankenstein creations: a running shoe upper on a basketball sole, creating, say, an indoor running shoe. He would request a range of sole sizes for further experiments. That his letters weren't crumpled up on receipt speaks more to a need for market feedback than to any desire to humor an eccentric track coach from the Pacific Northwest. From a shoe company's perspective, here was an obsessive artisan come to you, for free, suggesting how to make your product better. If his advice was sound and you followed it, not only might you sell him more shoes, you'd have a much better shoe on the market than your research and development budget could buy. That became even more important if your competitor happened to be located in, say, the same tiny Bavarian town.

In the 1960 Rome Olympics, Bowerman achieved another career milestone: having coached an Olympic champion. Two years after testing Bowerman's first shoe, Otis Davis collected gold medals in both the individual 400 meters and the 4×400-meter relay. Davis's photo finish in the 400 meters against the diving German sprinter Carl Kaufmann was published in *Life* magazine, both men breaking 45 seconds for the first time. Both were wearing white Adidas spikes. Bowerman's shoe experiments were getting more refined, but they had yet to match the technological sophistication major players such as Adidas could muster. On the grand stage of the Olympics, even his test pilot was taking no chances.

Adidas' reign on the track was assured, but not for long. By the end of the 1960s, a powerful new player would emerge in the sneaker game. It had started that evening in 1958 when Buck Knight slipped on a pair of Bill Bowerman's spikes.

6

SWOOSH

Like many other twenty-four-year-olds, Phil Knight didn't know what to do with his life. He had sold encyclopedias. Badly. He had worked as an accountant. Unenthusiastically. He had tanked an interview with a corporate recruiter by blowing his nose in a sock that he had mistaken for a pocket handkerchief. Not knowing what else to do, he asked his father for a loan to travel the world.

While in Tokyo, he wandered into a Japanese sporting goods store, and his interest was piqued when he saw a pair of knockoff Adidas track shoes that came highly recommended by the store's clerk. He asked the clerk who made them. Then he booked a train to Kobe to meet with representatives from Onitsuka Tiger.

Knight wasn't just any wayward kid out of college making a round-the-world trip. He was a Man of Oregon. After graduating in 1959 with a degree in journalism, he had attended the Stanford Business School, where he had written a paper for an entrepreneurial class titled "Can Japanese Sports Shoes Do to German Sports

Shoes What Japanese Cameras Did to German Cameras?" The graduate student saw a parallel between the high-quality Adidas shoes admired by Bowerman and their cheaper Japanese counterparts. German 35 mm Leica cameras were considered the professional standard following World War II, especially as Leica's chief competitor, Contax, found itself on the wrong side of the Iron Curtain. Leica seemingly had the market to itself. On the other side of the world, the Japanese company Nikon was reestablishing itself after making binoculars, bomb sights, and periscopes during the war. Nikon became very good at copying Leica lenses much more cheaply. During the Korean War, photojournalists discovered the Nikon lenses because they were more available in the region, and within a decade, Nikon and its Japanese competitors such as Canon were competing globally. Knight argued that Japan, with its cheaper labor and material costs, could also produce shoes that could compete favorably with the German brands.

Knight wore a green Brooks Brothers two-button suit—as he tells it, the only suit he had taken on his worldwide trip, and arrived late at the Onitsuka headquarters after having mistakenly taken a taxi to the showroom instead of the manufacturing facility on the other side of town. As Knight was led through the accounting room, all the accountants stood and bowed to the man they thought was an important American businessman but who was in fact a recent college graduate who, between his suit and airline ticket, had all of his assets on his person. About half a dozen executives were waiting for Knight when he stepped into the conference room at the back of the factory.

Not knowing what else to do after such a warm reception, Knight told them he was an American shoe importer. To Onitsuka, he was convincing as a dynamic young tycoon promising a way into the US market. In 1962, Japan was exporting $49 million worth of footwear to the United States. Onitsuka, whose most successful product was a flat-soled distance running shoe, had only one distributor in the country. When asked the name of his company, Knight made up the name Blue Ribbon Sports on the spot. When Knight asked his father to wire him $37 to order a few samples, his just-concocted company became Onitsuka's second US distributor.

Knight knew what he was going up against: Adidas clearly ruled the track spike market. But Adidas spikes were often expensive and sometimes hard to get. Knight planned to sell Tiger shoes for less, undercutting Adidas to gain a foothold in the market. Onitsuka's executives excitedly showed Knight product samples: there were a training shoe called the "Limber Up," a high-jump shoe called the "Spring Up," and a discus shoe called the "Throw Up." Knight did his best to stifle a laugh.

The Limber Up seemed promising, and Knight held it aloft. "This is a good shoe," he said. "This shoe—I can sell this shoe." There was one more opinion he needed to get.

Knight would have to wait more than a full year for the samples to arrive for his old coach Bill Bowerman to look at. When the two sat down for hamburgers on a dreary Eugene day in January 1964, Knight just wanted Bowerman's blessing and thought he'd maybe sell a few dozen shoes to the Oregon track team. But Bowerman had bigger plans: he wanted in.

Bowerman and Knight each chipped in $500 to fund Blue Ribbon Sports, and soon afterward they were importing Tiger track spikes from Japan. Bowerman's clout made an easy sell to other track coaches in the western half of the country. Bowerman couldn't resist ripping the shoes apart, of course, and he soon had ideas for how to improve them. Americans had longer and heavier bodies than the Japanese, which translated into different feet; Bowerman went to work on "Americanizing" the Tigers. "During the autumn track season of 1965, every race had two results for

Bowerman," Knight wrote in his memoir more than fifty years later. "There was the performance of his runners, and there was the performance of their shoes. Bowerman would note how the arches held up, how the soles gripped the cinders, how the toes pinched and the instep flexed. Then he'd airmail his notes and findings to Japan." Onitsuka sent back a sample that had a wedge to reduce stress on the Achilles tendon, a soft inner sole, and more arch support, all of which drove Bowerman wild. Finally, a shoe company was really listening to his ideas.

BEFORE THE OCTOPUS WAS SERVED to him, Kihachiro Onitsuka had a problem. His basketball shoes just weren't working.

Japan after World War II was in a state of reorganization, restructuring, and rethinking. No longer an empire, the island nation was in the midst of finding its postwar identity. For the thirty-two-year-old Onitsuka, the solution to building communities and uniting people, as the company history put it, was through physical activity—so he started a shoe company. Making shoes would help rebuild the smoldering cities and towns leveled by US bombs. Onitsuka made the lasts for his first line of basketball shoes by pouring hot wax from Buddhist candles over his own feet. He was hoping that the sport that was popular with the American GIs would take off in his country. Basketball shoes themselves were difficult to find at the time; Onitsuka stood to have the market all to himself if he was able to produce a popular model. The shoes, though, didn't sell. They were too slippery, not gripping the court the way they should.

When his dinner arrived at his mother's house one hot summer evening in 1951, as the story goes, he realized that the cold cucumber and octopus salad had the solution to his sole problem. One piece of octopus was stuck to the bottom of his bowl, and

Onitsuka studied the suction cups at the bottom of its tentacles. If he could mimic the concave surfaces for the sole of his shoes, they'd solve the start-and-stop problem. He adapted the new sole to a pair of Onitsuka Tiger 1950 OK Basketball Shoes, which proved just the thing to help the first high school team to wear them to win their championship. The name "OK" came not from the shoes' being merely adequate but from the creator's initials.

Onitsuka Tiger had solved its basketball problem, but the company soon found that its main strength was in the running shoe market. It helped that Japan had a strong culture of running. Like the boarding schools and colleges of Great Britain and the United States, Japan's schools served as an incubator of sports. Since the early twentieth century, high schools and colleges in Japan had sought to produce the top teams to compete in the *ekiden*, a class of relay race that can often last more than a hundred miles, in which each team member runs roughly half a marathon.

There was a new problem to be solved: long-distance runners wearing his shoes often complained of blisters developing on their feet. As the company tells it, the imaginative Onitsuka found the answer in the bathtub. He noticed that his feet would become wrinkled in a steaming hot bath and realized that heat was causing the blisters inside the shoes. Onitsuka's designers studied the way a motorcycle engine uses the air passing through it to cool itself. When perforated holes were added near the toe and sides of the shoe, similar to a motorcycle engine's air intake, the blisters started to disappear. Other new designs included a marathon shoe with a cleft toe, inspired by Japanese *tabi* socks worn with sandals. Before long, Onitsuka's shoes were gracing Japan's top athletes. The Olympic marathoner Kenji Kimihara credited his 1968 silver medal to his countryman's Magic Runner model of shoes, which he wore for each of his thirty-five races.

That was the company Knight and Bowerman had bought

into. Onitsuka hoped that Japanese technology would appeal on the other side of the Pacific.

VERY SLOWLY, BLUE RIBBON ADDED an employee here and there, almost always ex-athletes of Bowerman. The going rate for the new part-time sales reps was $1.75 for each pair of running shoes sold and $2 for each pair of spikes. It wasn't much, but the commission per pair could buy nearly a dozen hamburgers at McDonald's, the kind of thing young men fresh out of college might want. A physical store opened in 1966 in Santa Monica to lessen the need for Blue Ribbon's salesmen to sell out of the trunks of their cars.

As business picked up, Knight was well aware of the precariousness of selling other people's shoes. For one, even with his old track coach's recommendations and notes sent back to headquarters, Blue Ribbon had to move whatever Onitsuka shipped to them. Then there was the danger of the supply line from Japan to Oregon being so long; orders arrived dangerously late and were often wrong. There was also the distribution rights issue. Blue Ribbon had the West Coast to itself, but that created a paradox: if it got too good or too big, if it couldn't match pace with demand or didn't do so cheaply enough, headquarters could bring in another distributor. That was the danger Blue Ribbon's employee number one, Jeff Johnson, raised in a frantic 1970 letter to Knight: the Cortez, Blue Ribbon's first big original shoe, was getting too popular.

The shoe had come out of Bowerman's tinkering. Taking yet another page from Dr. Frankenstein, he'd ripped apart two models of Tiger shoes, one of which had an outsole that melted like butter but a midsole that remained intact and another that had a stronger outsole but poor midsole. He had stitched the best parts of each one together and inserted an arch cookie, a half circle of leather to cushion fallen arches or flat feet. The early version of the shoe was the same one he had prepared for the recuperating Kenny Moore. The design was mailed off to Japan for approval. When the company sent the prototype in 1967, it looked like the shoe of the future; there was cushioning, there were bold colors and clean lines. But what to call it? Adidas usually released an athletic shoe just prior to the Olympics, naming it after something to do with the host country. When Knight and Bowerman named it the Aztec, Adidas shot back a cease-and-desist letter, saying that its new pre–Mexico City Games release had the name Azteca Gold. Trying to come up with a new name, Bowerman took off his baseball cap, put it on again, and rubbed his face.

"Who's the Spaniard that kicked the shit out of the Aztecs?" Knight recalled Bowerman asking.

"Cortez," Knight responded. "Hernando Cortez."

IN THE TURBULENT year of 1968, the Olympic Games in Mexico City in October seemed to offer a brief respite. Martin Luther King, Jr., and Robert Kennedy had both been killed by assassins' bullets earlier in the year. In August, four Warsaw Pact countries, including the Soviet Union, had invaded Czechoslovakia, quashing the reforms of the Prague Spring. Student movements around the world were protesting for civil rights, democracy, and university reform and against the Vietnam War. Dozens of nations threatened to boycott the Olympics if apartheid South Africa was allowed to compete. In the end South Africa, and fellow apartheid-supporting nation Rhodesia, were barred from competition. Days before the Olympics began, in what became known as the Tlatelolco Massacre, Mexican police and military fired on a group of mainly student protesters, killing at least forty-four.

There is little surprise that one of the most indelible images from the 1968 Games was one of protest. On October 16, the American sprinters Tommie Smith and John Carlos won gold and bronze, respectively, during the 200-meter sprint, with Smith turning in a world-record time. During the medal ceremony, Smith and Carlos walked toward the award podium wearing black socks, their hands solemnly clasped behind them, each holding a single Puma sneaker. Smith mounted the top of the medal stand and raised both his arms in a victory pose. His right hand was clenched in a fist, and his left held his sneaker. He set the shoe on the podium and bent down to receive his gold medal. As "The Star-Spangled Banner" played, Smith and Carlos, heads bowed, each raised a black-gloved fist and kept it aloft during the duration of the national anthem. The third runner on the podium, Australian Peter Norman, did not raise his fist but showed solidarity with Smith and Carlos by wearing the same Olympic Project for Human Rights badge as the Americans did.

Each aspect of Smith and Carlos's Black Power salute was planned in advance and held a symbolic meaning. The sprinters had chosen the black socks without shoes to represent black poverty. The black scarf represented black pride, and the beaded necklace stood in for victims of lynching, while Carlos's unzipped track jacket, a breach of Olympic etiquette, symbolized the working class.

Olympic officials quickly condemned the sprinters' protest. At a press conference afterward, Smith and Carlos explained that their actions had stemmed from the unequal treatment of blacks in the United States, even in the wake of the progress made by the civil rights movement. For their efforts, Smith and Carlos were booed, insulted, and racially abused as some in the crowd threw things at them and shouted insults such as "Niggers need to go back to Africa!"

"If I win I am an American, not a black American," Smith

told reporters. "But if I did something bad then they would say 'a Negro.' We are black and we are proud of being black. Black America will understand what we did tonight."

IOC president Avery Brundage, who had advocated against boycotting Hitler's 1936 Berlin Games, and the eight other members of the IOC's Executive Council had them expelled from the Games. In a note of irony, suspecting that the politically active sprinters were going to do something during the medal ceremony, the IOC had dispatched Jesse Owens, whose gold-medal performances had rebuked Hitler's racist views, to try to talk Smith and Carlos out of making any political demonstration at the Games. After the protest, the sprinters again met with Owens, who asked why they had used the black gloves.

"Well Mr. Owens," Carlos said. "These gloves are to let you know that we are representing black people before we represent anyone, anything, any symbol, any flag, or any nation. This is Technicolor, sir. We want to be very clear about who we are representing." The protest and the resulting expulsion made headlines worldwide. Some of the coverage was sympathetic, but much more of it was critical and condemned Carlos and Smith for making a political statement at a supposedly nonpolitical event such as the Olympics. One columnist divided black US sprinters into "militants" and "nonmilitants."

"When I saw those two guys with their fists up on the victory stand, that made my heart jump. I thought that was beautiful," said Margaret Lambert, formerly known as Gretel Bergmann, the Jewish high jumper who had been forced by the Nazis to train with the 1936 German Olympic team as a ruse to show how supposedly tolerant Hitler's regime was. She had been unceremoniously cut from the team as soon as it became clear there would be no boycott. In 2005, Smith and Carlos's protest was memorialized by a statue of the two sprinters at San Jose University, their alma mater. The black-gloved fist is the protest's most highlighted image, but the sculpture also includes the symbol the sprinters used to underscore black poverty: an empty blue sneaker.

Along with the political messages, viewers at home were getting a whole new perspective on the Olympics. The 1968 Games were the first to be broadcast live in color. US audiences tuning in to ABC could see the Australians' yellow frocks, the Hungarians' electric-pink uniforms, and the red jackets of the Canadian delegation during the parade of nations. In a sign of the times, the crowd in the Estadio Olímpico Universitario rose to their feet and cheered as the Czechoslovakian team entered the stadium, out of respect for the events following the Prague Spring earlier that year. Not all of ABC's forty-three hours of telecasts were live, but satellite technology allowed the network's viewers to see much of the Games as they happened. Four years earlier, during the Winter Olympics in Innsbruck, Austria, ABC producers had to send the taped black-and-white coverage by plane to the United States each day for broadcast.

Much to the delight of Bill Bowerman, the Dasslers, and everyone else who wanted to see faster running times, the 1968 Olympics were the first to use an all-weather rubberized running track, similar to what Bowerman had been experimenting with. Prior to this, Olympic tracks had been more or less the same since Jesse Owens's day; 3M, the company that had made the new track, even hired Owens himself to help persuade Olympic officials to install the modern, manufactured running surface. Though the innovation improved times, it also introduced a new problem: instead of the spikes just grazing the track, as they used to, there was a split second of resistance as they became stuck in its surface. That obviously took precious time and energy away from the runner. A track shoe now needed to grip and release the track, rather than impale it. Onitsuka's solution would be to produce a shoe with a more flexible spike plate, which allowed the longer spikes just beneath the ball of the foot to drive into the track while the shorter spikes near the toe would provide traction as the foot impacted and left the ground.

The prospect of falling world records combined with expanded television coverage heightened the stakes for shoe brands. Color broadcasts helped viewers easily spot Adidas' three stripes or Puma's Formstrip; it was more critical than ever that the winner have the right shoe, no matter what it took. The above-board, nonbribery measures still involved finding remarkable athletes and giving them a free pair of shoes. Adi Dassler, now in his late sixties, continued to seek out Olympic track stars to wear his shoes. High jumper Dick Fosbury was originally laughed at by coaches and athletes for sailing over the bar belly up instead of using the more common scissor-kicking or roll/straddle methods, but just before the 1968 Olympics, a package arrived from Adidas containing handmade spikes—for each shoe a different color, as Fosbury preferred. "It was just amazing that this German cobbler would spend hours on spikes just for me," Fosbury said. "I was extremely grateful and certainly wouldn't dream of accepting cash to wear them." Fosbury would go on to win the gold medal, and his "Fosbury flop" technique would change high jumping forever.

With so much at stake, the Adidas-Puma rivalry devolved into less savory tactics. Olympic rules still prevented competitors from accepting sponsorships, but surreptitious brown envelopes of money were more and more a part of securing an athlete's shoe loyalty. More deviously, shoe reps' hotel reservations were mysteriously canceled. Adidas had a shipment of Puma shoes impounded, and Puma countered by having runners smuggle the shoes out of the impound yard. One American Puma rep was even thrown into a Mexican jail by undercover policemen without explanation and released only through intervention from the State

Department. In the end, Adidas prevailed: more than 80 percent of the athletes wore the three stripes.

Plenty of Olympians were training in Tiger shoes, but few were actually competing in them. The Tiger Cortez was selling well for Blue Ribbon, but as a thick-soled training shoe it was too clunky to match up against a track spike. A sneaker with a different sole was just around the corner, one that would bind the young Blue Ribbon Sports to running for decades to come and fuel a new exercise phenomenon that only a few, including Bowerman, would see coming.

IT STARTED WITH BREAKFAST.

"We were sitting out there, having waffles on the front deck as we often did," recalled Bowerman's wife, Barbara, in a 2006 documentary. "And he suddenly looked over at the back of the waffle iron. He jumped up, went to town, and got two cans of urethane and poured them into the waffle iron, and of course it wouldn't even come apart after that."

Another version of the story has Barbara Bowerman going to church on a summer Sunday in 1971. Bill, who always stayed behind, was sitting in the kitchen, not on the deck, when he eyed the waffle iron. Flats in the early 1970s had next to no tread on the bottom, which meant that the shoe was light but lacked much in the way of cushion or grip. Bowerman had been racking his brain trying to come up with a light tread that could be used on many different terrains. Sprinting spikes were no good for running on grass or mud. Staring at the square-shaped studs of his waffle iron, the idea hit him. He poured molten rubber into the iron but ended up fusing it together.

He went out and bought two more waffle irons, one to replace the one he had ruined and one to make a plaster mold. He ruined a good many more in making test molds based on the pattern. He eventually realized that the waffle iron was only the inspiration, not the answer. He took a piece of stainless steel with wafflelike indentations to the Oregon Rubber Company and ordered a pliable surface with hard rubber nubs. After years of experimentation, he had produced his greatest innovation: a waffle sole. The pattern provided grip on any surface and was cheap to make once the right mold was finalized. Bowerman saw possibilities beyond racing flats. Training shoes, including Blue Ribbon's own Cortez, had only a ribbed sole, which didn't help much on wet grass or mud. Flat-soled shoes such as the Converse All Star and the Keds Champion might be fine on a flat court but were useless for running on uneven or wet ground. The spikeless running shoe that Bowerman had been searching for since the days of the cinder track was finally here.

As was his practice, Bowerman used his athletes as human guinea pigs. Geoff Hollister, a miler under Bowerman in the late 1960s, was one of the first to wear a test pair of the waffle shoes and noted that the "urethane spikes" worked on grass, mud, pavement, or track. Hollister had been hired as Blue Ribbon Sports' third employee, responsible for handling the distribution of the Tiger shoes throughout Oregon.

Decades later, several old waffle irons were found at the Bowerman ranch in such disrepair they had to be thrown out. Likely figuring they could've somehow been useful one day, the track coach had held on to them, their experimenting days long behind them.

THE YEAR 1971 was a big one for Blue Ribbon Sports. It was ready to break away from Onitsuka Tiger. The Cortez had, as Jeff Johnson had warned, become almost too popular; Onitsuka was satisfying its local customers first, and shipments were of variable quality and, more often than not, late. He knew that Blue Ribbon would need a bold logo to compete with Onitsuka's crisscrossing lines, Adidas' three stripes, and Puma's side-of-the-shoe Formstrip. That same year, while teaching accounting at Portland State University, Knight met a graphic design student named Carolyn Davidson. Knight hired her to come up with a logo, "something that evokes a sense of motion." Davidson presented the Blue Ribbon Sports team with what looked like a chubby check mark, for which she was paid $35.

Next came a new name. Out of the dozens of choices the Blue Ribbon insiders came up with, two floated to the top: "Falcon" and "Dimension Six." The latter was Knight's own idea, and he wasn't going to let it go easily, no matter how much the rest of the staff hated it. Normally when the hypercompetitive Knight refused to budge, the staff would change the subject and convince the boss of a better idea later. But since a new name was needed by nine the next morning, Blue Ribbon was at an impasse.

At seven the next morning, Jeff Johnson phoned Bob Woodell, employee number four, with the new name, which had come to him in a dream and caused him to sit straight up in bed and say it out loud: "Nike." The name, he explained, was that of the Greek winged goddess of victory. It had a distinctive, strong-consonant double syllable, like Xerox and Kleenex.

Woodell wasn't convinced by Johnson's energetic pitch but told Knight anyway.

"What happened to Dimension Six?" Knight asked.

"Nobody seems to like that one but you," Woodell said. "You know, this Nike thing does fit the shoes."

"I guess we'll go with the Nike thing for now," Knight said after he sent the final decision off by telex. "I really don't like any of them, but I guess that's the best of the bunch."

7

COURTING STYLE

lmost every night, Walt Frazier would wash his sneakers with soap and a brush. The next morning, when they had dried and become a crisp white, he'd lace them up meticulously. They had to be just right when the eleven-year-old went to play basketball on his school's dirt playground. Frazier liked looking down and seeing how they looked as he walked. The rocks and pebbles of the playground would send the ball bouncing up at odd angles, sometimes hitting Frazier in the nose. It was the best playing surface his all-black school could offer in deeply segregated 1950s Georgia. Whatever way the ball bounced, he wanted to look good.

A little more than a decade later, Frazier had traded that dusty schoolyard court for the hardwood floor of Madison Square Garden, but he'd lost none of his sartorial flair. In the late summer of his rookie season the Knicks were in Baltimore, and to kill time and get his mind off the game, he went shopping. He stopped dead in his tracks at the sight of a wide-brimmed, brown velour Italian hat. "Well, I ain't playing good but I still look good!" he thought to himself. When he wore the hat, he was immediately laughed at—by both the other team and his own. Two weeks later, the gangster movie *Bonnie and Clyde* hit the theaters and his teammates made a connection between Frazier's flashy dressing and Warren Beatty's dapper bank robber, Clyde Barrow. Newspapers also picked up on Frazier's tendency to steal the ball, making his new nickname, "Clyde," stick for good.

Frazier was going through his pregame ritual while preparing for another performance as a point guard for the New York Knicks. He'd tape his ankles while still in his underwear so as not to wrinkle his uniform, donned ever so carefully to avoid bulges or creases. His Pumas were laced just so, as his playground sneakers had been. While he was examining his hair in the mirror, combing down any stray hairs that might be sticking out from his mustache or sideburns, one of the Knicks ball boys walked by. "Hey, get Clyde some ice, his head is swelling up," the ball boy said.

Shoes also played an important part in Frazier's ritual. "Just before going onto the floor I like my hands to be dry," he said. "So what I do is rub them on the bottom of my shoe." It was superstition as well as style; like many players, he was careful not to change any detail while on a winning streak. "I've had good games and my sneakers need to be changed because they're wearing down, slippery almost, but I won't change them now. Not until I have a bad game." When not in Pumas, Frazier favored white Chuck Taylors, sometimes with orange laces on one foot and blue laces on the other.

CHUCK TAYLOR'S basketball evangelizing extended into the 1960s. His relentless promotion, which included a stint as a US Army Air Forces coach during World War II, helped solidify the Converse

All Star as the top sneaker at all levels of the sport. It was not without competition: the PRO-Keds Royal, a look-alike canvas shoe right down to the inner ankle patch, was promoted by player and coach George Mikan with some success. But by 1969, the year of Taylor's death, Converse had sold 400 million pairs of his signature All Stars.

Meanwhile, the phenomenon of athlete endorsement was becoming more sophisticated and more lucrative. For decades, when ticket sales had been the primary source of revenue, athletes in general hadn't made all that much money. Even in major spectator sports such as baseball and football, many players had side jobs in the off-season. As televised broadcasts became more common, athletes' salaries rose along with the sponsorship dollars that poured in to support those broadcasts. Early sports agents understood the value of associating their player with a certain brand. Arnold Palmer's line of signature Wilson golf clubs in the late 1950s netted the player tens of thousands of dollars in royalties and the company much more in added sales. The benefit of each deal wasn't just the revenue stream, it was the added exposure, which, if the athlete remained relevant, could turn into other sponsorship deals. Palmer would go on to create his own line of self-designed clubs, star in commercials for United Airlines and Hertz Rent-A-Car, and become well known to non–golf fans who enjoyed mixing iced tea and lemonade. It was in some ways exactly what The Babe had done decades earlier, but now there was room for a lot more stars to cash in.

Not all boats rose with the advent of broadcasting. In addition to the Olympics, tennis and college athletics had strict rules against amateur athletes getting paid. After the Technicolor 1968 Olympics raised the international profile of Adidas and Puma, both brands were quick to look to other sports to lock in athletic endorsements. One of the problems of their under-the-table brand war had been that without a contract to lock them down, athletes were free to play companies against each other and collect envelopes containing escalating amounts of cash (a strategy the savvy 100-meter champion Armin Hary had pioneered).

Horst and Armin Dassler, the sons of Adi and Rudolf, respectively, assumed more prominent roles in their companies and continued the rivalry started by their fathers. The 1970 World Cup was the next big international sports tournament, and the cousins competed to secure athletes in the world's biggest sport. Neither side wanted a repeat of the dirty tricks of the 1968 Olympics, though, and they knew there was one player who could trigger that scenario: Pelé. Signing the Brazilian hero would be costly for both brands; first, he wouldn't be cheap. Second, other players would demand more from their shoe deals, triggering an arms race neither brand could afford. The cousins devised an informal "Pelé pact": any player was fair game except the world-famous forward. Many of the Brazilian players had Puma contracts, though, and Pelé kept hassling the Puma representative as to why he wasn't offered one. The temptation was too much for Armin Dassler, who signed off on the deal. Seconds before the start of the final between Brazil and Italy, Pelé asked the referee for a momentary delay while he tied his shoes. As he crouched down, the camera caught the unmistakable horizontal white Puma stripe. The whole world, including Horst Dassler, now knew what shoes the greatest player wore.

The peace of the Pelé pact was over, and the age of the celebrity athlete was unequivocally here.

EVEN BEFORE THE PELÉ INCIDENT, Horst Dassler understood the value of finding the right name. His father was still busy running the family business out of Bavaria with his wife, Käthe. Unwilling to pass the full reins of the company to his only son just yet, in 1959, Adi instead offered Horst the chance to turn around an ailing shoe factory in France. Horst, age twenty-three, hatched a plan not just to save the factory but to turn his tiny slice of control into a major component of the company. Adidas France would release its own lines independently of the German operation, which was encouraged to be viewed not as a parent company but as a competitor. Horst's first moves would be to expand beyond his father's focus on soccer boots and track shoes, cracking open new markets in tennis and basketball by introducing, for the first time, leather versions of those shoes.

Horst set his sights on the US market, which wasn't a top priority for the Europe-centric Adidas headquarters. Professional basketball was an unlikely first target; it had yet to achieve the cultural status of professional baseball or football in the United States, much less the popularity of soccer in the rest of the world. There was no Pelé to go after. College basketball had no trouble attracting an audience—a 1968 regular-season game between the University of Houston and UCLA was the first nationally broadcast regular-season matchup, as 120 stations across the country interrupted network coverage to broadcast the "Game of the Century." But the NCAA amateur rules made student athletes off-limits to endorsements. In contrast, the NBA didn't broadcast a nationally televised regular-season game in prime time until 1970. But under the radar was exactly where Horst wanted to be, for the moment.

In 1964, Horst's subsidiary came up with the Supergrip basketball sneaker and a high-top variant called the Pro Model. The Adidas shoes sought to correct a design flaw in the canvas shoes: their tendency to slip on the court. The leather provided better support than flimsy canvas, and the Supergrip's wider base, as the name implied, provided better traction on the hardwood.

The only problem was that there weren't many takers. "They had played in canvas all their lives; [the shoe] looked completely alien to them," said Chris Severn, one of Horst Dassler's most important consultants. "They weren't even getting paid by Converse."

Severn shopped the shoe around to NBA teams, but only one took a gamble on Adidas. San Diego Rockets coach Jack McMahon had his hands full with the lowest-ranked, lowest-paid, most injury-prone team in the league. Many of McMahon's players hurt themselves by slipping, and a shoe literally named the Supergrip seemed like the answer. At first the players were skeptical, but they ended up liking the extra support the leather provided. By the end of the season, the Supergrip fared better than the Rockets' losing record. The team exposed the rest of the NBA to the odd-looking sneaker, prompting players on other teams to want to try it for themselves. The following year the Boston Celtics won the championship in Adidas and brought an abrupt end to the canvas sneaker's dominance. Severn also convinced Horst Dassler to sign Kareem Abdul-Jabbar, one of the league's biggest young stars and already famous from his college days, for a hefty-for-the-time $25,000 a year.

The name of the company's shell-toed sneaker was changed to Superstar, a name fitting to challenge the All Star. A leather version of the Chuck Taylor shoe never caught on, and by 1973, 85 percent of professional players were wearing Adidas and college teams were following suit. It was all a product of the Horst-led French operations—but as basketball shoes pulled in 10 percent of the company's sales, Horst had to downplay how swiftly his exports were rising compared with the operation in Germany, lest his mother, who was in charge of international operations, think he was trying to peel off business from her.

Horst's other focus was tennis. Unlike the NBA, which was slowly gaining mainstream popularity through the 1960s, international tennis stars had existed since the beginning of the century. But both were new to endorsements: whereas basketball needed to convince sponsors it was worth investing in, tennis needed to be convinced that sponsors were worth it. Just as in the Olympics, professionals could make money at the sport but were barred from the top amateur-only tournaments such as Wimbledon and the French Open. It was as if a baseball player could play for the Yankees but couldn't play in the World Series. Enforcing an athlete's amateur status was applied haphazardly, and this era of tennis was one of "shamateurism" as players made a living by accepting payments under the table. Yet it was a tectonic shift in 1968 when professionals were finally allowed to compete in major tournaments, ushering in the Open Era. Finally prize money, above-board payments, and endorsement deals were allowed, joining tennis to basketball, golf, and other American sports.

Adidas had produced a tennis shoe in the 1950s, but it was due for an update. Robert Haillet, one of the top professional French tennis players, was Horst Dassler's choice for a signature leather tennis shoe. Haillet had turned pro in 1960, and, though unable to compete in the French Open, was able to accept endorsements. By the time Robert Haillet the shoe was released in 1965, Robert Haillet the person had led his country's Davis Cup team, reached the semifinals of the French Open as an amateur, and as a pro had made several appearances in the Wembley Championship, a tournament that was the lesser, professional equivalent of Wimbledon. The shoe itself was completely white, conforming to the sport's squeaky clean dress code. The only distinct design feature was three rows of perforations on each side, which were meant to allow air in but also served to evoke the three stripes without actually featuring the stripes. By the end of the decade, Haillet retired and Dassler needed to find a fresh name to fill his shoes.

The surest way for Adidas to break into the US market was

by signing an American player. The rising star Stan Smith was suggested. The six-foot-three, 200-pound Smith was a hulking presence on the court, all business and rarely smiling, but he had several big wins to his name and seemed more accessible off court as a wispy-haired, mustachioed Californian. Adidas approached him in 1971, the same year Smith won the U.S. Open, to start wearing the Haillet shoe in competitions. Horst and Smith met at a nightclub in Paris and by 11 o'clock it was agreed that the American would be the new face of the German shoe from France. On the strength of Smith's 1972 Wimbledon win and his number one ranking, sales took off.

So had tennis's popularity. The hard-surfaced courts that popped up at schools and recreation centers offered an alternative to the expensive grass ones that only country clubs were in the financial position to maintain. Tennis still retained its upper-crust connotations and was a sport that people aspired to, whether they played it or merely dressed as though they played it. Wearing a Lacoste shirt with its iconic crocodile, for example, didn't necessarily mark someone as a tennis player, but it did carry certain connotations of the country club set. The same held true for tennis shoes.

Among professionals, the Adidas shoe was such a success that in the early 1970s, half of the Wimbledon field of about eighty players was wearing it. "I got really annoyed the first time that I had lost a match against a guy who was wearing my shoes," Smith said. When Smith first began wearing the shoe, he had been promoting something named for another player, but as he found success, Haillet's name, once on the shoe itself, gradually began to evolve off it. Smith would go on to win three more Grand Slam doubles titles and help the United States win several Davis Cup titles, and by the end of the decade his association with the shoe would be complete. Like the Chuck Taylor All Stars, Smith's name (and signature) was right there on the sneaker—along with a picture of his face on the tongue. Also like Taylor, Smith the shoe would become more famous than Smith the tennis player.

AT MADISON SQUARE GARDEN, the Knicks were so bad that whenever the circus was in town, it was the team that had to move out of the Garden. There were more paying customers for elephants and clowns than for the league's perennial bottom-feeders.

Despite that, interest in Big Apple basketball wasn't dead. Quite the opposite: the game was wildly popular on playgrounds across the city. Part of this was a space issue: inner cities were not the sorts of places to find enough open fields for football or suburban baseball diamonds, but concrete basketball courts fit easily into city parks in every neighborhood and required relatively few players and little equipment. New York had more public parks than any other city in the country.

In predominantly black neighborhoods such as Harlem and Bedford-Stuyvesant the park game developed its own ecosystem, with a distinct code of conduct and its own stars with names such as Earl "The Goat" Manigault and Herman "Helicopter" Knowings. In this world, the Madison Square Garden equivalent was Rucker Park on 155th Street and 8th Avenue, near the former site of the Polo Grounds stadium. Spectators unable to afford a ticket to the pros still had access to great summer-league games, especially if they could score a spot at the famed Rucker Tournament. People sat on the tops of buildings, in trees, on the fences, or on the nearby Macombs Dam Bridge just to catch a glimpse of play. It was showy, and it was aggressive. You couldn't see slam dunking on TV, but you could see it at the Rucker. "I wouldn't even try to compare it with college ball, because the games down here are more physical," said Julius Erving of his time sneaking off to the

Rucker as a high school player. Erving's nickname, "Dr. J," came from those playground games. For the impressionable fans, the top players were hugely influential, not just for how they played but for what they wore.

Back at the Garden, the Knicks' fortunes started to improve when the team registered back-to-back winning seasons. Walt Frazier's chance to prove himself on the Knicks would come at the end of a third straight winning season during the 1970 NBA finals, which pitted New York against its cross-continental rivals, a Los Angeles Lakers team led by greats Wilt Chamberlain and Jerry West. The Lakers had been to the finals in six of the last eight seasons, while the Knicks were slowly shaking off their reputation as a team that had gone nearly a decade with a losing record. The 1969–70 Knicks were led to the championship by captain Willis Reed, a dominating center who was also the top scorer, but when he injured his leg in game five, it threw New York's chances of winning its first championship into doubt. He sat out the following game, and the Lakers stormed over the Knicks, bringing New York to the brink of defeat. Much attention had been placed on whether Reed would return for game seven. The rest of the Knicks were warming up when Reed took the court, only minutes before the tip-off. Waves of cheers spread though the Garden, giving the Lakers pause. Though the captain played only long enough to score the first two baskets of the game, it was enough to energize his teammates. Frazier stepped up and put in a career-high performance of 36 points, 19 assists, and 5 steals, pushing New York to victory. Forty years later, ESPN would name that game the greatest game seven in finals history. "If we played the Lakers ten more times, we would not have won," Frazier recalled. "But for this one game, everything came together."

Frazier, Reed, and the rest of the championship Knicks became the toast of the city—which, being the media capital of the country, pushed the players' stardom much farther than had they played in, for example, Milwaukee. The players wrote best-selling books about the experience. Frazier and two of his teammates appeared on *Sesame Street*. All that new exposure heading into the NBA's twenty-fifth season gave the league a big boost. In a few short years the Knicks had gone from getting bumped for the circus to being one of the driving forces of their sport's ascendance on the national stage.

The attention also turned the Knicks into fashion icons across the city. "If you didn't dress, the guys got on you about it," remembered the small forward Cazzie Russell of the world of big hats, gold chains, pearl cufflinks, and turtlenecks. Knicks forward and future US senator Bill Bradley's fashion sense, and the Princeton grad's propensity to carry books in his coat pocket, was deemed so dull that teammate Dick Barnett was drafted to improve his style. Barnett gave up after a couple of months. Of all the New York players, though, Frazier's look reigned supreme.

"After the game, we come out, going on the bus, and all these guys and girls would be around the bus just to see what I was wearing," Frazier said. "We were always competing to see who could outdress the other on the team." But it was no competition. Decked out in fur coats, tailored suits, and gold-chained medallions, sideburned or bearded, behind the wheel of his Rolls-Royce or walking down the sidewalk, Frazier's "Clyde" persona became iconic. The point guard was the subject of magazine photo shoots that involved the round bed and mirrored ceiling in his high-fashion, high-living apartment. Even standing in a filthy, graffiti-adorned New York City subway car for a photo shoot, he looked sharp in a dark suit, light tie, and wide-brimmed hat.

Frazier's mix of celebrity, style, and star power on the court began to attract a new kind of notice. Former New York Jets football player Bill Mathis went to Frazier one day and told him that

Puma wanted him to wear one of its shoes. The company would provide all the sneakers Frazier could want, plus $5,000. Frazier agreed. The only problem was that the basketball shoe Puma made, blandly titled Basket, was too heavy for its new marquee player's liking. He suggested a lighter, more flexible shoe, so Puma modified a version of the Suede, the same model used in Tommie Smith and John Carlos's 1968 Olympic protest.

With that, the 1973 Puma Clyde sneaker was born, making Frazier the first NBA player to have his own signature shoe. That was groundbreaking for a number of reasons. Chuck Taylor might've had a sneaker named after him, but this was well past his playing days. And there were other professional players endorsing sneakers at the time, but having a shoe named after a current player provided a certain level of free advertising. Anytime Clyde came up in conversation, it gave a small boost to the status of the shoe and vice versa. This was the consumer's chance to buy a small slice of the stylish, man-about-town image Frazier had cultivated.

The ad campaign highlighted both of Frazier's personas—cool, flashy "Clyde" and court-dominating Walt. One ad featured a picture of the basketball star in a geometric-patterned button-up shirt. Another offered a page of basketball tips such as how to take the ball from your opponent under the headline "I steal for a living." At the bottom of that ad, Clyde said, "If the shoes feel right on your feet, then you're going to feel better playing in them." This type of advertisement recalled Taylor's approach, the sales pitch disguised as a skills clinic. Frazier's shoe straddled old and new eras in sneaker marketing: advertisements with long copy such as this one, especially ones offering practical advice, were beginning to die out, replaced by simply a photo of the star himself, like other ads of his. The straightforward implication: if these shoes are good enough for Frazier, they're good enough for you.

Frazier in Clydes on the court was one thing, but Frazier in

Clydes on the street was something else entirely. For most people in New York, the Puma Clyde was the first suede sneaker they had seen. The Knicks' second championship title in 1973 raised the profile of the team and, by extension, the shoes. For many people in Harlem, it wasn't until they saw top players at Rucker Park wearing them that Clydes became "it" shoes. But once they were, they were *really* cool, with the one-two tastemaker punch of a high-rolling player like Frazier and neighborhood playground stars.

Brands were slow to capitalize on the phenomenon of people buying sneakers because they saw them elsewhere in their neighborhood, but with the Clyde, Puma was sitting on a eureka moment: it had a shoe that had made the leap from court to casual on the back of a recognizable player. By the mid-1970s, not many ballplayers were wearing the Puma Clyde anymore, but the shoe remained popular on New York City streets as casual wear. The Clyde's toughest opponent was now New York's weather. The city would spread salt on the winter snow to speed melting, but the salt ate away at the shoe's suede exterior. "We'd see a snowstorm and get happy," commented one Puma executive. People wanting to avoid buying replacement pairs sometimes carried a toothbrush around with them to brush off the street stains.

The sneaker's transition from sportswear to streetwear came from the bottom up—you wore what you saw in the neighborhood—as well as from the top down: you wore what you saw in the culture. Throughout the 1970s, Adidas' Stan Smiths, for one, were showing up on trendsetters far from the tennis court. In a promo photo for the Beatles' "Penny Lane" 45, John Lennon is wearing white Adidas sneakers, and he was photographed casually wearing a pair more than once. Walter Matthau wore a beat-up pair of Stan Smiths in *The Bad News Bears*. David Bowie wore a pair of the same shoes in press photos in his mid-1970s *Station to Station* period. Bringing it full circle back to sports, fans of the Liverpool soccer team started wearing Stan Smiths in the 1970s instead of team scarves or jerseys, partly in an attempt to avoid being singled out by rival football hooligans intent on beating up Liverpool supporters. Other models were catching on in pop culture as well. Rolling Stones Keith Richards and Mick Jagger wore Adidas Gazelles in the early 1970s. The young Michael Jackson was sometimes photographed in a pair during his Jackson 5 days.

By the end of the 1970s, Frazier had been traded to the Cleveland Cavaliers; his playing career had been downgraded, as had his sneaker endorsing. He left Puma to sign with Spalding, a company that, despite making an early sneaker, was known more for its basketballs. Frazier again had a signature shoe: the suede Spalding Clyde Frazier.

So much had changed in the sports and sneaker world in a few short years. As many sports shook off the rules of amateurism, athletes were becoming brand spokespersons. Thanks to televised broadcasts, sports audiences were expanding, as was the public's conception of when and where sneakers could be worn. Sneaker companies and their stars weren't the only ones driving this shift. Throughout the 1970s, a social movement was taking shape that emphasized a revolutionary idea: that anyone can be an athlete.

8

EVERYONE IS DOING IT

One Sunday morning in 1962, Bill Bowerman went for a jog in the lush hills of New Zealand. Earlier in the year, he had led his Oregon Ducks track and field team to its first NCAA championship, but now, after a minute of running, he was winded.

Bowerman had crossed the Pacific Ocean to seek the advice of Arthur Lydiard, New Zealand's Olympic track coach, who had trained three medalists at the Rome Games two years earlier. They had been corresponding for years about shoes, track surfaces, and coaching strategy, and now Bowerman wanted to see Lydiard in person and learn firsthand how the Kiwi coach was training so many distance and cross-country greats. How could a tiny island nation of 2.5 million produce two Olympic running gold medalists at the 1960 Games when Great Britain, a country of 52 million, had produced only one?

To loosen the Oregon coach up from the previous day's flight, Lydiard invited Bowerman to join his running club on a light run. The idea of the run hardly seemed of any concern to the six-foot-two, 200-pound Bowerman, a former college football player and track star. Even at fifty years old, the crew-cut Bowerman still looked the part of the confident military man he had been two decades before. More than a hundred people had gathered at a residential park in Auckland for the weekend run—men and women, young and old. Bowerman noticed that a majority of them were, like him, over forty. The Auckland Joggers Club had been among the first jogging clubs in the world to be established, and on that particular day, its members were set to run around One Tree Hill, a 600-foot volcanic peak in the middle of the city draped with a layer of green grass. Lydiard assured Bowerman that he would be just fine with the slow group. With that, hundreds of Aucklanders took off in what to Bowerman resembled more a cross-country race than a light Sunday jaunt.

"I went about a hundred yards and I'm huffing and puffing and they're laughing and running on ahead," Bowerman said.

The pack of runners turned.

"Then we started going up this hill," he recalled years later. "God, the only thing that kept me alive was the hope that I would die."

A seventy-six-year-old jogger who had survived three heart attacks took pity on Bowerman and ran at his pace while making polite conversation. The track coach was too out of breath to respond. The jogger led him down a shortcut to meet up with the rest of the group. Stunned that he was so out of shape, Bowerman spent the rest of the trip jogging before breakfast, sometimes with Lydiard, sometimes with other runners. When he returned to the United States a few weeks later, his wife noticed that he was ten pounds lighter than when he had left.

Lydiard was considered one of the best coaches in the world and had developed a training philosophy still widely used today, in which intensive workouts are interspersed with lighter, easier ones to give the body time to rest and recover. His "Train, don't strain" maxim gelled nicely with Bowerman's "hard-easy" method of alternating strenuous workouts with lighter recovery ones. At the base of that training was an aerobic conditioning exercise that was just starting to catch on; Lydiard called it "jogging," popularizing the term for the trotting pace of his slowest runners. He had come to appreciate jogging the same way Bowerman had: by being bested at it by someone much older. Bowerman was fascinated. He held the highest respect for Lydiard's coaching, but he realized that one reason so many great distance runners were coming out of New Zealand was that the culture was already there, even for those who would never compete in the Olympics. New Zealanders were putting themselves at the top of the running world by running en masse.

Upon his return to Eugene, Bowerman started a jogging club. He was surprised at how many locals, of varying physical condition, turned out. At the time the most popular physical leisure activities were bowling, golfing, and tennis. Bowerman recruited his University of Oregon runners to lead the groups and partnered with a local cardiologist to come up with a training regimen for nonathletes. Many Eugene residents came to jog in whatever they happened to be wearing: gardening shoes, trousers, or, in one woman's case, a Sunday hat and trench coat. "You yourself are the only equipment necessary," Bowerman would later write. "Many fitness programs cost a great deal before the first workout. Not so with jogging. Ladies with only high heels will need a pair of flats."

IN THE 1960S, RUNNING IN PUBLIC was reserved for athletes and eccentrics. Early joggers were often harassed by motorists who threw beer cans or taunts. One Nike employee was told to "get a horse." "It wasn't popular, it wasn't unpopular—it just was," Knight recalled years later. "To go out for a three-mile run was something weirdos did, presumably to burn off manic energy. Running for pleasure, running for exercise, running for endorphins, running to live better and longer—these things were unheard of." Big-city joggers sought out secluded areas and early-morning hours; one Chicago executive used his sports car's odometer to plot a two-mile course for himself before taking up the sport. Even South Carolina senator Strom Thurmond was said to have been stopped by the Greensboro, South Carolina, police in 1968 for jogging.

THE JOGGING BOOM IN OREGON was helped along by clubs run by Bowerman's athletes. One of the most talented was a runner from Coos Bay named Steve Prefontaine, who joined the Oregon team in 1969. "Pre," as he was known, had already shattered high school records when Bowerman wrote him a letter courting him to the team, a rarity for the Oregon coach. "It blew my mind," Pre said of the letter. "Just two paragraphs. It said something like if I want to go to Oregon, under his guidance and supervision, there was no doubt in his mind that I'd be the greatest distance runner in the world. Man, all I could think of was where's the dotted line, I'll sign."

Pre never missed a practice or a race, but his cockiness sometimes clashed with Bowerman's way of doing things. In one exchange, Pre told the coach he didn't want to run the 2 mile. Bowerman replied, "Where are you going to run next week?" Pre turned and walked away. A few steps later, he reconsidered. "Well, I'll run the 2 mile, but I'm not going to like it." He ended up setting a school record in the event.

Pre's profile blew up in June 1970 when the freshman runner was featured on the cover of *Sports Illustrated*, decked out in Oregon green and yellow. (Opposite the contents page in that issue was a full-page ad for the reigning American sneaker company of the day: "All Stars for all stars.") In the 1970s, track and field occupied more of the American sports appetite than it would four decades later. A month after the Pre cover story *Sports Illustrated* featured distance runner Frank Shorter shaking hands with his Soviet rival Leonid Mikitenko after Shorter's upset win in Leningrad. A friend and training partner of Prefontaine, Shorter described their races as being so intense that they became friends again only after crossing the finish line. In all, track and field stars were featured on the cover eighteen times that decade. The 1970 Pre article was as much about his talent and promise as it was about Bowerman's legendary reputation. But though the coach and Phil Knight had been selling shoes for several years, nowhere in the article were Blue Ribbon Sports or Tiger shoes mentioned. In other words, the sports-watching public in 1970 knew more about an Oregon freshman than they did about Bowerman's side business.

Pre attracted crowds of thousands to Oregon's Hayward Field, many locals now excited about the sport thanks to Bowerman's clubs. Pre, a running evangelist himself, conducted jogging sessions, visited schools to talk to kids, and even coached inmates at the Oregon State Penitentiary, a detail only his closest friends knew. It wasn't for nothing that *Runner's World* compared Pre to Muhammad Ali in 2016; nothing seemed to stop him from working to be the fastest distance runner of all time. He once raced the 5,000 meters with a lacerated foot that bled through his shoe—and still managed to win. Audiences in Oregon lapped up each victory.

Around this time, pockets of grassroots runner mania were popping up outside of Oregon. In New York City, a Romanian immigrant named Fred Lebow made his money by making cheap knockoffs of designer fashions. He made his name by organizing a 26.2-mile race in Central Park in 1970. The first New York City

Marathon had only fifty-five finishers and was so far down on the city's radar that the runners had to dodge baby strollers and bicycles. Under Lebow's direction, the marathon course grew beyond Central Park and set the model for other urban marathons to follow. Runners snaking through the city directly exposed the sport to the city's five boroughs, chipping away at the idea that running long distances was only for the elite.

The 1974 New York City Marathon winner, Norbert Sander, recalled racing again two years later, the first time the marathon extended through the whole city. He passed a homeless man who seemed inspired. "He said, 'Next year, I'm going to do it,'" Sander said. "That is the beauty of it."

The New York City Marathon became so successful that in 1981, the organizers of the first London Marathon looked to Lebow for advice on how to set up a race that wove through the streets of a major city. The road, once a jog-at-your-own-risk area, became the center of the growing movement. To accommodate that interest, the New York City Parks Department installed twenty jogging tracks in 1968. Shorter, more approachable races sprang up throughout the 1970s, and the heightened visibility attracted a diverse audience, one that suddenly *wanted* to be seen jogging. One New York Road Runners board member said, "The park became the best singles bar in New York and all you had to do was show up in the evening and say to a guy or a girl, 'gee, where'd you get those shoes?' and bang, you had a relationship." "Fun runs" introduced the concept that racing could be more about participation than running fast or even finishing. Jogging was the "anyone can do it" sport. Sears, Roebuck even sold a brightly colored jogging outfit for children that came with a log to chart progress.

With one major asterisk: though running attracted both men and women, women were long excluded from competition. Women had been marginalized from organized competitive activity ever since the end of World War I, when sports programs in schools had all but disappeared, and misguided conceptions about the fragility of women's bodies persisted. They were excluded from most of the large established races, especially marathons, for reasons stemming from a long-held Victorian view on the effect of exercise on women. An 1898 article in the *German Journal of Physical Education* summarized: "Violent movements of the body can cause a shift in the position and a loosening of the uterus as well as prolapse and bleeding, with resulting sterility, thus defeating a woman's true purpose in life, i.e., the bringing forth of strong children." Views hadn't changed much in the intervening years. In 1966, when twenty-three-year-old Bobbi Gibb opened an envelope from the race director of the Boston Marathon, she expected to see her race number. Instead a note from the race director said, "Women aren't allowed, and furthermore are not physiologically able." Gibb, numberless, ran the race anyway.

Gibb was hardly alone, of course, in challenging this notion of sports not being for women. The following year a twenty-year-old Syracuse University journalism student named Kathrine Switzer skirted the issue by registering for the Boston Marathon as "K. V. Switzer." In the middle of her race, one of the officials, seeing that she was breaking the strict gender rule, charged at her and screamed, "Get the hell out of my race and give me those numbers!" Switzer's boyfriend shoved the official out of the way while press cameras caught the whole ordeal. Switzer finished the race and made sympathetic headlines—the photos of the distressed Switzer being lunged at by an angry man helped—but despite the bad press, the Boston Athletic Association didn't allow women to compete until 1972.

In 1973, Waldniel, West Germany, held the first all-women's marathon, and in 1979, the New York City Marathon added a women's division, which was won by the Norwegian Grete Waitz in a record time of 2:32, a drop of about an hour off the women's record of fifteen years earlier. A women's race was finally included in the 1984 Los Angeles Olympics and won by the American Joan Benoit, bringing added attention to the sport in the country as well as to the fact that US women could be fierce competitors on the world stage.

THE SNEAKER INDUSTRY WAS STILL in such an early stage in the 1960s that sometimes all it took to create a successful company was a single well-executed idea. In 1906, the New Balance Arch Support Company was founded in a small town outside Boston. Initially the company manufactured arch supports and orthopedics and was content enough to remain small with modest growth. In 1960, it hit upon a novel idea: foot length had always determined the size of a mass-produced shoe, but what about foot width? That year it introduced its ripple-soled Trackster running shoe, available in a range of half-inch widths. It was a revolutionary idea, but very little effort was put into marketing the shoe; most Trackster sales consisted of mail orders to colleges and high schools. A little more than a decade later, New Balance Shoes (Arch Support had been dropped from the name) was sold to a twenty-eight-year-old sales manager named Jim Davis for $100,000, the same amount as the company's annual sales. Davis inherited a company with a loyal customer base but only six employees churning out a few dozen pairs of Tracksters from a garage in Watertown, Massachusetts.

Davis was determined to take his well-fitting shoes to a market beyond New England. "Show me a runner whose shoes don't fit and I'll show you a loser," he would later be quoted as saying in a New Balance magazine ad. Davis wondered how much of a facelift the brand needed to attract a wide audience. "Do I need a new name?" he asked his designer, who responded that "New

Balance" was just fine, but the "nursing home Adidas" look of the shoes would have to go. Instead, an italicized capital *N* would grace the sides, and each model of the shoes would be known by a number, not a name.

Davis's dream of nationwide recognition came much sooner than he could've expected. The jogging boom's tidal wave raised the fortunes of every company in the running shoe game, but none more than New Balance. The brand received a mention in a 1975 issue of *Runner's World*, which was exciting enough, but the real reward came in the magazine's October 1976 issue, which named the New Balance 320 model the best running sneaker in its inaugural shoe guide. Just like that, everyone wanted the little shoe that could from the Northeast. The company had taken seventy years to reach a sales level of $100,000, and in 1976 alone sales registered $1 million. The following year New Balance recorded $4.5 million in annual sales. The brand had arrived.

The jogging boom was also fueling Nike. The Waffle Trainer was first sold to the public in 1974 and caught on nearly instantly, selling so many pairs that the company had to borrow money to produce more shoes. That year the company's total sales were $4.8 million. The following year, it was pulling in $8 million, $3.3 million from the Waffle Trainer and other racing flats alone. Early ads for the shoe played up the origin story: a picture of the shoes inside a waffle iron was captioned with large black letters reading "Hot Waffles."

Pre was an early wearer of the waffle shoes. Nike put him on the payroll for $5,000 a year and had business cards made up to read "National Public Relations Manager," making Prefontaine the young company's first paid athlete. Far from being stuck behind a desk, Pre contributed in the form of his many trips to Europe for races and his network of friends among international elite racers, many of whom were sought out for opinions on a particular model of shoes. Often a fellow runner would receive a box of Nikes with a note from Pre reading "Try these. You'll love them." At the same time, Pre couldn't be tied down. He usually raced in Adidas but sometimes wore Puma, Onitsuka Tigers, or even North Star, a Canadian brand.

The Nike job was partly for Bowerman to get Prefontaine out of a bartending job he thought didn't gel with the runner's role-model status. But Pre was going to do what he wanted to both on the track and off. He once announced to his fans that he would race a mile at Hayward Field and a thousand people turned out, despite the fact that Eugene's farmers had chosen that day to torch their fields to burn off weeds. When the winds changed, the black smoke blew over the city, an incident later known as "Black Tuesday." Rather than disappoint the people who had come to see him, Pre ran the mile anyway, clocking 3:58.3 minutes and hacking up blood from the soot in the air.

Nike's sales continued to climb year after year. People were snatching up jogging shoes almost as quickly as they could be produced. But—crucial to the lasting success of Nike, New Balance, and Adidas—not all of them were being used for running. The Converse All Star and Keds Champion had outlived their usefulness in competitive sports, but the companies were able to sell the same model of shoes year after year because they had managed to make the leap to casualwear. Jogging shoes such as the Cortez and the New Balance 320 had comfort on their side and had even started to become cool.

Sneakers, especially Nikes, were showing up more and more in pop culture. Nike had a guy in Hollywood handing out the shoes to any actor who would take them. The shoes made appearances in *The Incredible Hulk*, *Starsky & Hutch*, and *The Six Million Dollar Man* before their big break: Farrah Fawcett-Majors. A poster of the twenty-nine-year-old actress wearing a red swimsuit launched her career from bit parts in commercials to a starring role in the detective show *Charlie's Angels*, the most iconic part of which was Fawcett-Majors's blond, blown-out hairdo. In a 1977 episode, Fawcett-Majors's character escaped from a bad guy by riding away on a skateboard while wearing a pair of Nike Senorita Cortezes. Fawcett-Majors paired the white sneakers with bell-bottoms and a red top that matched the red of the sneaker's swoosh. A poster of that moment in the episode was soon available, Fawcett-Majors posing on a skateboard, her Nikes on full display.

The company couldn't have dreamt of better advertising. Here was a young, attractive star exposing Nike to an entirely new segment of the population: one that didn't necessarily have an interest in jogging but wanted to look like a famous actress. After the episode aired, stores had trouble keeping "the Farrah shoe" on the shelves. The effect compounded: the more sneakers found their way into magazines, TV shows, and photo spreads, the more accepted it became to wear gym shoes outside the gym.

THE 1972 OLYMPIC GAMES IN Munich will never shake off the horrific images of the hostage standoff and massacre by Palestinian terrorists that left eleven Israeli athletes and coaches and one German policeman dead. But when the games resumed after a period of mourning, America's eyes were on its distance running team. After leading much of the 5,000-meter race, Pre placed a disappointing fourth, leaving the hopes of American running in the hands of Pre's wiry, mustachioed twenty-four-year-old teammate Frank Shorter, and Kenny Moore, who ran at Oregon under Bowerman. Shorter won the marathon, becoming the first American to do so in sixty-four years, while Moore finished fourth. *Life* magazine ran a cover of Shorter, calling him "the happy exception" to the "Haywire Olympics."

Shorter's victory did more than just contribute to the United States' medal tally.

"When Americans saw an American could win this race," he recalled years later, "I think it kind of planted the seed . . . people started to think about the marathon differently. In a way I was kind of demystifying it, because I don't think people saw me as, sort of, any kind of physically imposing or different type of athlete. I came from sort of a standard American middle class background." It was just the spark his countrymen needed to spur the next phase of the jogging boom: getting serious.

It was still the "anyone can do it" sport, but average runners now wanted to see just how good they could get. *Runner's World* saw its circulation jump from 35,000 in 1975 to more than 200,000 in 1978, and a number of books made up the sacred texts. In 1967, Bill Bowerman partnered with a cardiologist to write a book titled simply *Jogging*, which sold more than a million copies. The following year, air force colonel and doctor Kenneth H. Cooper published *Aerobics*, which promoted exercises such as jogging to improve cardiovascular health. Also in 1967, a thirty-five-year-old magazine editor from Connecticut named Jim Fixx pulled a tendon playing tennis and took up jogging to rehabilitate his injury. When Fixx, a 220-pound, two-packs-a-day smoker, ran his first race, he finished dead last in a field of fifty. The winner, much to Fixx's amazement, was sixty years old. In 1977, Fixx published *The Complete Book of Running*, a guide that, in his words, would "first . . . introduce you to the extraordinary world of running, and second . . . change your life." Fixx's own life had changed dramatically; by the time his book hit the shelves, he had dropped 61 pounds and kicked his smoking habit. The book spent eleven weeks at the top of the best-seller list.

Americans had latched onto the idea of running as transformation, or at least as a way to slim down and get healthy. The cardiologist George Sheehan's half-dozen books on running and fitness emphasized the health aspects of running, as Fixx's did, but added the additional dimension of running as a way of people "finding themselves." His many articles and books focused as much on philosophy, religion, and introspection as they did on running. The doctor frequently traveled the country for speaking engagements at various conventions, corporate gatherings, and running groups to spread the Gospel of Jogging.

As a testament to how far the activity had come, the July 4, 1977, cover of *People* magazine featured a jogging Farrah Fawcett-Majors and her husband, *Six Million Dollar Man* star Lee Majors, beside the headline "Everybody's Doing It." Even Jimmy Carter joined the trend, declaring a National Jogging Day in October 1978 and positioning himself as the first "jogging president," notwithstanding his collapse during a 10K road race.

AFTER HIS PERFORMANCE in the 1972 Games, Steve Prefontaine quipped that Eugene, Oregon, would name a road after him: Fourth Street. The disappointing finish fueled his motivation for a better showing at the next Olympics. In May 1975, he invited the Finnish track and field team to Oregon for a special track meet, hoping that Olympic gold medalist Lasse Virén would agree to a rematch in the 5,000 meters. When Virén couldn't make it, Frank Shorter stood in for him; Prefontaine handily beat him to clock the second-fastest American 5,000 meters ever, 2 seconds off his own record time. After a going-away party for the visiting athletes, Prefontaine gave Shorter a ride home. After Pre had dropped his friend and training partner off, his butterscotch-colored MGB convertible swerved on a twisty road, hit a rock wall, and flipped over, killing the twenty-four-year-old runner.

It's tough to say what Pre would've accomplished had he lived.

In his lifetime, he held every US record from 2,000 to 10,000 meters, yet never set a world record or won an Olympic medal. Pre attracted a cult of admirers after his tragic young death in a way that's usually reserved for rock stars. "Pre's rock," the rock his convertible hit on Skyline Boulevard in Eugene, has become a place of pilgrimage for runners of all abilities, where many leave race numbers, medals, and sneakers. His records have long since been broken but his legacy has continued: two decades after his time at Oregon came dueling biopics, *Without Limits*, starring Billy Crudup and Donald Sutherland as the athlete-coach pair, and *Prefontaine*, featuring Jared Leto and R. Lee Ermey. He has featured heavily in Nike ad campaigns over the years, whether they happened to be about a rereleased Waffle Trainer, the Nike Air, or just the company in general. Nike even sold a shirt with the runner's face, stenciled like Che Guevara's, above the words "Pre Lives." Pre's image, forever to sell Nikes in the afterlife.

Bowerman retired from coaching at Oregon in 1972 but remained on the Nike board until 1999, the year of his death. (Late in life he suffered from nerve damage from inhalation of toxic chemicals during a lifetime of poorly ventilated shoe experiments.) Over the years he made numerous threats to resign from the board over design issues, suggesting in one of thirty-one such letters that an unsatisfactory running shoe be renamed the "shit shoe." But those letters were taken less as grievances and more as reminders that the company's early success had been due to good design. At the height of the jogging boom, Bowerman reflected on one tangible benefit of his life's work: just how much weight running shoes had shed over the years.

"You can bet there wouldn't be so many people running today," Bowerman said in 1979, "if they had to carry all the extra baggage we had back then."

9

MEANWHILE, ON THE WEST COAST

Millions of people saw Patti McGee perform the most difficult trick in skateboarding. The blond, nineteen-year-old San Diego native placed both hands on either side of a wooden skateboard and flipped herself up into a handstand, her bare feet in the sky with the board in motion. A photographer snapped the picture of the national girls' skateboard champion, which ran on the May 14, 1965, cover of *Life* magazine. With the magazine's circulation of more than 7 million, the cover encapsulated skateboarding in the mid-1960s: McGee's breezy California style, the headline "The Craze and the Menace of Skateboards," and even the small bandages on McGee's red-soled feet.

Skateboarding traces its roots directly to California surf culture. The first surf shop opened in 1956 under a Huntington Beach pier as the sport was becoming a regional phenomenon, but it was popular culture that elevated surfing from obscurity to the definition of cool. In the hit 1959 movie *Gidget*, the young Sandra Dee finds her way into the world of the Kahuna, Moondoggie, and other California surfers. To the Beach Boys, the "Surfin' Sa-fari" began "at Huntington and Malibu [where] they're shooting the pier" and quickly spread across "Surfin' U.S.A." to "all over Manhattan and down Doheney Way." The group's first four out of five singles mentioned surfing; Jan and Dean's 1963 single "Surf City" promised a world where there were "two girls for every boy." Almost from the start southern California's wave culture was as much lifestyle as sport. A sunny world filled with surf, sand, and scantily clad beachgoers was an easy fantasy to sell.

The term "sidewalk surfing" began to appear around the same time "Surf City" was climbing to number one on the charts. Skate-boarding began as little more than a dry-land adaption of surfing, with early boarders borrowing everything down to the polished wooden boards of their aquatic counterparts and the lingo; "eat-ing it" meant falling off your board in both sports. The first rid-ers, surfers who took to the land if the waves were flat that day, rode barefoot; sneakers would've dulled the feel of the board that only skin on wood could provide. The result was to be expected: mangled and bloodied feet.

Skateboards were mass marketed beginning in 1958, though the construction was so simple it was easy to find DIY instruc-tion guides. Boards then were little more than an eighteen-inch-long hunk of wood with a pair of disassembled metal roller skates fastened to them—much smaller and thinner than the typical skateboard of today, which measures about thirty-one inches. Surfboard manufacturers added skateboards to their lineup and classed them up a little from the simple board and wheel design by mimicking the look and feel of their marquee products with lami-nated redwood or oak surfaces. They had little experience with the new sport's mechanics, though, and the clay and metal wheels of early boards were slippery and didn't turn very well. And a "wipeout" on pavement was much more painful than in the water.

Beyond the bored surfers of California, the skateboard caught on as a faddish toy, a variation on roller skates. Skateboard competitions even caught the eye of major broadcasters such as ABC and of national magazines, such as *Life* magazine, which published the cover shot of Patti McGee.

By the mid-1960s, however, public perception had started to shift. Instead of an activity "associated with conformist, simple Middle America" as it had been, skateboarding was, as *Life* succinctly put it, a "menace." In 1965, skateboards, the California Medical Association reported, caused more childhood injuries than bicycles. By that August, twenty US cities banned the practice from their streets and sidewalks. "Is skateboarding going the way of the hula hoop?" Charles R. Donaldson wondered in the *Los Angeles Times* in 1966. Yet those few who stuck with the fad long after it crested helped drive the rise of a new subculture.

In 1965, the Massachusetts-based Randolph Rubber Company hit on a then-novel idea: a sneaker made specifically for skateboarders. The Randy 720 was a blue suede low-top featuring a soft sole made from a rubber compound marketed as "Randyprene." The reinforced boat shoe was sold for $14.95 (about $90 today) at the first US skate shop, Val Surf in North Hollywood. Mark Richards, a co-owner of Val Surf and an early skater, appeared in an advertisement for the shoe, which departed from the usual white or black color. "Being the first to wear a blue shoe was pretty brave," Richards said. "I remember taking quite a bit of flak for it."

"WE'RE GOING TO BE FINE," Paul Van Doren told his family when he explained how their lives were about to change. "He lined the five of us kids up," recalled middle child Steve Van Doren, who was ten years old at the time, "and he just said 'hey, I quit my job; we're going to start a new company. There can be no 'can I's,' can I have this, can I have that." It wasn't as shocking a decision as it might have been—Van Doren had worked in the shoe business his entire life—but it would be a huge gamble. Luckily, that was Van Doren's specialty. He had left school in eighth grade, opting to instead spend time at a horseracing track. He would offer odds on the races in the mid-1940s for a dollar, big money at the time, and his boldness earned him the nickname "Dutch the Clutch." When Van Doren's mother found out what he had been doing instead of going to school, she hauled the young Paul into the Randolph Rubber Company, where she worked, and got him a job making shoes.

In the years before "Randy's" introduced the first skate shoe, Van Doren had worked his way up to executive vice president. He faced a new challenge: turning around a factory in Garden Grove, California, that was leaking millions of dollars each month. He enlisted his brother Jim and longtime friend Gordon Lee to help revamp the shoe production in the Golden State. It took them only eight months to make the factory profitable. Three months after that, Dutch the Clutch reassured his family that everything would indeed be fine.

In the mid-1960s, any new sneaker company had to go up against the juggernaut brands of the time: Converse, Keds, PF Flyers, and Van Doren's old company, Randy's, which had grown to be the third largest manufacturer in the United States. Amid that tough competition, the brothers Van Doren, Lee, and a Belgian associate of Paul, Serge D'Elia, established the Van Doren Rubber Company.

Paul's confidence stemmed from years of watching Randy's sell hundreds of thousands of shoes, but on a margin of only a few cents per pair. Retailers received most of the per shoe profit. If he could operate both the factory and the retail stores, Van Doren reasoned, he'd effectively remove the middleman and enjoy a far more comfortable margin. Plans were made to open a combination factory, office, and retail store called the Van Doren Rubber Company at 704 East Broadway in Anaheim, California, at the beginning of 1966. Old shoe-making machinery was shipped in piece by piece from across the country, and all through 1965, a sign out front read "Opening January!" As the schedule ran tight, a smaller "Would you believe February" was added to the sign, borrowing a recurring joke from the TV comedy *Get Smart*, in which the bumbling spy would revise his bluff when it wasn't convincing.

Setting up his own company was more complicated than Van Doren had anticipated. When opening day finally came in March, the problems multiplied. Their store was lined with shoe boxes, but the boxes were empty. The only thing yet produced was samples of the three different styles available, which were so new that the Van Dorens had not named them yet. The traditional boat shoe was style #44, available in four colors and selling for $4.49 a pair. All the Van Dorens could offer the twelve customers who showed up was a promise: pick out the style and color of the shoes you want, and they'd be ready for pickup later that afternoon. No one had thought to put cash for change into the register, so those first customers had to return another day to pay.

The opening-day supply hiccup would prove to be an opportunity. Once the factory was up and running, it took only a few days to fill the empty boxes. As Steve Van Doren tells it, not long after, two women came into the store, one wanting pink shoes and decided the pink sneakers available weren't bright enough for her. Paul Van Doren shook his head; the pink available was the only shade he had. Her companion wanted a yellow shoe, but in a softer tone. Van Doren knew he couldn't afford to carry so many different colors, but it got him thinking. "Ladies, go down the street about half a mile, there's a fabric store," Van Doren's son

Steve remembers him saying. "Buy half a yard of fabric and bring it back and I'll make you a pair of shoes out of whatever color you like because I can't have nine different colors of pink here."

Those original customers had come back to pick up their orders of sneakers, so why not offer the chance for people to custom order whatever shoe they wanted? At a time when the Converse All Stars were available in only a handful of colors, Van Doren was offering a unique deal. Want plaid shoes to match your Catholic school uniform? We can make them. Want red-and-gold sneakers to match your high school colors? We can make them too. Want leopard print, corduroy, Hawaiian shirt print, or any other fabric on your shoe? Why not, we'll give it a shot.

Word of mouth was the marketing strategy Paul Van Doren liked, not least because it didn't cost anything. In addition to the customizability, Van Doren wanted to build shoes so tough that customers would have to tell other people about them. On the surface, there wasn't much to visually differentiate a white Van Doren #44 from the simple design of Keds Champion tennis shoe. The canvas used for the first Vans was heavier than the kind used for Keds or the Converse All Star at the time, though, and the rubber sole was twice as thick as the one on PF Flyers' plimsolls. After hearing customer complaints that the sole cracked around the ball of the foot, Jim Van Doren (who, as a mechanical engineer, had set up the company's machinery), went to work recreating an indented wafflelike sole pattern.

During the first year, Vans was opening stores on an almost weekly basis around the region, and sales kept pace. The company's early success also had to do with California's year-round warm climate. In New England, where winter temperatures might just scratch above freezing, sneaker sales dipped as heavy boots replaced canvas. In Los Angeles, where January temperatures hovered around the sixties, sneaker season stretched nearly year-

round. California's "endless summer" also shaped its sports landscape, much the same way cold winters helped basketball spread
among gymnasiums across New England and the Midwest. Unbeknownst to Vans' founders, their company would become as
synonymous with a sport as Converse was with basketball and
Nike with jogging.

"OKAY, YOU CAN COME OUT for a while, but first you have to do Rat
Patrol," Tony Alva remembered the surfers telling him.

"Rat Patrol" was Alva's ticket to the hottest surfing spot in
Los Angeles, an abandoned amusement park in a rundown part
of town. Barely a teenager, Alva and his friend Jay Adams would
protect the area from interlopers until the older surfers deemed
them worthy enough to join them in the water.

"We'd sit up on the pier with these wrist rockets and this pile of
polished stones, and just bombard anyone who was from outside
our territory with whatever was available," he recalled. "Rocks,
bottles, rotten fruit."

By the end of the 1960s, surf rock had run its course, as had the
first skateboarding craze. The "endless summer" brand of surfing
imagined by the Beach Boys was gone, replaced with a rougher,
more gonzo version idolized by the young Alva and Adams. A
relic of the past became the headquarters of the new wave. Pacific
Ocean Park was a sea-themed amusement park built on a pier in
Santa Monica, once so well known it had been given equal bill-
ing with Disneyland in a Beach Boys song. The park shuttered its
gates in 1967, and as its roller coasters and boardwalks crumbled,
the surrounding Ocean Park neighborhood decayed with it, earning the area the nickname "Dogtown." Local surfers soon found
it to be a prime spot owing to its natural swells. Dogtown graffiti
proclaimed "Locals only" and "Death to invaders," two directives

Alva and Adams were meant to enforce. Now empty of crowds, the biggest thrill the old POP offered was below its pier: a hidden spot nicknamed "the Cove" where brave boarders attempted to weave along a wave under the derelict pier's wooden supports, dodging not just the dock pilings and rebar but pieces of detritus below the water's surface. "You could get impaled on a fallen roller coaster track or, like, a piling," said Alva years later.

· When the waves were flat, Alva and his friends looked for the next best thing: a place to try out their surfing moves on a skateboard. Some of the POP surfers talked about a high school in nearby Brentwood that had been built on a hillside and featured fifteen-foot concrete retaining walls, perfect for re-creating the low-to-the-surface moves Alva watched his favorite surfers do. "To a 12-year-old kid it was awesome," Alva says. "The asphalt had just been repaved, so the banks were really smooth and pristine—just these huge, glassy waves."

Alva and the other long-haired Dogtowners hung out at the nearby surf shop Jeff Ho Surfboards and Zephyr Productions. The shop sponsored first the Zephyr Surf Team, of which Alva and his fellow POP surfers were a part, and in 1975 the Zephyr Skate Team. The twelve so-called Z-Boys (including one Z-Girl, Peggy Oki) skated low to the ground, gliding and carving curves with a well-placed hand plant much as they did when surfing. Their moves were made possible by the polyurethane wheels that had replaced the old metal and clay ones, which provided faster rides and sharper corners over more surfaces.

Higher speeds and more elaborate tricks meant that barefoot riding was out and sneakers were in. The Randy 720 may have been designed for skating, but it stood up to the sport's rigors only to a point. A skateboard's brake is the shoe itself, the rubber often making an abrupt and blunt or slow and skidding impact with the pavement. As a result, one shoe would often wear out faster than the other, and well-worn shoes were sign of a veteran rider, not an inexperienced or careless one. "Trashed shoes are like a war wound, evidence of how hard you skate, not something to be embarrassed about," as one rider put it. How a shoe was worn down also acted as a kind of shibboleth to other skaters: those in the know could tell what style of skater someone was by the type of damage a pair of sneakers had sustained. Deep pockets for replacement shoes are not a hallmark of teenagers, so solutions to a holey sole or ripped upper came in the DIY form of duct tape or a sealant such as Shoe Goo.

Skateboarding was coming back out of obscurity, and the Z-Boys' first big test was the April 1975 Bahne-Cadillac National Skateboard Championships, which attracted hundreds of skaters from across the country to Del Mar, California. The skate team stood out in their uniform of a blue Zephyr T-shirt and matching blue Vans deck sneakers. Dressed in a flamboyant purple Hawaiian shirt, Z-Boys manager and Zephyr shop cofounder Skip Engblom stood out, too.

"There's our entries and there's our check," Engblom said when he reached the registration desk. "Where's our trophies?"

Early skateboard competitions often took place in parking lots, the skate area, a flat rectangle in which riders would perform their tricks, cordoned off by bales of hay. The scene resembled a figure skating competition with wild-haired teens in place of sequined outfits and ice. The Z-Boys' surfing-style tricks, with their fluid spinning and turning, made a sharp contrast to the other skaters, who were performing more of the gimmicky upright tricks and handstands popular a decade earlier when Patti McGee had made the cover of *Life*. "It was like Ferraris versus Model-T's," said Z-Boy Nathan Pratt. Rowdy behavior further set the Zephyrs apart from the other skaters. As no one really knew how to score the Z-Boys' style, Jay Adams and Tony Alva placed third and fourth, respectively, in the junior men's freestyle. Z-Girl Peggy Oki fared better, winning the women's freestyle event. Their moves caught on fast; at each subsequent skate competition there were more people emulating, and trying to dethrone, the Zephyr team.

By the mid-1970s, more brands were seizing on the community of serious skaters, who also happened to be impressionable young consumers. Makaha Sportswear released a shoe in 1976, the Radial, that promised to "break the deck/shoe barrier." The Radial featured a stiff sole with suction-cup-like circles on the bottom, as if, like Kihachiro Onitsuka, they'd been contemplating an octopus. Hobie, another California board brand, created a blue suede high-top with a small tag sewn on the back of the tongue: "For skateboarding use only / not designed for other activities." Skaters appropriated other brands, too, especially high-top basketball shoes. In Germany skaters gravitated to the Adidas Handball shoe, though skateboarding's countercultural status conflicted with the comparatively more mainstream (for Germans of a certain age, anyway) handball. "My father was also wearing 'Handball' shoes," recalled the half-pipe specialist Claus Grabke. "He was actually a handball player. Skateboarding was an escape from the world of the parents, so there was no way I could have worn those."

HISTORY IS FULL OF the outsized effects of seemingly minor events, and, as we've already seen, nowhere is that truer than in the development of sports, that corner of culture where backyard games become multimillion-dollar industries. Strange confluences are at the heart of the story of sneakers—Charles Goodyear had no idea how many innovations would depend on his discovery of vulcanized rubber. Robert Moses and his New York City Parks Department could hardly have foreseen how building city parks with basketball courts in them would provide the environment for urban basketball, hip-hop, and streetwear fashion to thrive in. Whoever made the griddle pattern on Bill Bowerman's waffle iron inadvertently contributed to the modern running shoe. And one of the pivotal moments in the rise of skateboarding, and its sneakers, was something no one could have seen coming: a change in the weather.

As wild an impression as the Z-Boys made at the 1975 Del Mar skate competition, it was the statewide drought the following year that would make the group's true influence felt. The backyard pools installed across the Golden State mostly sat empty as strict measures to conserve water were put into place. Per design trends, the pools generally had a smooth drop-off to the deep end and an angle-free bowl shape, which helped boarders skating in them pick up speed and rocket up the sidewalls—a step up from the concrete slopes of local high schools and drainage canals. Throughout 1976–77, all those perfectly shaped bowls were just sitting there, ripe for the taking and allowing boarders to get closer than ever to surfing on dry land. For the Z-Boys, finding the perfect pool was like finding the perfect wave at POP's Cove; once you came across a vacant house, you kept your find quiet lest other boarders crash your party. The Z-Boys would even bring pool-draining equipment or spend hours digging out dirt and debris if the prospective pool promised high curves and big air (and big falls).

The pools offered an exclusive, "members only" feel that the paved slopes of Santa Monica area schools hadn't, and they became laboratories of innovation as boarders swapped tricks and one-upped each other. In just a short time, those backyard guerrillas changed the sport in ways few other sports have experienced. Doing handstands or weaving between orange cones wasn't the height of excitement anymore; vertical-based, or "vert," tricks were.

One of the first things vert skaters discovered was the next-level beating their sneakers were taking. Vans' "Sherman tank" deck shoes, with their sturdy canvas, became L.A. skaters' first choice. Vans was quick to pick up on the new audience. Steep ramps and pool walls often flung errant boards skyward, only to bring them back down on a skater's feet and ankles; Vans patented an $8 cufflike Velcro-and-vinyl ankle guard to combat the problem. The company also began to distinguish itself by working directly with skateboarders. In 1976, in consultation with Z-Boys Tony Alva and Stacy Peralta, the company released its first skate-specific shoe, the #95, now known as the Era. Later that year Vans debuted a new logo: wedged in a cartoon skateboard appeared the words "Vans 'Off the Wall,'" referring to the moment when skaters shot off the side of a pool and into the air. For skateboarders, who wore one shoe out faster than the other, Vans' customization came in handy; you could just buy a replacement left shoe if you wanted to. In 1977, Vans paid Stacy Peralta $300 a month to advertise for it, making the twenty-year-old, who had had a cameo role in an episode of *Charlie's Angels*, the first skateboarder to cash sneaker endorsement checks. (Alva, meanwhile, left his association with Vans to start his own skateboard company.)

Then Hollywood stepped in. In 1981, Universal Studios asked Vans' PR rep for some sneakers to use on an upcoming movie set in a California high school. The rep sent the studio a newish slip-on model in a loud checkerboard pattern. The producers of that movie, *Fast Times at Ridgemont High*, liked the shoes so much that they became key to the wardrobe of the long-haired, laid-back slacker Jeff Spicoli, memorably played by the young Sean Penn. The film, released in 1982 and inspired by screenwriter Cameron Crowe's book of the same name, instantly became a teen movie classic. Spicoli's antic stoner was the face of the film, and his checkerboard Vans were his calling card. In one scene he takes the sneakers out of a blue shoe box (marked with Vans' "Off the Wall" logo) and hits himself over the head with them to demonstrate how high he is. The shoes were on all the posters as well as on the movie's sound track album cover, ensuring plenty of exposure for a brand still virtually unknown outside southern California. "We were about a $20-million company before the movie came out," reflected Paul Van Doren's son Steve, "and we were on track for $40 million to $45 million after that."

FOLLOWING THE *FAST TIMES AT RIDGEMONT HIGH* windfall, it was time for Vans to take another gamble. What had allowed the Van Doren Rubber Company to thrive up to this point was a reputation for producing a durable product, a loyal fan base, and a level of customization that companies relying on economies of scale couldn't afford. Vans didn't have the household-name athletes or design technology of brands like Nike, Adidas, or Puma. Now Jim Van Doren, who had been the president of the company since 1976 (Paul had assumed the chairman position and was dialing back his involvement), had a plan for Vans' next bet: diversification.

By the early 1980s, skateboarding's comeback wave had started to break. The skate parks that had popped up featured halfpipes and bowls mimicking swimming pools, but those elements proved to be injury magnets. Tricks got only more dangerous, and insurance rates spiraled higher even as overall attendance fell, forcing many of the parks to close. The market for skate sneakers tumbled, too. Nikes and Converses had simply been repurposed for the sport, but companies that relied on skate-specific shoes, such as the sporting goods manufacturer Wilson, saw the prices of their products tumble in a short amount of time. The price stickers on one box of Wilson shoes showed a markdown from $17.99 to $10.79 to $8 to $4 to $3 before the shoes ended up in a storage garage.

Jim Van Doren was looking to avoid that fate, and he knew the interest in checkerboard slip-ons wouldn't last forever. In 1982, he invested almost all of Vans' profits into a line of performance shoes named Serio. It seemed like a sure thing; the Olympics were coming to Los Angeles in 1984, and he felt the brand's "Made in the U.S.A." status could capitalize on sports-fueled patriotism. The line got off to a promising start when one of the company's jogging shoes received a five-star rating from *Runner's World*. Vans introduced Serio wrestling shoes, boxing shoes, break-dancing shoes, and even a skydiving shoe.

The same reasons for Vans' early success proved to be their undoing. Athletic shoes required a different production process than Vans' rubber and canvas plimsolls did, so the company had to rent space for a new factory. Taking a page from New Balance, the Serio shoes were available in a range of widths, and, as with Vans' traditional line, customers were able to choose from a variety of materials, sizes, and colors. All of that drove production costs up, as did the lack of inexpensive overseas labor. (It also didn't help that federal immigration agents rounded up 140 undocumented workers from Vans' Anaheim factory in 1984.) With no mainstream professional athletes or teams wearing the shoes, much less endorsing them, and no national advertising campaign, Vans couldn't hope to match the exposure or cachet of the larger brands. By Steve Van Doren's own admission, the Serios were only semisuccessful in Vans' own retail stores and nationally sold hundreds, not thousands, of pairs.

In 1984, nearly twenty years after its founding and two years since *Fast Times* put it on the national radar, Vans filed for Chapter 11 bankruptcy protection. The company's $12 million in debt prompted the bankruptcy court to remove Jim Van Doren as president. Echoing another pair of shoemaking brothers, Vans' financial trouble caused a rift in the Van Doren family. Like the Dasslers, the Van Doren brothers were not on speaking terms in the years after the split; also like the Dasslers, each Van Doren continued to run an athletic shoe company: Paul once again became the chief executive of Vans, while Jim started a company called Now of California. The latter business quickly fizzled, but Paul managed to pull his company out of bankruptcy by 1988, at one point telling employees to bring their own pens from home to save the expense.

After only a couple of years skating together, the Z-Boys went their separate ways. Some, like Alva, started their own companies. Stacy Peralta became a filmmaker and founded the legendary skate team the Bones Brigade, which included a young skater named Tony Hawk. The resurrected Vans returned to form by dropping the plan to compete with the Adidases and Nikes of the world in favor of returning to its roots: offering simple, custom-made shoes to a small but devoted market. As Nike had with the jogging boom, Vans had successfully capitalized on a niche sport—but it was going to stay niche for now. As with the surf, there was always another wave of skateboarding on its way. Another company, meanwhile, was hitting it big in a much larger untapped demographic.

10

LET'S GET PHYSICAL

A mostly shirtless Rice University track team carried Billie Jean King on a feathered throne to the biggest tennis match of her life. By September 1973, King had won ten Grand Slam singles titles and more than twice as many doubles titles, but more people were about to watch this exhibition match than any of those championships. More than 30,000 fans packed the Houston Astrodome to watch her play fifty-five-year-old Bobby Riggs, who, like the twenty-nine-year-old King, was both a former Wimbledon winner and number one–ranked player. The $100,000 match was billed as the "Battle of the Sexes," and the circuslike spectacle (Riggs made his entrance into the stadium accompanied by buxom young models) was broadcast to about 90 million worldwide viewers, opening, appropriately enough, with the song "Anything You Can Do, I Can Do Better."

The King-Riggs match was hardly the first time men and women had faced off in tennis. In a mixed-sex match in 1933,

Helen Wills had beaten the former NCAA champion Phil Neer in straight sets. Riggs had handily beaten the then–number one player Margaret Court in an earlier "Battle of the Sexes," but he had long been after King as an opponent. King had resisted Riggs's propositions because she felt a loss would set back the fragile progress women had made in the Open Era. Women's professional tennis had been around for only three years, and women's tennis circuits were fewer and far less lucrative than those of their male counterparts. Even in the biggest tournaments women played for less; King had walked away with £750 for her 1968 Wimbledon win, while Rod Laver, the men's champion, had won £2,000. But King eventually agreed to play Riggs.

"I can't play for money," King said in a press conference before the match. "I've got to play for a cause."

Riggs, meanwhile, doubled down on the chauvinism angle: "My goal is to keep our women at home, taking care of the babies, where they belong."

In the early 1970s, sneaker companies, especially those that made athletic shoes, weren't really paying attention to women. The jogging boom was unequivocally coed, but many early training shoes advertised to women, such as the Senorita Cortez, were built on a men's last. Keds' simple canvas shoes had staying power as casual wear, but their days as athletic shoes had passed many decades before, and PRO-Keds were popular on playgrounds in middle America and on New York City park basketball courts, but they were marketed mainly to men and boys. Few female sports stars had attained household-name status; King and her fellow tennis players Chris Evert and Margaret Court were more or less it. One reason for this was dismal school funding for women's and girls' sports. Prior to 1971, less than 1 percent of college athletic budgets went to women's athletic programs. Roughly 7 percent of varsity athletes were female. Companies such as the juggernaut

Adidas and the growing Nike followed the culture, essentially ignoring women as a viable audience.

King beat Riggs, winning the "Battle of the Sexes" in dramatic fashion. After winning in three straight sets, she tossed her racket straight up into the air as Riggs hopped the net to congratulate her and the crowd roared. King's victory came just when things were starting to shift for women in sports. Just a year earlier, in 1972, the revolutionary education amendment known as Title IX had paved the way for more equitable representation and funding. Under Title IX, there could be no discrimination based on sex for "any education program or activity receiving Federal financial assistance"—which meant, among other things, that every dollar spent on a men's high school or college athletic program had to be matched in a women's program. A lot of things were going to change.

On April 1, 1980, millions of people reached for their sneakers. At 5:30 that morning, New York City mayor Ed Koch was at a meeting in the fourteenth-floor office of the city's police commissioner to discuss what was to be done about a strike by the city's transit workers, which had brought subways and buses to a halt. The strike came as the city was just beginning to get back onto its feet following a disastrous near bankruptcy, famously exemplified by the 1975 *Daily News* headline about a proposed federal bailout: "Ford to City: Drop Dead." (The bailout ended up happening.) While the police commissioner was speaking about freeing up parking spaces to ease traffic congestion, Koch looked out the window at the Brooklyn Bridge and saw tens of thousands of people walking over it into Manhattan.

"This is going to save us," he thought.

The mayor left the meeting, the press in tow, and went down to the exit of the bridge. "Walk over the bridge!" he told his city, well aware that press cameras were recording this bit of political theater. Behind him people streamed into the borough for their Tuesday-morning work, applauding the mayor's words. "Walk over the bridge! We're not going to let those bastards bring us to our knees."

The strike lasted eleven days, during each of which Koch stationed himself at one of Manhattan's bridges to cheer on the pedestrian commuters. His constituents needed no encouraging; in a mess that coined the term "gridlock," they were doing what they had to do to get to work. Koch noticed their strange but practical uniform: suddenly the sight of men and women wearing sneakers with their business suits, often carrying tote bags with their dress shoes inside, became common.

"It looked a little weird at first, but it was sure better than wearing three-inch heels," recalled Kim Stroman, who wore white sneakers with her stockings as she walked over the Brooklyn Bridge to her job in lower Manhattan during the strike.

The explosion of interest in jogging, tennis, and basketball during the 1970s had made sneakers more varied and readily available than ever, and during the eleven-day strike New York stores saw an uptick in snap purchases. The transit strike demonstrated the reigning appeal of sneakers outside sports: they were the shoe you reached for if you needed to be comfortable. By the time of the 1988 movie *Working Girl*, the sneaker's place among working women, especially, was cemented enough to be a one-stop signifier of class division. Melanie Griffith's secretary character commutes via the Staten Island ferry in a pair of puffy white Reeboks, while her boss, who can afford to be impractical, arrives by hired car in a pair of stylish heels.

There was another story behind Melanie Griffith's sneakers. It was the story of how companies finally realized there was a serious demand for women's sneakers—as in sneakers actually designed for women, and not just for walking around. Farrah

Fawcett-Majors skateboarding in her Senorita Cortezes in 1977 had been a red herring (or maybe, considering her fan base, an indication that Nike had been targeting men all along). The next big innovation in American sneaker culture, like many before it, would have its roots abroad.

THERE WERE LEG LIFTS. There were pelvic thrusts. There were flailing arms and lunges that resembled a scarecrow blowing in the wind. There was even a move where one would plant both feet on the ground, bend down, slap the ground, swing the arms through open legs—and repeat. Above all, there was counting. Lots of counting.

The actress Jane Fonda saw all that after she fractured her foot in 1978 while filming a movie. By that point she was well known to audiences, not only for having won one Best Actress Academy Award and being nominated twice more but for her protests against the Vietnam War. The foot fracture prevented her from practicing ballet—which she had used to stay in shape for the past twenty years—even after the foot had healed. As an alternative, her stepmother recommended an exercise instructor in Los Angeles.

"Her class was a revelation," Fonda wrote later. "I entered so-called adult life at a time when challenging physical exercise was not offered to women. We weren't supposed to sweat or have muscles. Now, along with forty other women, I found myself moving nonstop for an hour and a half in entirely new ways."

Jogging may have been the first great exercise fad to sweep the nation, but for many people looking to get into shape, cardio work, especially when done in public, only held so much appeal. The workout routine that captured Fonda's attention was more intimate—just an instructor leading a small group in a series of stretching, stepping, and reaching routines. In 1979, Fonda and the fitness instructor opened their own aerobic exercise studio in Beverly Hills; Fonda herself even led some classes. The studio joined several others springing up across Los Angeles (notably Richard Simmons's Slimmons workout studio in 1974) offering gymgoers an alternative to weights or the treadmill.

In just a few short years, the fitness and aerobics movement wormed its way out of California and into pop culture. Olivia Newton-John's video for her 1981 song "Physical" had the unitard-wearing singer leading a gym full of pudgy men in weight lifting and aerobics as they transformed into scantily clad beefcakes. Also that year, Fonda published a book detailing her workout regimen, which featured the svelte actress's legs pointed straight up into the air. *Time* magazine ran a cover story in November of that year featuring a shot of five people holding pictures of their former "unfit" selves.

Aerobics also attracted those who wanted to skip the gym entirely. The late 1970s had seen the introduction of home video systems, and following the success of her book, a producer approached Fonda with the offer to produce a VHS version of her workout. It was the first video of its kind in a market still focused on providing feature films on demand—but you could watch a tape of *Jaws* only so many times. When *Jane Fonda's Workout* was released in 1982, it quickly became one of the top-selling video-cassettes up to that point, outselling its closest competitors, *Star Trek II: The Wrath of Khan* and *An Officer and a Gentleman*, and opening the door to a whole genre of "self-help" videos.

Baby boomers too shy to do leg lifts, neck rolls, or step and kicks in public could now do so in the privacy of their living rooms, while overscheduled stay-at-home moms and career women could avoid the hassle of attending fixed-time classes. By featuring a household-name celebrity such as Fonda, the exercise routine came into American homes with a familiar face. Her workout videos included a bold, if unspoken promise: yes, you *can* look like me, and I'm going to show you how. Fonda wasn't just another lithe ingenue, either; she was in her mid-forties when *Workout* first appeared. It was the final piece in her more or less single-handed elevation of aerobics to a national fad: here was a middle-aged woman with a very unstereotypically middle-aged body. But amid the leg warmers and the high-cut striped unitards Fonda and her companions wore in the video, one detail had gone overlooked: they were all barefoot.

Angel Martinez noticed that. He was a sales rep on the West Coast for Reebok, a British brand introduced to the United States only a few years before. He was driving back to San Francisco after a failed sales trip. Reebok was producing a few models of well-received running shoes, but now that the running boom had crested, stores were paring back their offerings, often carrying only established brands such as Nike, Tiger, and Puma. On the way home, Martinez paid a visit to his wife's new exercise class, which he'd heard was a fad growing out of the West Coast. The attendees complained of leg and foot pain; many exercised barefoot on carpeted floors, hardwood, or concrete. The answer clicked. "Aerobic shoes," he said to himself.

When participants in aerobics classes did wear sneakers, they were appropriated from other sports. "Shoes must allow for sideways movement," said the fitness pioneer Jacki Sorensen in 1981. Jogging shoes were totally inadequate; tennis shoes were better. When Martinez, an avid runner who knew the importance of purpose-built footwear, presented his idea of an exercise shoe to Reebok chief Paul Fireman, it was rejected. Fireman had never heard of aerobics. Martinez persisted and sketched a sneaker on a napkin; he took it to another Reebok executive, who ordered a prototype to be manufactured in East Asia. Martinez took the prototype to fitness instructors, who loved it. After more cajoling,

Fireman was convinced. The first shoes came back from the factory with a wrinkle around the toe, which the factory owner apologized for in a letter, saying they were working on correcting the mistake. The Reebok executives loved the wrinkles, however, which made the shoe resemble a ballet slipper. They ordered the factory to put the wrinkles back in, a process that took months.

Meanwhile, Nike was working hard to ignore the fitness boom. In 1980 Judy Delaney, a product developer at Nike's East Coast factory, repeatedly brought up the idea of an aerobics shoe for women, but her ideas were dismissed in favor of more models of running shoes. Two wives of Nike higher-ups took an exercise class together and asked their husbands to push for a proper aerobics shoe. Nike's corporate lawyer was having a postwork beer at a Portland bar when a group of men and women walked in after attending a class; afterward the lawyer phoned his boss, Phil Knight, excitedly claiming that "the future is aerobics," but nothing came of the call. Even Bill Bowerman had been writing memos saying the company should be making aerobic shoes, but to no avail. Nike exec Rob Strasser was heard to say the company would never "make shoes for those fags who like aerobics." With Nike determined to ignore the new market, the stage was set for Reebok to step in.

In 1982, the Reebok Freestyle fitness shoe hit the shelves. The Freestyle didn't look like anything Nike, Adidas, or Puma was making at the time. For one, it wasn't bulky, especially showy, or packed with technological gimmicks; in fact, it appeared flimsy. It came in white but was also available in the unfamiliar shades of pastel pink and blue. The upper was made of garment or glove leather, much softer and more pliable than the leather used for other sneakers at the time, hence the wrinkles around the toe. Freestyle wearers found them so comfortable that they didn't need to be broken in. The most distinctive feature of the high-top variation of the sneaker was the three poufy ankle supports and the two thin Velcro straps to keep them in place. Nike's designers at one factory laughed at the Freestyle when they first saw it.

Fireman ordered 32,000 pairs of the Freestyle, a big gamble. Sales were quiet the first week, until Martinez came up with a promotion that offered two free weeks at a Richard Simmons fitness class with each purchase. The 32,000 pairs sold out in a matter of days. Next the company used a strategy Martinez had thought up when he was dropping in on his wife's fitness classes.

"If on Monday the instructor was wearing a pink headband, by Wednesday, everybody was wearing a pink headband," he said. Rather than try to match the advertising budget of a Nike or an Adidas, Reebok began handing the Freestyle out for free to aerobics instructors. For the thousands of women who took aerobics classes, those ordinary endorsers provided a level of trust not present with a celebrity athlete. Reebok didn't even have to court aerobics' one bona fide celebrity, Jane Fonda; she was already wearing the Freestyle in her later exercise videos because they happened to be the most popular. Sales begat sales.

Two other factors came along at the just the right time to help the Freestyle succeed. The first was the retail sneaker stores that were suddenly popping up at shopping malls across the country. Before the 1980s were out, Foot Locker and the Athlete's Foot had become mainstays in the same way that stores such as JCPenney and the Gap had a few years before. Shopping malls, and the culture that came with those "pyramids to the boom years," as Joan Didion called them, were in many ways a throwback to the days of the town square. Just as the village shoemaker had once been the only place to get your shoes, now the mall's athletic shoe store was the place to get your sneakers. No longer would a shopper have to go to an obscure specialty store or resort to mail order.

The malls themselves helped. An innovation of the 1950s,

indoor suburban shopping malls really came into their own in the 1970s and '80s; they kept customers comfortable inside and milling around with air-conditioning, fountains, open spaces, restaurants, and music. The 1978 zombie movie *Dawn of the Dead* riffed on the idea of malls as sanctuaries—places containing everything one could need, undead apocalypse or not. For suburban teens of the '80s, that was more or less true, as malls became the cool places to hang out. *Fast Times at Ridgemont High* opens not at Ridgemont High but at the local mall, where a montage shows the real social scene in action. Mall-going teens unwittingly subjected themselves to a barrage of repeat marketing. Even if you have no intention of buying a certain product, walking by its display in a store window enough times will make you aware of it.

There were plenty of mom-and-pop stores across the country selling athletic shoes, of course, but the accessibility and familiarity of stores such as Foot Locker, the Athlete's Foot, and Champs Sports lent a certain legitimacy to the evolving sneaker industry. Foot Locker employees were dressed in black-and-white-striped referee uniforms, subtly underlining that you, the consumer, were the athlete. In 1982, the same year the Reebok Freestyle and Jane Fonda's first workout video came out, the first Lady Foot Lockers begin to appear in Canada and immediately proved that the market for female-specific sports shoes was strong enough to support a spin-off store. By the end of the decade, Foot Locker and Lady Foot Locker would alone sell 20 percent of all brand-name athletic footwear in the United States.

The second factor in Reebok Freestyle's success lay in the shoe's jump from the exercise studios to the street. Though the tennis and running booms had injected their respective sneakers into fashion throughout the 1970s, sneakers as everyday wear didn't happen overnight. People laughed when the designer Karl Lagerfeld featured tennis shoes with his 1976 couture collection.

But as the 1980 New York City transit strike demonstrated, more and more people were wearing comfortable shoes everywhere; the Freestyle was a perfect candidate for ubiquity. Part of this was that they didn't scream "SPORT!" the same way the Nike Cortez did—the Reebok logo and adjacent Union Jack were little more than a centimeter high, minimalist compared to the Nike Swoosh or Adidas stripes made purposely large enough to be seen on TV screens. The Freestyle's white and pastel palette also paid off, as people bought multiple pairs to have a choice of colors. "We made shoes that matched the color of clothes," Angel Martinez said. "It was not brain surgery."

The Freestyle rocketed Reebok's sales from $1.5 million the year before the shoe hit the market to nearly $13 million the year after. New Yorkers later nicknamed the shoe "5411s," after the price of $49.99 plus tax. Other models followed that took notes from the Freestyle. The year 1983 saw the release of the Reebok Classic running shoe, which quickly made the leap to a casual shoe thanks to its soft leather, clean lines, and all-white look. A tennis variety called the Newport Classic took off as well. Reebok also produced a men's version of the Freestyle called the Ex-O-Fit, which featured a thick Velcro strap across the ankle, replacing the two thinner ones on its feminine counterpart. By 1987, Reebok's sales had reached $1.5 billion, putting it ahead of Nike, as well as Adidas and Converse, in domestic shoe sales.

Sneakers such as the Converse All Star and Keds Champion had long been worn casually, thanks to bobby-soxers, greasers, and punk rockers, but only after those models had outlived their usefulness on the competition field. Keds, in particular, owed much of its business to the lifestyle market. Now it found its niche threatened; if consumers were perfectly happy wearing a pair of trendy white Reebok Classics, why would they reach for a pair of simple Keds? To avoid sliding into irrelevance, the company launched the "Keds. They Feel Good" marketing campaign in 1989, which played up the sneakers' comfort while giving a nod to their sports roots, with a focus on women. In one ad, a mother balances her smiling child on her Keds-wearing feet, the tagline cheekily proclaiming "Keds introduces weight-lifting shoes." The campaign helped triple the brand's sales that year.

Reebok had found success by marketing to both men and women, while its competitors missed the opportunity. Aerobics may have ended up being a passing obsession in the decade of big hair and leg warmers, but companies that didn't embrace exercise that fell outside the realm of "traditional" sports played by "traditional" athletes risked falling behind companies that did. Major brands began using women-specific lasts to build their shoes. New Balance's W320 running shoe featured a narrower heel that gave a snugger fit. Smaller companies sprang up, including Rykä, which catered exclusively to women, in 1987.

As the accepted definition of sports and the people who played them expanded, sneakers grew to become a legitimate fashion item across genders—but not yet an iconic one. A basketball player who seemed lighter than air and a rap group from Queens were about to change that forever.

Meanwhile, within sports, the fight continued not just for recognition but for equality. In the summer before her win against Bobby Riggs, Billie Jean King founded the Women's Tennis Association, an organization that would oversee all of professional women's tennis. A month later, thanks to her lobbying efforts, the U.S. Open became the first Grand Slam event to agree to equal pay for men and women. King, who had a model of Adidas tennis shoes named for her, continued to use her platform to promote equal pay for men and women.

"It wasn't about tennis, it was about social change," she said later of the "Battle of the Sexes." "I knew that going in."

11

STYLE AND FLOW

The inventor of a new American art form was a teenage transplant from Jamaica who dropped his accent to fit in. Clive Campbell emigrated from the tiny Caribbean nation when he was twelve years old. As a teenager in the early 1970s, Campbell, who went by the name DJ Kool Herc, and his sister would host parties in the building rec room at 1520 Sedgwick Avenue in the West Bronx. Herc played music that the party's high school–aged guests wanted to hear: James Brown, Booker T and the MGs, or the Jimmy Castor Bunch. Only about forty to fifty people were able to pack into the space; there was so little room that Herc's sound system was in the rec room while the teenage DJ himself watched the party from an adjacent space. But people weren't coming to his parties for the location, with its linoleum floors, radiators, and fluorescent lighting; they were coming for the music. To conceal his prized set list from rival DJs looking to see what music he played, Herc would soak off the record labels, a common practice in Jamaica's competitive dance halls.

At one such party in August 1973, as the legend goes, eighteen-year-old Kool Herc was doing what he normally did, scanning the crowd to see what parts of the record they danced to and what parts they didn't. "I was noticing people used to wait for particular parts of the record to dance, maybe [to] do their specialty move," he recalled years later. Keeping his audience engaged was key. Since most of the dancing seemed to happen during the break beat, the rhythmic section between verses that sometimes included only a drum and bass, Herc surmised that that was what his audiences really wanted. As he exchanged the rec room for outdoor park jams and clubs, he began to experiment with isolating the break beat. In a technique he called "The Merry Go Round," he would play the break on one turntable and, when that was nearly finished, cue up a second, identical record on a second turntable to replay the drum break when the first record had finished. Then he would move the first record back, switch to it, and replay the break, creating a loop of the part the crowd *really* wanted to dance to. The young DJ's selection of obscure funk tracks could be played for as long as he saw fit while a friend added improvisational rhymes and shout-outs over the breaks.

In 1973, New York City was riding high on Walt Frazier's championship-winning Knicks, but there was little good news in the Bronx. Hundreds of thousands of manufacturing jobs had left, the average per capita income dropping to the lowest in New York City. Forty percent of the South Bronx was on welfare, and 30 percent were unemployed, with youth unemployment hitting 60 percent. Property values had plummeted, partly as a result of Robert Moses's Cross Bronx Expressway, which had cleaved neighborhoods and deterred new development. Thousands of police officers and firefighters had been laid off as a potential city bankruptcy loomed; drug commerce and petty crime had soared. Slumlords hired arsonists to torch their buildings for insurance money; between 1970 and 1980, seven Bronx census tracts lost 97 percent of their buildings to fire and abandonment.

Violent crime also featured heavily. Youth gangs with names such as Black Spades, Savage Skulls, and Seven Immortals carved up the Bronx block by block, gaining and losing turf to rival gangs as lethal collateral damage piled up. In 1977, President Jimmy Carter toured bleak streets to shouts of "Give us money!" and "We want jobs!" He called the trip "sobering." The borough's woes were summed up during game two of the World Series a few days later, when a helicopter shot of Yankee Stadium showed a raging building fire a few blocks away. ABC announcer Howard Cosell supposedly uttered the now-famous phrase: "There it is, ladies and gentlemen. The Bronx is burning."

Kool Herc's West Bronx outdoor parties were in a comparatively tamer area than the troubled South Bronx. But there were DJs there, too, including a member of the Black Spades, the biggest gang in the borough, who called himself Afrika Bambaataa. Bambaataa was the Black Spades' warlord, a leader responsible for expanding territory and attracting recruits, who was skilled at crossing lines and forming relationships with rivals. A 1971 truce between the gangs coincided with Bambaataa's shift toward apprenticing as a DJ. "When I did become a DJ, I already had an army with me so I already knew that my parties would automatically be packed," he later said.

In 1975, Bambaataa had a change of heart following the shooting death of his cousin. He formed an organization that transformed into the Zulu Nation, a nonviolent community group that counted among its membership former gang members who wanted to straighten their lives out. Inspired by Herc's dance parties, Bambaataa organized massive block parties that featured himself on the turntable, advancing Kool Herc's breakbeat innovation by mixing in such varied source material as portions of Grand Funk Railroad, the Monkees, and Malcolm X speeches. The resulting mashup of styles was like nothing anyone in the Bronx River area had ever heard. The Zulu Nation's parties weren't a sideline to its efforts to promote peace but rather the main event—and they worked. With the common denominator of fresh music, the scene gained more and more popularity and legitimacy as an alternative to gang membership, reaching eventually not only black neighborhoods in the Bronx and Harlem but also the Puerto Rican community in East Harlem.

While DJ Kool Herc brought out the break beat and Afrika Bambaataa mixed genres, another Bronx teenager named Joseph Saddler was catching on. "I had never heard sound, let alone music, that loud in my whole life," he would write years later. "I could feel the boom of the bass coming up through my Super Pro Keds." The teenage Saddler, who would become better known by his stage name Grandmaster Flash, began tinkering with turntables, receivers, capacitors, amplifiers, and anything else he could find abandoned in alleyways and built his own setup.

"I was a scientist looking for something," he recalled. "Going inside hair dryers, and going inside washing machines and stereos and radios, whatever you plugged into the wall."

Grandmaster Flash took the next step in hip-hop's development. Like Herc, Flash's family had Caribbean roots, his parents having immigrated from Barbados. Also like Herc, Flash's interest in music came from his father's record collection, which he'd get into trouble even for touching. Flash admired Herc's switching from one break to the next but felt that his dropping the needle to find the beginning of the break was too inelegant. He developed a way to seamlessly continue the loop by using a crayon to mark the break on the record, so he knew how many rotations he had to spin it back—using his hand, a taboo at the time. Flash could add elements of one song with one hand and "rewind" the break with the other, editing a song on the fly and turning the turntable into an instrument in its own right.

In Flash's first appearance in the early morning hours at Disco Fever, a South Bronx club a few blocks north of Yankee Stadium, five hundred people showed up. His sets grew more popular each week, and the mostly teenage crowd grew more unruly. The club's owners set a new price at the door to cover the additional security: one dollar for everyone wearing shoes, five for anyone wearing sneakers.

BY MASTERING THE BREAK, this "Holy Trinity" of Kool Herc, Afrika Bambaataa, and Grandmaster Flash gave rise to a new form of dancing, called breaking, in which sneakers would play a large part. Break boys weren't like disco dancers of the time, who moved to the whole song; b-boys waited for the extended instrumental break to show off their unpredictably fast, James Brown–inspired footwork, their pivoting and twisting, and their martial arts–like dance moves. B-boys (and b-girls) could show off moves perfected in living rooms and hallways to audiences at house parties, block parties, and clubs, often traveling to other parts of the city to challenge rivals for dance floor supremacy. Confrontation was at the heart of breaking; dancers proved their dominance, nonviolently, by pulling off moves that opponents couldn't match or top—the more stylized, fluid, and in tune with the music, the better.

The b-boy movement coalesced in the mid-1970s, populated by kids too young to get into clubs and encouraged by the increasing presence of outdoor jams. To establish and maintain reputations, breakers formed themselves into crews. The surest way of setting your crew apart was having a look as cutting edge as your moves. "Fresh" b-boy style, down to the sneakers, stood in sharp contrast to the grungy look of youth gangs, who often wore beat-up Converse All Stars or PF Flyers along with their customized jean jackets. Stylish breakers liked things flashy and branded—track suits, Kangol hats, Lee jeans, or T-shirts, maybe with the name of their crew in Old English lettering.

Good sneakers were necessary for the acrobatics of break dancing, but brand and style were also key. Breakers adopted what was popular on the streets: Puma Suedes and Clydes, Converse All Stars, Adidas Superstars, PRO-Keds, Nike Cortezes. As sneaker brands released more models, colors, and styles in the later 1970s, crews expanded their tastes. "We liked [the Adidas Superstars] because they looked fly and sort of armored," said Jorge "Popmaster Fabel" Pabon, a member of the Zulu Nation and the b-boying Rock Steady Crew. "Plus, white on white low top Shell toes could match with anything."

Members of the four-cornered world of hip-hop youth culture (MCs, DJs, graffiti artists, and b-boys) were at the forefront of street fashion, beginning to rival professional and playground basketball players as influencers. Each New York City borough and neighborhood had its own subtle ways of dressing. If you saw someone wearing a velour sweat suit that matched the brand of his sneakers, you were in early-'80s Harlem. Clarks shoes and Cazal glasses with thick black frames were popular in Brooklyn. PRO-Keds 69er sneakers, basketball shoes that, at a distance, could be confused with Chuck Taylors, were known as "Uptowns" because they were especially popular in the Bronx and Harlem. Afrika Bambaataa often wore Uptowns when DJing in the park. The dancers were the style ambassadors—like bees cross-pollinating from flower to flower, b-boys from Brooklyn neighborhoods such as Bed-Stuy, Fort Greene, or Flatbush heading uptown to do battle would bring new styles with them and imitate what their rivals in the Bronx wore.

If you wanted to stand out at a basketball court or block party,

Rubber overshoes, like these circa 1830s, protected the wearer's shoes from the elements. Pre–vulcanized rubber had a tendency to melt in the heat and turn brittle in the cold.

Smith College class of 1895 basketball team, taken only a couple years after the sport's invention. Basketball gained popularity as a wintertime alternative to dull gym calisthenics.

Beachgoers, like these swimmers in Deauville, France, in August 1913, wore an early style of canvas sneaker called a plimsoll.

Converse salesman Chuck Taylor tosses a basketball behind him, circa 1927.

COACH FRANK LEAHY SAYS,

"WIN IN KEDS!"

"In very fast game and for all sports, you'll do better for your team, and have more fun, if you wear correct athletic shoes. I was happy to advise on the design of new Frank Leahy Keds, so that your footwear can help you get the most from healthful, manly sports."

—FRANK LEAHY

Here's how Frank Leahy told us to build the new Keds named for him:

* Rugged construction; note those burly, non-slip, ground-grip soles.
* Cool, light uppers that "breathe" when you move — they're washable.
* Speed-built in — note the no-bind, short-cut tops, the lace-to-toe design that braces arch and ankle, and the special arch-supporting straps.
* Scientific construction for stamina — the Shockproof Arch Cushion and Cushioned heels give you resilient footing, so legs and feet don't tire out, get tired. You'll enjoy staying in the game longer.

Yes, you'll get speed and sports enjoyment in every pair of Frank Leahy Keds. Treat yourself to them soon!

Ask your store for 1951 44-page Sure Football of Sports and Games.

Natural Support!
KEDS SHOCKPROOF ARCH CUSHION AND SCIENTIFIC LACE

u.s. Keds
The Shoe of Champions

UNITED STATES RUBBER COMPANY
Rockefeller Center, New York

Along with Converse, Keds were some of the most widely sold sneakers in the middle of the twentieth century.

Tennis grew in popularity when it moved from athletic clubs to public parks, though footwear was often an afterthought. Note the heels in this casual game in Brooklyn in 1940.

Adolf (Adi) Dassler examines a soccer shoe with screw-in studs. Adi would found Adidas while his estranged brother, Rudolf, started Puma.

University of Oregon track coach Bill Bowerman building his own shoes for his athletes. With Phil Knight, one of his former runners, he cofounded Nike.

One of Bill Bowerman's more famous experiments involved pouring liquid rubber into his wife's waffle iron in an attempt to create an outsole with better grip.

While receiving a bronze medal at the 1968 Mexico City Olympics, American sprinter John Carlos (*right*) raises a sneaker as part of a demonstration for racial and economic equality. He and teammate Tommie Smith (*left*) were forced from the Games after raising a Black Power salute.

New York City's street and playground basketball courts helped grow the game and the sneaker's popularity. Here kids play on a makeshift court on East 109th Street in 1968.

"Z-Boy" Tony Alva rides down the side of a swimming pool wall, wearing Vans. California's mid-1970s drought enabled skaters to develop daring aerial tricks in newly emptied pools.

Charlie's Angels star Farrah Fawcett-Majors wearing a pair of Nike Senorita Cortezes in 1976.

Runners snake their way through New York City's Central Park during the L'Eggs Mini-Marathon, circa late 1970s/early 1980s. The jogging boom expanded the public idea of just who could be an athlete.

Reebok capitalized on the aerobic and fitness boom of the 1980s with shoes such as the Reebok Freestyle Hi. The shoes became popular outside the gym as well as in.

Run-DMC were the first nonathletes to get a sneaker contract, partly thanks to "My Adidas," an ode to their beloved Superstars.

A rash of sneaker- and sports jacket–related crimes led to this May 14, 1990, *Sports Illustrated* cover story.

Michael Jordan in action at the 1988 NBA Slam Dunk Contest.

Sweatshop protesters outside a Chicago Niketown in 1993.

Designer Jeffrey Ng, aka jeffstaple, holds a pair of his Nike x Staple Design Dunk Low Pro SB Pigeon, which nearly caused a riot upon its release in 2005. The shoe now sells for several thousand dollars on the secondary market. *Dale Algo/@daleknows*

Sneakerhead and shoe designer Jazz Bonifacio with some of his collection. Some estimates put the secondary sneaker market at more than $1 billion a year.

Basketball shoes of eras past, including the Adidas Jabbar, Superstar, Puma Clyde, and Pro-Keds hightop, on display in a traveling museum exhibition in 2015.

In parts of Ghana, it is typical for the style of a coffin to reflect the personal identity of the deceased—in this case embodied in a Nike sneaker. *Paa Joe* (abbreviated). Coffin in the form of a Nike Sneaker.

Triathlete Sarah Reinertsen runs in an Össur Flex-Run prosthetic with a Nike Sole attachment. Advances in technology and design have pushed athletic footwear far beyond its humble origins in the mid-1800s.

Sneaker arms race: in 2017, Adidas and Nike each developed special shoes to aid marathon runners in an attempt to break the two-hour mark.

every detail counted, even the way you wore your shoelaces. Fat laces were hard to come by over the counter in 1970s New York, so kids took the laces out of their PRO-Keds or Converse, stretched them out, starched them, and then ironed them, a process that could take half an hour. Next there was an art to how you laced your shoes. Manufacturers would thread the lace first under, then up. By lacing in the opposite direction, pushing the lace aglet in from the top, a wearer showed he at least cared enough about his shoes to change the way they had been laced when they came out of the box.

For now these were the codes of a group of youths in one city. But street fashion was about to reach a wider audience as hip-hop grew and expanded.

AN AFRICAN AMERICAN DOCTOR NAMED Gerald W. Deas makes one of the unlikeliest cameo appearances in sneaker history. Besides his day job as an internist at Jamaica Hospital Medical Center in Queens, Deas wrote plays, poems, and songs revolving around social ills. His play tackling poor diets, titled *Oh! Oh! Obesity!*, was staged on Manhattan's Lower East Side in 1984. In 1985, the same year the FDA gave Dr. Deas an award for his advocacy of nutrition labeling, a poem of his was turned into a rap song. "Felon Sneakers" was Deas's take on what he saw as the troubling trend of kids wearing sneakers without laces, as prison inmates did. One couplet read, "You shoot and kill / You wearing those sneakers but you lost your will." Deas felt that imitating the way inmates wore shoes would hold young black men back. That caught the attention of a hip-hop group called Run-DMC, who didn't like anyone slighting the way they wore their Adidas Superstars.

By the mid-1980s, hip-hop had moved on from DJ-centric outdoor parties and jams as the music itself focused more on the MC aspect than the man behind the turntable. Grandmaster Flash saw the shift early and enlisted not one but five MCs to rap over his beats. Grandmaster Flash and the Furious Five, along with the rival group Cold Crush Brothers, transitioned hip-hop to performances that were more concerts than neighborhood dance-a-thons.

Hip-hop groups started to appear in trendy Manhattan clubs and to sign record deals. In 1982, Afrika Bambaataa & Soulsonic Force released the electro-funk single "Planet Rock," influenced by the German electronic band Kraftwerk, James Brown, and Sly and the Family Stone. The Zulu Nation founder performed in spacy costumes that resembled a meld of Flash Gordon and Funkadelic. That same year, Grandmaster Flash and the Furious Five released the influential hit "The Message," which painted a bleak, realistic portrait of inner-city poverty to the refrain "It's like a jungle sometimes / It makes me wonder how I keep from going under." (DJ Kool Herc, the third member of the "Holy Trinity," by then had faded from the scene.)

Run-DMC marked another chapter in hip-hop's evolution. The rhymes of the trio's two MCs, Joseph "Run" Simmons and Darryl "DMC" McDaniels, were harder and more rock-oriented than those of other acts, and the group's DJ, Jason "Jam Master Jay" Mizell, relied on drum effects and scratching rather than the disco-adapted samples favored by the genre's pioneers. As with "The Message," Run-DMC sang about the world around them. "Unemployment at a record high / People coming, people going, people born to die," the two MCs sang on their debut 1983 single "It's Like That."

Their stripped-down sound was what one might actually hear on the street, not produced in a studio with expensive equipment. This went for their look, too: after dropping their original geeky plaid outfits, Run-DMC adopted leather jackets, black velour hats, Adidas track suits, and gold chains—something fans might see on their native Hollis Avenue in Queens, not the futuristic con-coctions of Afrika Bambaataa or the disco glam–inspired looks of Grandmaster Flash (chest-baring leather, rhinestones). Run-DMC's "uniform" was more reminiscent of the matching b-boy crew outfits of a decade earlier. "What we wear onstage is just what all the youth wear," said DMC. "That's what, you know, all our fans wear. So dressing this way lets them know, 'Oh, he's just like me.'"

Like any good b-boy gear, the shoes were essential. Capping off Run-DMC's appearance was a pair of crisp black-and-white Adidas Superstars, unlaced.

In part because of its mix of hip-hop and rock, the group achieved a newfound level of mainstream success for rap music. Its 1984 debut album was the first hip-hop record to be certified gold, its second, platinum. 1986's *Raising Hell*, Run-DMC's third album in as many years, changed the game for good. As with the two that had preceded it, *Raising Hell* would set a new sales re-cord, becoming the first hip-hop album to go multiplatinum.

Two tracks were breakout hits. The first had started with Def Jam Recordings' founder, Russell Simmons—Run's older brother—noticing how many people were buying Adidas Super-stars just because the members of Run-DMC were wearing them. In DMC's telling, Simmons, high on angel dust, suggested that the group record a song about the shoes.

DMC immediately had ideas. "We're going to flip the stereo-type," he said. "We're going to say, 'standing on Two-Fifth Street in our Adidas' and we're going to talk some positive stuff." They would make the song a return shot to Dr. Deas's "Felon Sneak-ers": kids in laceless sneakers could hang out (Two-Fifth was slang for 205th Street in their Queens neighborhood) without being criminal. "And Russell was like, 'Whatever, just make sure you say, "My Adidas." ' "

"My Adidas" was the first single released from the album and directly addressed the image issue: "My Adidas only bring good news / And they are not used as felon shoes." Run's and DMC's pounding, interchanging vocals rapped over a simple drum track punctuated by horns. Elsewhere in the song, Run and DMC sing about how many different colors of Adidas they have ("Got blue and black cause I like to chill"), how they "won't be mad when worn in bad weather," how they are used to do anything like "travel on gravel, dirt road or street" and so superior that they "won't trade my Adidas for no beat-up Ballys."

Raising Hell's other hit was an unexpected cover of Aerosmith's 1975 song "Walk This Way," a call-and-answer with Aerosmith's Steven Tyler trading lines with Run and DMC and Joe Perry's guitar trading riffs and scratches with Jam Master Jay's turntable. In much the same way that Blondie's "Rapture" was the first taste of hip-hop for many white listeners during the disco era, the new version of "Walk This Way" found an expanded audience in Aerosmith's fan base. The song became an international hit, and the video played on heavy rotation on MTV, telegraphing hip-hop sensibility and style to millions for the first time. Run-DMC's white, unlaced Adidas Superstars received several close-ups.

On July 19, 1986, Run-DMC played Madison Square Garden. Betting that there were more than free shoes and track suits to be had from the group's favorite brand, their road manager invited Adidas executives to the concert. One of the executives, Angelo Anastasio, was a former soccer player (he'd been on the New York Cosmos with Pelé) who the year before had made a deal to get Rocky Balboa out of his Nikes and into Adidas in time for *Rocky IV*. He was curious why a musical act would adopt a brand the way Run-DMC had. In a display of clever stagecraft, before launching into "My Adidas," Run-DMC asked their fans to hold their shoes up in the air. The crowd of tens of thousands obliged.

"Everybody had on new Adidas," DMC recalled years later. "There was nothing but three stripes in there and that made Adidas say, 'Yo, we giving y'all a deal."

From his vantage point onstage hidden behind a speaker, Anastasio was amazed. He went to Horst Dassler to convince him that three African American rappers singing about the conservative German brand was a good thing, as evidenced by all those three-striped sneakers he had seen held in the air at the concert. Shortly after the Madison Square Garden show, Run-DMC marked another first for hip-hop: the first million-dollar contract with an athletic shoe company. The deal was the first between any athletic apparel company and a non–sports star or team. An important line had been crossed: suddenly you no longer needed to be a basketball star to endorse basketball shoes. Musicians and other celebrities had worn sneakers, but with its sponsorship of Run-DMC a major brand was now willing to pay for that star power.

Run-DMC didn't invent the practice of flashing a particular brand, of course; it had been a staple of hip-hop as a way to differentiate your b-boy crew. But by capitalizing on it, they ushered in a new era for music, especially hip-hop, in which an artist's image and look could be just as profitable as his songs. Other hip-hop groups began to ally themselves with sneaker brands. MC Shan, who had rocked Puma since his b-boy days, started a beef by rapping "Puma's the brand cause the Klan makes Troops" on his 1988 track "I Pioneered This"—which angered LL Cool J, the poster boy of the brand Troop which was (falsely) rumored on the street to be made by the KKK. Heavy D & The Boyz recorded a tinny track titled "Nike" on their 1987 debut album. Doug E. Fresh swore by the Swiss brand Bally and, possibly upset by the Bally diss on "My Adidas," featured a pair of his sneakers blowing away a pair of Superstars in a Wild West–style music video segment. Meanwhile, Adidas was busy releasing special-edition Run-DMC shoes. The Eldorado and the Fleetwood were named after the groups' favorite cars, and the Ultrastar had an elastic tongue that made it easier to wear laceless.

In the same year *Raising Hell* dropped, 1986, Run-DMC's Def Jam labelmates the Beastie Boys released a bombshell album of their own. *Licensed to Ill* sold more than a million copies within three months of its release and was the first hip-hip album to top the *Billboard* album chart. A white rap trio from Brooklyn, the Beastie Boys' Ad-Rock, MCA, and Mike D had begun as hard-core punk rockers, even playing at legendary Lower East Side club CBGB. When they started to incorporate hip-hip into their act, they brought a punk, frat-boy flavor to it, their T-shirts and shorts mixed with gold chains and baseball caps stylized with graffiti. With a fan base whiter than Run-DMC's, the success of the Beastie Boys' debut album again introduced a new audience to hip-hop and the styles that came with it.

The Beastie Boys weren't synonymous with a specific shoe, but if they had a sneaker of choice, it was the Adidas Campus, a low-top suede shoe similar to the Puma Clyde. Like the Clyde, the Campus had begun life as a basketball shoe in a slightly different form when the Boston Celtics wore them in 1971. When the Campus hit the streets in 1983, it was quickly adopted by b-boys and b-girls. Incidentally (or not), after the group achieved mega-success with *License to Ill*, the Campus was deemed by the New York street fashion-conscious to be "played out." Other parts of the country could imitate the white boys from Brooklyn if they wanted, but those on the cutting edge had moved on. Mike D was still wearing the Campus on the cover of the group's 1992 album *Check Your Head*.

Yet the Beastie Boys were serious about sneakers in their own right. In a 1992 interview on MTV's *House of Style*, Mike D and Ad-Rock explained their aesthetics. "We have a certain respect for a certain era of utilitarian design," explained Mike D. "If kids out there are into the new sneakers, that's cool. We just lean toward the classic, functional design." Ad-Rock showed off his green Campus to the MTV interviewer and explained the subtle differences between that shoe and the Adidas Gazelle. To the layman the shoes appear identical, but in fact the Gazelle sports a narrower, more pointed toe. By that point the Campus was being phased out, and compared to the Gazelle it was far less widely available. The interviewer, astounded that anyone would want old shoes, asked how the group even got them.

"You gotta find them, like records," said Ad-Rock. "It's like a hobby. You gotta search for it, find the real McCoy." The Beastie Boys employed a crew member to scour sporting goods stores looking for boxes of "deadstock," or fresh-in-the-box sneakers, models that had failed to sell when released years earlier. The job of the "sneaker pimp" would be to find rare models for the band that no one else had, which, in turn, would drive fans to hunt for rare pairs themselves. That time-consuming process often involved sifting through retail storage areas or garages. It certainly wasn't common practice, but it marked the beginnings of the lengths some people would go to to have a sneaker no one else had.

Sneakers had made the transition from sport to casual wear before break beats and b-boys hit the scene, but hip-hop elevated them to something new. MCs made sneakers a status symbol, a carrier of cool for an audience that was concerned first and foremost with how a shoe looked, not how it performed on the court or field. Sports stars, however, weren't to be counted out. At the same time Run-DMC was telling fans to hold up their Adidas shoes in Madison Square Garden, a former Adidas fan was on his way to becoming an American icon.

12

HIS AIRNESS

Phil Knight knew it. Jeff Johnson knew it. Everybody at Nike knew it. It was 1984, and Nike was in trouble. Yes, it had a strong presence in the running market it had helped create, but that segment was in decline. The company had missed the women's fitness craze that Reebok, the new kid in town, had cashed in on. Converse was the brand to beat in basketball, followed by Adidas, which was also still the Goliath of the global athletic shoe market. Nike had posted its first quarterly loss. Four years after the company had gone public, there were layoffs.

There was only one solution: gather the Buttfaces. Thrown around as a joke during an early meeting, the name had stuck to the key members of the company's management team as a term of endearment. Buttface meetings were often rowdy, loud, and booze-filled—and they determined the direction of the company. The Nike execs convened at their Oregon lodge, the place where they always met when big decisions needed to be made. The focus would be on what to be done about the 1984 NBA draft.

The company had half a million dollars budgeted for endorsements for new NBA stars, and Knight had decided that it needed to make a big play in the basketball market lest it be relegated to just being a running shoe company. Horst Dassler, as Knight was well aware, had skirted his parents' business inclinations in using the French branch of Adidas to enter the US basketball market. Now Dassler, only two years older than Knight, was less than a year away from becoming chairman of all of Adidas. If there was a time to take on the world's number one athletic shoe company, this was it.

Breaking into the top ranks of the NBA required a gutsy wager on who would make it big. The decision was tough: the 1984 NBA draft was stacked with college talent. There was Akeem "The Dream" Olajuwon, a seven-foot-tall Nigerian-born University of Houston center known for his effortless dunks. The powerfully built, bullet-headed, mouthy Charles Barkley, an Auburn forward, led the Southeastern Conference in rebounds each season he played. Sam Bowie, who towered at seven foot one, had been on the basketball radar since high school. Gonzaga point guard John Stockton led his conference in scoring, assists, and steals his senior year. Any of those athletes seemed worth an endorsement deal, but Nike had learned the hard way that talent wasn't enough to guarantee sales.

Knight, Johnson, and the other Nike brains debated the various options. Joining them was a rotund man named Sonny Vaccaro, who didn't look like he played the game so much as he resembled a basketball himself. Vaccaro was at the meeting because he helped Nike get to the point of approaching pro players. In 1965, he had helped organize the Dapper Dan Roundball Classic in Pittsburgh, the first All-American showcase of high school talent, which attracted college coaches from across the nation on the hunt for new prospects. He had gotten to know the game from the bottom up, and, not unlike Chuck Taylor with his basketball yearbook, had an eye for who would be great. At that time in recruiting, there were few opportunities to see a lot of young players at once; Vaccaro was their gatekeeper.

Then there was Rob Strasser. Like Vaccaro, Strasser wasn't the athletic type. The lawyer was six foot two, weighed 300 pounds, eschewed exercise, and loved Hawaiian shirts. Unlike Vaccaro, Strasser didn't have an encyclopedic knowledge of the game, but he'd participated in his share of scrappy negotiations for new talent. He also had a sense of the marketing mold a young Nike star should fulfill, something he had summed up in a 1983 memo: "Individual athletes, even more than teams, will be the heroes; symbols more and more of what real people can't do anymore— risk and win." A few years earlier, Nike had courted the cult of personality by signing stars such as tennis's John McEnroe and track's Carl Lewis. Strasser was on the lookout for the basketball version—someone with outsized talent plus that something extra.

STRASSER AND VACCARO were at the heart of how Nike had decided that basketball's rookie ranks were its best, indeed its only, hope. In 1977, Vaccaro had approached Nike with a burlap sack full of shoes of his own design, including a basketball sandal. When the Nike executives finished laughing, they found that Vaccaro had a wealth of contacts with college basketball coaches around the country. Knight hired Vaccaro on the spot and paired him up with Strasser for a new mission: to get college teams into Nikes. The task was easier said than done, as most of the big schools were already wearing Converses or Adidas, but Knight's reasoning was simple: Nike didn't have the money to snag big-name talent in the pros. Converse didn't have Adidas-level money either, but it had a history Nike didn't. "If you had gone to a playground and asked kids what sneakers they wanted," recalled Nike designer Peter Moore, "they would have said Converse." The seeds of Chuck Taylor were still bearing fruit.

Both top brands had star power behind them. One Converse ad featured Philadelphia 76ers legend Julius Erving dunking over the competition while vocalists chanted, "Hey, hey, Dr. J, where'd you get those moves?" The ad's tagline: "Shoes of the stars." Adidas' biggest name was the Lakers' Kareem Abdul-Jabbar, who had just won his fifth Most Valuable Player award at the end of the 1976–77 season. In contrast, Nike's biggest NBA prospect had been rookie Marques Johnson, taken third in the draft by the Milwaukee Bucks. Strasser offered him $6,000, but once news of the deal reached Adidas headquarters, Horst Dassler upped the amount to $10,000, plus royalties. The Germans took it a step further and introduced a new shoe by the end of the decade, the Top Ten, which was worn by ten players in the NBA, including Johnson. Every time Strasser made a smaller deal for Nike, he'd ask the sports agent David Falk, "Am I getting fucked on this deal?"

Nike wasn't ready to give up. By the end of 1977, its sales were approaching $70 million and Nikes were in more places than they had ever been, often gaining exposure in unexpected ways. In December, the Houston Rockets were playing the Los Angeles Lakers when a fight for the ball broke out at the beginning of the second half. Kareem Abdul-Jabbar, Kermit Washington, and Houston's Kevin Kunnert came to blows after a rebound. As Abdul-Jabbar tried to restrain Kunnert, Houston forward Rudy Tomjanovich ran to center court to help his teammate. Washington punched Tomjanovich hard, shattering his jaw and face, and Tomjanovich hit the floor, unconscious, in a pool of his own blood. Abdul-Jabbar later said the sound was like a melon being dropped on concrete. Tomjanovich was rushed into emergency surgery, where he barely pulled through. Washington was suspended for twenty-six games. Later that night, Phil Knight received a phone call from his father, who had watched the game on TV. "Oh, Buck, Buck, it was one of the most incredible things I have ever seen," the elder Knight said. "The camera kept zooming in and you could see quite clearly . . . on Tomjanovich's shoes . . . the swoosh! They kept zooming in on *the swoosh!*"

"The punch" wasn't an isolated incident in professional basketball at the end of the 1970s. Besides the occasional on-court violence (Abdul-Jabbar punched a player in another incident that same season), the newly merged NBA and ABA had a reputation for rampant drug use. In 1978, New Jersey Nets star player Bernard King was arrested for drunk driving and cocaine possession. In 1983, Michael Ray Richardson, once called "the next Walt Frazier," checked into rehab for cocaine addiction. That same year the league set up an antidrug policy that would ban players for egregious violations (Richardson would be the first player banned). With low television ratings, the league's relevancy was also in question; it wasn't uncommon for some finals games to be broadcast on tape delay. All of that had racial undertones, made explicit in a 1979 comment by an executive of a charter NBA team to a *Sports Illustrated* reporter. "The question is are they [black players] promotable?" he asked. "People see them dissipating their money, playing without discipline. How can you sell a black sport to a white public?"

In short, professional basketball wasn't in the best place.

Still, pro ball was pro ball. Nike didn't have the capital to start poaching its competitors' clients or snag top prospects, but maybe getting lower-tier college players into Nikes early would establish brand loyalty. The company had learned from the lessons of Chuck Taylor and his grassroots clinics. NCAA amateurism rules prevented any payment to the university players it was trying to court, but Strasser and Vaccaro had a quick work-around: they could pay the coaches, who would give the players the shoes for free. Coaches would get $10,000 and shoes for each of their players, who didn't have to wear them—but the coach should encourage them to. A first-year head coach might make only $25,000; an extra ten grand in the bank would make a huge difference. As far as Nike's ambassadors were concerned, it was a win-win for everyone.

One month after being sent out on the task, Strasser excitedly reported back the schools that had signed on to the swoosh: University of Nevada, Las Vegas; Arkansas; Houston; Georgetown; and many more. By 1981, about eighty college teams were wearing Nikes. The small investment of a few thousand dollars and a few dozen pairs of shoes was more cost-effective than advertising; on TV, it was easy to see which players were wearing the swoosh.

Meanwhile, sneaker money in the NBA was starting to climb. The $10,000 for Johnson in 1977 seemed like small change a mere four years later, when the top pick in the 1981 NBA draft landed a $65,000 contract. In 1982, Adidas reupped its deal with Kareem Abdul-Jabbar for $100,000. That same year, New Balance, which had once touted that its shoes were "endorsed by no one," upped the ante further by signing the number one draft pick and future Hall of Famer James Worthy for a shoe contract worth $1.2 million over eight years. On its own roster, Converse had who might be the best three players of the early 1980s: Larry Bird, Earvin "Magic" Johnson, and Isiah Thomas.

This compounded a problem for Knight and Co. Strasser and Vaccaro's success aside, the top college players weren't necessarily sticking with Nikes when they broke into the big leagues. Big shoe contracts still lured them to Converse or Adidas. By the early 1980s, Nike did have a lot of players on the books—more than 120, or about half of the NBA—who were being paid anywhere from $8,000 to $50,000. On paper, it might have seemed like a success that half the professional basketball players were wearing the swoosh. But all those lesser-known players were costing Nike money it didn't have, while Converse and Adidas seemed to have figured out the formula of doing more with fewer (albeit megastar) deals. Strasser and another Nike exec came up with a plan: let all those small contracts expire to free up money to build a campaign around a young, talented up-and-comer.

THAT WAS THE POINT AT which the Nike team found themselves in 1984, putting their heads together at the Oregon retreat. The consensus seemed to settle on spreading the endorsement money across Olajuwon, Barkley, and Stockton. Then a fourth name came up: Michael Jordan.

Jordan was a promising young forward coming off his junior year at North Carolina. As a freshman, he had sunk the game-winning shot in the 1982 NCAA championship game. That particular basket had impressed Sonny Vaccaro enough to push hard for Jordan during the meeting. To him, it didn't make sense to place a low, safe bet on several players when you could go all in on Jordan.

The story was all in the shot. Here was a young player, new to the North Carolina Tar Heels, on a team stacked with the likes of James Worthy and Sam Perkins. That same young player had happened to get the ball while his team was one point down with seconds left in the championship final against a powerful Georgetown team led by Patrick Ewing, one of the best college players of his day, later to be selected as one of the fifty greatest NBA players of all time. Against that pressure, who was the lanky, nineteen-year-old Jordan to try to score? But he didn't just make the seventeen-foot basket, he did it with such ease that it seemed as though it took no effort at all, as though anyone could do it. Even his tongue was out. That was who should represent the company. Vaccaro told the others at the meeting that he would bet his entire career at Nike on it.

The decision was settled. The swoosh would put all the eggs, all $500,000 of them, into the Jordan basket. Not only that, Jordan wouldn't wear an existing Nike, he'd wear a line made especially for him. Jordan was in LA as cocaptain of the 1984 US Olympic basketball team, so Vaccaro arranged a meeting with the player at a Tony Roma's steakhouse in Santa Monica. The first problem: Jordan didn't particularly like Nikes. North Carolina was a Converse school, and he himself preferred Adidas. But Converse and Adidas weren't matching Nike's effort in wooing Jordan. Converse was too invested in the one-two punch it had with Magic Johnson and Larry Bird, and Adidas was still under the leadership of the matriarch, Käthe Dassler, who was trying to ease the inevitably rocky transition to her son, Horst, and four daughters. Vaccaro presented Nike's offer to Jordan.

Strasser and David Falk, the sports agent the Nike exec had hashed out many deals with, sat down to draw up the terms. Falk had negotiated a $3 million, five-year contract with the Chicago Bulls for Jordan and also wanted lucrative endorsements for his young star. With most sneaker contracts, a player chose the shoe he liked, secured a deal to wear it, and received a load of shoes to hand out to friends and family. Walt Frazier's Puma Clyde had ushered in the era of the signature shoe, but the Jordan deal would take player endorsements to another level. Nike offered its star-to-be royalties not only on each pair of Air Jordan sneakers sold but also on any Nike Air basketball shoes, in addition to Nike stock and a percentage of sales on any Air Jordan apparel. All told, the deal was worth $2.5 million over five years. What's more, Jordan would be the new face of Nike's advertising, fitting in with Strasser's vision of marketing individual athletes as heroes. Whatever magic he had would be the real appeal of the brand.

Still, Jordan needed convincing just to meet with execs at Nike headquarters after the Olympics. Jordan complained to his mother, Deloris, that if Nike wanted him, they should come to him. She put the matter into stark terms for her son. "Michael," she said, "you promised to go. When the plane arrives at Raleigh-Durham in the morning, you be on it because your father and I are going to be on it and we're all going to Portland."

Falk was surprised at how his client sat stone-faced during the Portland pitch meeting, which seemed to impress Jordan's parents much more than the young star. Sonny Vaccaro even appealed to Jordan's demand for a car by sliding two toy cars across the table to him. Still Jordan's face was inscrutable. "From what I understood and perceived," he said in an interview decades later, "[Strasser] really didn't know the type of player and the type of person I was. He was looking at whoever he could find to fit that mold from what he was trying to do from an Air Jordan standpoint."

Peter Moore, Nike's creative director, went to work designing the shoe. Moore didn't know who Jordan was but knew the shoes had to make a splash. The design featured a high, padded ankle collar and a look that somewhat resembled the earlier Nike Dunk shoe. The logo would feature a basketball surrounded by wings, reminiscent of those worn by pilots. Yet the most distinctive feature was the bold color scheme. When Moore showed the player a sketch of the red, black, and white of the first Air Jordan, Jordan said, "I can't wear that shoe. Those are the Devil's colors." When reminded that they were the colors of the Chicago Bulls, he still insisted that his shoes be Carolina blue, his UNC Tar Heels college colors. Meetings with Converse and Adidas didn't turn up a deal anywhere close to Nike's, however. Finally Jordan agreed to sign with the swoosh.

The team that would be taking Jordan was less promising than the shoe deal. To call the 1984 Bulls a bad team would be putting it mildly. Despite playing in a big city like Chicago, the Bulls rarely had a winning season; just before Jordan arrived, the team had won a dismal twenty-seven out of eighty-two games. Five years earlier, it had lost the opportunity to draft Magic Johnson because of a coin flip, which seemed fitting. The team had sold only 2,047 season tickets for Jordan's first season. Yet only a few months after he began play, attendance at Chicago Stadium had doubled.

Jordan's play wasn't the only thing that called attention to himself. At the time, NBA rules stated that players had to wear shoes conforming with the team's uniform. Though the Nike shoes Jordan wore at first shared the Bulls' black and red, their flashiness was deemed too much for the league's dress code and Jordan was fined $1,000. Nike's designers and advertisers were stuck; what good was a shoe if your star player couldn't even wear it? The Air Jordan wouldn't be released to the public until later in the season, but Nike wisely doubled down on the shoe color controversy, putting out a commercial that featured a slow pan down the player before settling on his shoes. Black "censored" bars covered the banned sneakers while a voice-over explained, "On September 15, Nike created a revolutionary new basketball shoe. On October 18, the NBA threw them out of the game. Fortunately, the NBA can't keep you from wearing them." Jordan continued to wear black-and-red shoes and Nike continued to pay the fine, a small price considering the exposure it was buying the company.

The Air Jordan went on sale on April 1, 1985, only a few weeks before the season's playoffs began, retailing for $65 in two variations—or "colorways," in sneakerspeak: entirely black and red, and white and red with a black swoosh. On the court, the shoes helped Jordan not only win rookie of the year (he led his team in points, assists, rebounds, and steals, the only first-year player ever to do so), but the Bulls managed to slip into the play-offs for the first time in four years. Nike could hardly have expected to find a better advertisement than a fresh face seemingly turning a failing team around by himself.

As electric as Jordan's debut season was, the big story of the NBA's 1984–85 season was the hotly anticipated finals rematch between the Los Angeles Lakers and the Boston Celtics. The series was more than simply two of the best teams meeting. It was a culmination of rivalries: West Coast versus East Coast, dynasty versus redemption, Magic versus Bird, black versus white. The sheer level of hype was significant—a signal that professional basketball was moving past the league's troubled reputation of the late 1970s.

Going into the best-of-seven series, the Lakers had lost to the Celtics eight times, most recently the previous year, though it hadn't been for lack of talent. Magic Johnson, Kareem Abdul-Jabbar, and three of their teammates would later enter the Hall of Fame. The two teams gave fans plenty to root for (or against), but closer to the floor the battle had already been decided. Magic and Bird were both signed with Converse; whoever won the 1985 finals, the Converse Pro Leathers, a response to the leather Adidas Superstars, were going to walk away with a champion.

The brand's television commercials gloated. Larry Bird, holding a white-and-red leather Converse, told the camera that the shoe was made for "the best pro player." Julius Erving then entered the frame and took the shoe from Bird's hand, spouting off about how the shoe's technical features meant the shoe was really made for the 76ers' star.

"It's reinforced for me," Dr. J said.

"And me!" Bird retorted.

"Hey, maybe it was made for both of us."

"Must be magic."

A tone sounded and Magic Johnson popped onto the screen, took the shoe, and said, "Now, that's who the shoe was made for."

The three superstars laughed as the commercial cut to a close-up of the shoe. Given that the Lakers finally bested the Celtics four games to two, Johnson, in the end, probably had the strongest argument.

The commercial showed what a gamble Nike was making in throwing everything behind Jordan. Anyone buying the Pro Leather had the endorsement of three of the game's most iconic stars: if one shoe was good enough for each of their individual playing styles, it was certainly good for the amateur player. Converse's dominance came with a small price, though: each star's sneaker looked identical to the next white sneaker with colored star. The Air Jordan was worn by only *one* player, and his name was right there on its bold red and black.

Within the first month of the shoes' hitting the shelves, it was clear that Nike's risk had paid off. Retailers moved nearly half a million pairs of Air Jordans and earned Nike more than $100 million in revenues. Through the following year, more than a dozen other colorways followed, some with decidedly non-Bulls colors, including black/blue and white/purple. Jordan's coveted Carolina blue shoes were eventually available. The shoe was a hit.

Other sponsors wanted to take advantage of the seemingly antigravity Jordan. Luckily for Nike, the shoes had already become so much a part of MJ's image that they appeared in other commercials with him. In a McDonald's TV ad from 1985, an air traffic controller voice-over goes though the final "flight check" as Jordan's hand lifts a Big Mac box from a paper bag and "refuels" with a sip of Coca-Cola. The "final equipment check" includes a close-up shot of Jordan palming a basketball and adjusting his shoes. The last thing the viewer sees as "Air Jordan: Flight 23" leaves the screen is his Nikes.

Jordan's second season was marked by a foot injury that kept him on the bench, though the Bulls still managed to make the 1986 playoffs. Not long after they were unceremoniously swept out of the first round by Larry Bird's Celtics, Jordan appeared on *Late Night with David Letterman*. The host, an avowed Adidas fan who had convinced the company to send him fifty pairs of sneakers earlier that year, pulled out a pair of Air Jordans, trying to cover the logo. "Now, why wouldn't they let you wear it? Just because it's ugly?" After the laughter died down, Jordan chimed in, "Hey, I agree with you, they are ugly." Letterman asked why the colors had violated the NBA's rules. "Well, it doesn't have any white in it," Jordan responded. Letterman looked mock perplexed for a few beats before retorting, "Well, neither does the NBA."

That was perhaps the most incredible thing about the rise of stars such as Dr. J, Bird, Johnson, and ultimately Jordan: they had managed to bring young star power to the NBA and become national celebrities in many ways not because of but in spite of their sport's place in popular culture—its 1970s controversies exacerbated by the unspoken (or not) racial biases. Stars like these, faces people everywhere trusted and wanted to *be like*, were crucial to pro basketball's ongoing rehabilitation from the game's struggling reputation at the end of the 1970s and early 1980s.

Though Magic and Bird had won championships in their Converse shoes and Abdul-Jabbar in his Adidas, the championship-less Air Jordans had proved a hit. Their success wasn't enough to keep the team that had helped make it happen stick with Nike, however—over the next few years, Strasser, Moore, and Vaccaro would all decamp to Adidas. But Nike was sticking with Jordan.

13

MARS AND MIKE

S pike Lee, dressed in a New York Mets baseball cap and bright red shorts, stood on a New York City street trying to get the attention of uninterested passersby.

"Tube socks. Tube socks. Three for five dollars," he said.

"When I'm not directing, I do this," he explained. "It pays the rent, puts food on the table, butter on my whole wheat bread."

For people going to the movies in the summer of 1986, it was their first glimpse of Lee. The young director, in his late twenties, wasn't really selling tube socks—he was introducing the trailer of his debut movie, *She's Gotta Have It*, which he had written, directed, produced, edited, and starred in. The movie tells the story of a young, independent Brooklyn woman named Nola who balances three very different boyfriends. Lee plays one of those suitors, the basketball-obsessed bike messenger Mars Blackmon, whose preferred look is an up-turned cycling hat with "Brooklyn" printed on it, a belt buckle bearing his oversized first name, and jumbo black-rimmed Cazal glasses, a flourish from the b-boy days. Even the prospect of sex with his beloved Nola isn't enough to get Mars to literally take off his even more beloved Air Jordan sneakers. Despite the shoes' prominence in the film, Lee himself had to use part of the movie's meager budget to buy two pairs; Nike agreed only to kick in a poster of Michael Jordan for Mars's room. Though Lee, a lifelong Knicks fan, was just as obsessed with basketball as the character he played in the movie, he knew better than to make the local team Mars's obsession. Jordan was just too transcendent.

After the black-and-white trailer concludes, Lee appears in color again. "So, you buggin' out, right?" he asks. "You gonna go? Gonna go? Gonna go? Gonna go? If you don't, I'll still be here on this corner! Tube socks! Tube socks! Three for five dollars!"

She's Gotta Have It exceeded its $175,000 budget to take in $7 million at the box office. It also caught the attention of film critics, whose condescension spoke more to how fresh Lee's film was than did their intended praise. "There's something genuinely different here," wrote Michael Wilmington in the *Los Angeles Times* in 1986. "A perspective we don't see enough—the joy and liveliness of an often neglected present." "These characters are well-grounded in a largely black neighborhood and, unlike black characters in most other films, speak black dialect *intelligently*," wrote the critic of *Film Comment* magazine. "The blacks in Lee's film are real people. As real people, they speak to us all." "Mr. Lee has said he worries about how black audiences will receive the film," wrote *New York Times* film critic D.J.R. Bruckner upon the movie's release. "He need not limit his concern to one audience; his characters will interest everyone."

One of those "everyones" was a creative director named Jim Riswold from Wieden+Kennedy, a Portland, Oregon–based agency known for its offbeat commercials (a recent one had featured 1970s street scenes in Manhattan's Lower East Side set to

Lou Reed's "Walk on the Wild Side" to sell a Honda scooter).
Wieden+Kennedy had just taken over the Air Jordan commercials from a much larger New York City–based ad agency. After
seeing the *She's Gotta Have It* trailer and film, Riswold filed away
the name of the promising young director just in case Lee might
be needed for just the right advertisement at just the right time.

HOW DO YOU FOLLOW A CLASSIC? You dress it up. Not many sneakers came with a tag that said "Made in Italy," and that was the
angle the Air Jordan II was going for: high flyer meets high fashion. Designer Peter Moore highlighted the shoe's sides with faux-
lizard leather. Viewed from the side, the red heel portion of the
sole gives the subtle impression of the raised heel of a men's dress
shoe. The then-unheard-of retail price of $100 underscored that
the AJII, in the words of a Nike spokesman to *Sports Illustrated*,
"would look great in a tux." The shoe was a technical step forward
from the original Air Jordan; there were a full-length air cushion,
extra polyurethane midsole padding, and more ankle support.
The most notable thing about the AJII, though, was that when the
shoe went on sale in November 1986, two years after Jordan debuted its predecessor, it didn't have the Nike swoosh anywhere. It
repeated the winged basketball logo used on the first Air Jordan,
but even the word "Nike" is visible only in small black letters on
the back of the shoe.

By not including the logo synonymous with the company,
Nike was taking a gamble that Jordan was logo enough. And why
not? He was already also endorsing McDonald's, Coca-Cola, and
Wilson basketballs. The company was sure that the man, not the
medium, was the message, despite what Marshall McLuhan might
have said. The Bulls star's unbelievable dunks ought to be enough
to sell any product. In the 1986 commercial for the Air Jordan II

a funky guitar plays as a wordless Jordan cradles a ball and jumps in slow motion toward a basket. As his arms pinwheel around, his shoes seem to hit an invisible step; the viewer isn't sure if the step is really there or if His Airness is sailing on his own toward the dunk. When the Nike logo and the shoes are shown at the end of the commercial, a voice-over says, "It's all in the imagination."

The problem: there was another Nike in town. At the beginning of 1987, Nike introduced the Air Max, and the everyman's sneaker with a plastic air cushion visbily embedded in the sole was soon the talk of the industry, not the $100 signature shoe. The AJII didn't get as much court time as everyone hoped, either, with Jordan's injury putting him out of commission for much of the season. Things compounded: as it became clear that the AJII wasn't selling as well as hoped, executives reluctant to spend more money on basketball shifted resources away from it and toward the Nike Air line. Jordan himself appeared in a blink-and-you-miss-it cameo in the Nike Air commercial. In that environment, it's easy to see why Jordan might have wanted to shift allegiances. He wasn't long removed from his days preferring Adidas and Converse. Wiser heads at Nike sensed that and hatched a plan to keep Jordan in swooshes for the rest of his career.

Rob Strasser, still with Nike at that point, knew that Knight would have to be convinced what to do about Jordan, but first, the player himself had to agree. In May 1987, Strasser, Peter Moore, Jordan, his family, and his agent met in an airport Sheraton in Charlotte, North Carolina, to discuss the way forward. Strasser presented two options. There was the business-as-usual, shoe-a-season approach. Or, he proposed, "we can take Michael where no sportsman has gone before. Take him out of the realm of colored sneakers and into style." The juvenile-looking basketball-and-wing logo was out. The "Jumpman" would take its place: a silhouette featuring a dunking Jordan with his hand raised skyward and legs splayed out in either direction like an inverted *Y*. That simple logo, like Ralph Lauren's polo player, could be put on an almost limitless line of apparel. Jordan liked the idea.

Before the plan moved forward, however, came a bait and switch. In the summer of 1988, Moore and Strasser approached Jordan again. They had left Nike to strike out on their own and, they hoped, convince MJ to go with them. The offer of making Jordan the centerpiece of an entire brand still stood. Jordan was still frustrated at the sales of the AJII and the slowness at making the Jumpman line a reality. In other words, he was susceptible to fresh ideas. Strasser and Moore's plan might've worked, if not for a former Man of Oregon and an up-and-coming film director from Brooklyn.

LIKE HIS FELLOW OREGON DUCKS, Tinker Hatfield was always being pulled into his track coach's makeshift cobbler shop under Hayward Field's bleachers for a pair of shoes that might or might not leave his feet bleeding. He had made newspaper headlines as a star high school athlete and earned his place alongside his fellow Men of Oregon, holding the school's pole vault record. In 1976, he placed sixth in the US Olympic trials for pole vault. A short time later, after making a jump during his sophomore year, he fell seventeen feet onto an uneven surface and ripped a muscle of his ankle. That night in his hospital bed, awaiting five surgeries, he overheard the doctors say his track career would be over. Bill Bowerman had other plans for him, though. The coach designed a pair of track spikes with a heel lift on one side to ease Hatfield's limp, saving him from being dismissed from the team and losing his scholarship. Hatfield was grateful—and also intrigued. He began helping Bowerman with his shoe designs, often drawing them, giving feedback, and performance testing them.

When Hatfield joined Nike in 1981 as its corporate architect, few could predict that he would one day hold the company's fortunes in his hands. His first four and a half years at Nike had him designing office spaces and showrooms. After taking part in a twenty-four-hour design contest that was partly a way for Nike to catch up with Reebok, he came up with "the perfect shoe to ride a motor scooter in." Two days later, he was told that he'd now be designing sneakers.

Hatfield's first high-profile project was the Air Max, which had an unlikely inspiration. While on a trip to Paris, one of Hatfield's must-visit sites was the Georges Pompidou Center—a building turned inside out sitting amid the mansard roofs of picture-postcard Paris. The Pompidou Center has no outer walls; oversized pipes, ductwork, and glass-enclosed walkways and escalators resembling human hamster tubes are all visible from the street. The building's innards weren't just exposed, they were highlighted. The architects had the pipes, ducts, and conduits painted bright colors to attract the eye to them. For many architectural critics at the time the building was a modernist monstrosity, but for Hatfield it was a revelation.

The 1987 Air Max solved a design problem. It had been years since the Air Max Tailwind, the company's first shoe to have an air cushion in the heel, debuted in 1978, and many of Nike's signature sneakers, including the Air Jordans, had them. The air pockets, pumped full of nitrogen, both provided cushioning and saved weight, a genuine technological advance. But as they were buried in the midsole, the benefits of the cushioning were difficult to communicate to the consumer. Thinking back to his visit to the Pompidou Center, Hatfield realized the answer: make it visible; let people see, and touch, the sneaker's hook.

"I'm fully convinced that had I not seen the building," he later said, "I might not have suggested that we expose this air bag and make it visual and let people see inside the shoe."

The 1987 Air Max, the centerpiece of the new Nike Air line, shunted the AJII out of the spotlight. Ironically, Hatfield's innovations with the sneaker also made him the perfect candidate to step into the design shoes left vacant when Peter Moore had left for Adidas. He would create the next Air Jordan. Jordan, being the name on the shoe, of course, was asked for input. He'd been doing a lot of thinking since the AJII: he wanted the Air Jordan III to be somewhere between a high-top and a low-top in order to keep it light and comfortable yet still provide some support. Hatfield later remarked that that wasn't what he'd expected to hear from an athlete; usually a player just put the shoe on, and that was that. Hatfield designed accordingly. The AJIII wouldn't be the high-fashion misfire of its predecessor—although Hatfield couldn't resist a couple design flourishes: he included the visible air cushion and, just for fun, an elephant-print heel and toe cap.

WHEN SPIKE LEE received a call from Jim Riswold, the Wieden+Kennedy creative director, he at first thought a film school classmate might be playing a joke on him.

"Do I get to work with Michael Jordan?" Riswold remembered Lee asking.

Riswold told him the deal: we want you to direct commercials in black and white starring Mars Blackmon and Jordan, for which we'll pay you $50,000. To a young director who had maxed out credit cards to make his first movie, it was an unbelievable offer. Not only would he make almost a third of what *She's Gotta Have It* had cost, he'd get to work with Jordan. There was just one catch: Jordan didn't know yet. Jordan hadn't seen *She's Gotta Have It*, and he definitely didn't know who Spike Lee was. Jordan ended up agreeing with the idea; after all, if Nike was going to step up its game in marketing him, its approach would have to be different.

A movie director filming a sneaker commercial was sort of full circle, considering how many movies quietly featured sneakers. The Converse All Star had graced every player's feet in 1986's *Hoosiers*—the blueprint for nearly all inspirational sports movies to follow—to attest to its 1950s setting. A similar-looking sneaker had popped up in the famous finger-snapping opening scene of 1961's *West Side Story*, which begins on an East Harlem basketball court. All of the white street gangsters, the Jets, wear light-colored sneakers, while their Puerto Rican rivals, the Sharks, sport darker ones. Mars Blackmon, wearing his Air Jordans even during sex, was in good company.

As in Lee's debut feature, the characters needed to stand out. Jordan, in previous advertisements, had been somewhat unknowable. Sure, he performed amazing dunks and had a winning smile, but until he was paired with Lee's everyman fanboy Blackmon, Jordan's affable and approachable side was left untapped. Lee knew, though, that Jordan had the clout to change whatever he didn't like about the commercial.

"If Michael had said he wanted the next man instead, that would have been it for me," Lee wrote in his memoir.

On their first meeting, Jordan looked the director over and said simply, "Spike Lee," as if challenging Lee to show him what he could do.

Released in 1988, Lee's first Air Jordan commercial begins with a black-and-white shot of Lee in character as Mars Blackmon, hanging on to the rim of a basketball hoop, asking "Do you know how I get up for my game? Do you know? Do you know? Do you know? That's right. Air Jordan. Air Jordan. Air Jordan." The camera pans down to reveal that Blackmon has been standing on Michael Jordan's shoulders. The player himself, dressed in a white T-shirt with a tiny Jumpman logo on one side, gives an "Oh, brother" grin, and walks off, leaving Blackmon hanging from the rim. Jordan reappears in the frame and dunks the ball on Lee as the image fades to a red-on-black Jumpman. There is a brief glimpse of Air Jordan IIIs in the commercial, but they aren't the primary focus. The Air Jordan brand itself is, with its fresh new logo.

Jordan's smirk at Lee is as good a moment as any to mark the point where Jordan the player began to change into Jordan the icon. Here, finally, is a glimpse of the new character: Jordan the Pitchman, that approachable yet otherworldly basketball player with the electric smile who not only manages to make the impossible possible but leaves the hint that you, too, might be able to do the same. With the right products, of course.

The same year as the first "Mars and Mike" commercial, Lee released his second feature. *School Daze*, a musical comedy–satire set in a historically black college, looked at the tensions that developed not only between the have and have-not undergraduates in fraternities and sororities but between less openly discussed differences such as hair and complexion prejudices. The movie's positive reception and box-office success (it brought in twice what his first film had) cemented Lee as a voice to watch in independent cinema. That most Americans' first taste of his work had come from his sharing a screen with Jordan didn't bother Lee; he had no problem mixing art and commerce. In 1991, he explained why he had done the commercials: "I thought it was important for me and Mike to do something together. Young black people in different fields hooking up."

A second commercial for the Air Jordan III again featured a motormouthed Lee-as-Mars who says that covering Jordan was "Impossible. Impossible. Impossible." Jordan covers Mars's

mouth, saying "However, it's easy to cover Mars Blackmon."
Lee and the ad agency Wieden+Kennedy knew to highlight the
story, the emerging narrative, surrounding the player. Jordan
proved himself to be a natural on camera, but the smartest decision in developing the Mars-and-Mike campaign was to give the
pitchman a pitchman himself. Blackmon's fanboy enthusiasm is
enough that the commercial didn't have to rely solely on the athlete's acting ability.

Sneaker campaigns before "Mars and Mike" could be effective, but they had lacked Nike's finesse in leveraging the person
behind the product—and when they did try to showcase athletes'
charisma, they were less persuasive. In one Converse Weapon
ad from the 1986–87 season, Magic Johnson appears holding a
yellow-and-purple sneaker while rapping "The Converse Weapon,
that's the shoe / That lets Magic do what he was born to do." Four
other stars bob onscreen one by one, each offering his own stilted,
off-key rhymes ("For the kind of moves that never fail / The Weapon's the choice of Kevin McHale"). Finally it's Larry Bird's turn:
"You already know what they did for me / I walked away with the
MVP." That was where the difference between Nike's and everyone else's ads was most apparent. In the Spike Lee commercials,
there's a sense of Jordan acting just as you'd imagine he would:
the commercials take place on a basketball court and feature Jordan doing what he does best: dunking. Lee draws out Jordan's
personality, but there's no forcing him into something that seems
unnatural—no Jordan rapping, for instance. The Converse ad is
packed with six times as many NBA stars, but there's little that
separates Magic from Bird from McHale. Who are they *as characters*? Who knows? They're telling you to buy a certain shoe—that
should be enough, right?

On the court, Jordan was more than keeping up his end of the bargain. In February 1988, he had one final attempt in the last stage of the NBA Slam Dunk Contest. He extended himself back to one corner of the court, as if stretching a rubber band about to be released. As he approacheed the free-throw line, his trademark tongue stuck out as he launched himself into the air, slamming the ball hard, earning him a near-perfect score and his second Slam Dunk title. Slow-motion replays seem to show Jordan sailing through the air, as if on wires. Schoolchildren everywhere tried to replicate the shot, leaping as far as they could from the free-throw line, tongues out. (Jordan would later warn kids not to add that last gesture to their game, lest they accidently bite it off.) The following night, he'd win All-Star MVP for his 40-point performance during the exhibition game. Though the Bulls failed to make it to the Eastern Conference finals that year, Jordan capped off the season as the league's leading scorer, leading defensive player, and, for the first time, Most Valuable Player.

Sales figures for the Air Jordan III proved that everything had lined up right. The shoe's success helped Nike pass $1.2 billion in revenue in 1988, a sign that the recent rough patch of sluggish earnings, restructuring, layoffs, and cost-cutting measures was finally behind Knight and Co. What was more, the successor shoe, the Air Jordan IV, repeated the same multipart model: a Hatfield-designed shoe (this time his inspiration came from World War II fighter planes), a Lee-directed commercial (this time with Mars Blackmon and a cameo by Nola from *She's Gotta Have It*), product placement in Lee's next film, the Oscar-nominated *Do the Right Thing*, and Jordan's dominating on-court performance. Once Nike demonstrated that this way of selling both the shoe and the player worked, its competitors went to work to try to replicate "the Jordan effect."

The new crop of star endorsements made the public more

aware of the diversity of sneaker options, as they saw their favorite athletes duke it out first on the court and then in dueling commercials. The following years would see companies trying more angles to win fickle consumers' loyalty. It's gotta be the shoes you can strap on, pump up, play multiple sports in, and make a fashion statement with. Continue along this trajectory, and it all resembled an arms race, each sneaker more desirable than the last.

Michael Jordan was a Nike man for good.

14

BATTLE OF THE BRANDS

When Dee Brown laced up his shoes in the Charlotte Coliseum locker room on February 9, 1991, he had no idea he was about to drop a culture bomb. At six foot one, he wasn't on the tall end of the NBA spectrum, but the twenty-two-year-old had several tools at his disposal that made him an interesting dunker to watch: his large hands, his long arms, and his new Reebok Pumps.

Midway through each season, the NBA holds a weekend extravaganza of all things basketball. Since 1951, it had evolved from just the All-Star Game to a chance for fans to see retired stars back on the court, as well as watch players sink shots from downtown in a three-point shoot-out. The night before Sunday's All-Star Game featured the Slam Dunk Contest, a kind of figure skating of dunking in which winners were based on the subjective scores of a panel of judges, usually made up of past superstars. Banned for nearly a decade in the 1960s and '70s, the dunk was to basketball what the home run was to baseball: a glory score destined for the highlight reel if well executed.

When Brown squeaked in to join the other seven contestants in the competition, the rookie Boston Celtics point guard was far from the favorite. That distinction went to Seattle's Shawn Kemp, who established himself as the front-runner by tossing the ball into the air well behind the free-throw line and letting it bounce once near the paint before leaping into the air to grab it. Kemp, seemingly eye level with the rim, slammed his first dunk so hard that the straining noise of the rim could be heard over the noise of the crowd.

As the announcers railed off some color commentary for Brown, the player's action stopped them short. Brown had bent over to press the little orange basketballs on his black-and-white high-tops.

"He's pumping his shoes up!" said one announcer.

"Oh, there you go," replied the other.

"That's worth about a million bucks to him right there."

Echoing Kemp's dunk, Brown stood outside the three-point line and tossed the ball into the air, catching it on the first bounce. Then he grabbed the ball with both hands and slammed it behind his head into the basket.

Immediately afterward he bent down again to let the air out of his shoes, pressing a valve next to the inflation button. The reverse dunk was enough to get Brown to the second round. Again he repeated the show of pumping up his Pumps, the camera focusing in on the shoes before he darted off to land a two-handed windmill reverse dunk.

Brown and Kemp both advanced to the final round. As Brown began the approach for the final dunk, he was still unsure what he'd do to clinch the win. "If I run up there, they're not going to know if my eyes are closed if they're behind me or on TV," he recalled years later. "It came as a progression while I was running that I was just closing my eyes, to hand over my eyes, to whole arm over my eyes."

Brown leapt off the ground at the bottom of the free-throw circle, looked down, and brought his arm over his eyes. He held that position as he sailed toward the basket, landing the ball cleanly through the net with his other arm.

"Oh my, that's the cherry on the sundae," said one of the announcers.

The other announcer couldn't help but laugh. The winner was clear. Kemp ran up to Brown to congratulate him on the "no-look dunk," a move instantly patented by the rookie.

At an after-party later that night, Brown was riding high. The Celtic player fans wanted autographs from wasn't Larry Bird, Robert Parish, or Kevin McHale, Brown's more famous teammates—it was him. Later that night Brown wound up in a VIP room with the All-Stars: Magic Johnson, Charles Barkley, and, of course, Michael Jordan.

Brown somehow found himself alone with Jordan, who was only months away from leading the Bulls to the first of their six eventual titles.

"Hey, you did a great job out there, young fella, nice show you put on," Brown recalled Jordan saying. "But, you know, you started the shoe wars."

Jordan was right, if also late. The shoe wars had been going on since Converse and Keds, since before the Dassler brothers had carved up their tiny Bavarian town. What was different now, and what Jordan seemed to allude to, was that athletes seemed more and more personally invested in the fight; product endorsements, whether they were for sneakers or hamburgers, weren't just paychecks, they were declarations of allegiance. Along with championships, wins, and stats, commercials and products had become just another metric to rate athletes against one another. A fan could declare loyalty to Nike, Reebok, Adidas, or Converse just as easily as he could the Bulls or the Celtics.

There was also a more direct battle brewing: Nike was not happy to see the Pumps on its turf.

WHEN PAUL FIREMAN WALKED INTO a Chicago trade fair in 1979, neither rejuvenating the women's sneaker industry nor launching an inflatable basketball sneaker was on the thirty-five-year-old camping and fishing supply marketer's mind. He was looking for a career change when he met Joe Foster, the owner of a company named Reebok, which was also looking for a different direction. For both men, the National Sporting Goods Association of America Show would end their search. At the time Reebok was a relatively small British brand focused on customized athletic shoes, with next to no presence in the United States. Fireman worked out a $65,000 deal to license and distribute Reebok in the United States. He didn't expect to upend the industry with his investment. "My goal was to have a respectable, small, quality company where I could get my two or three weeks of vacation a year, and pay to send my kids to school," he recalled years later. In his deal with Foster, Fireman found himself in command of a rich history, one that predated Nike, Adidas, and even Converse.

In 1895, Joe Foster's grandfather, Joseph William Foster, a fourteen-year-old member of the local Bolton, England, harrier running group, started making handcrafted spiked running shoes in his bedroom. When he visited his shoemaker grandfather's workshop, he saw how much of a difference in traction the shape of the pegs on a pair of cricket shoes could make. By the end of the nineteenth century, he perfected his spiked "running pumps" and founded his own company to sell the shoes, eventually partnering with his sons. Demand grew so high that he established the first sports shoe factory, one that invited athletes to get fitted for a custom pair, whether for running or cricket. The gold medal–winning runners featured in *Chariots of Fire* wore J. W. Foster and Sons shoes in the 1924 Paris Olympics. In 1958, two of J.W.'s grandsons split from the family business to form Reebok as a companion company and, two decades later, assumed ownership of J. W. Foster's original company.

For all his "respectable, small, quality" talk, Fireman had big plans for Reebok's American branch. In 1981, he introduced three models of top-of-the-line running shoes, hoping to capitalize on the connection to the film *Chariots of Fire*, which was released that year. Like Phil Knight before him, Fireman loaded the trunk of his car with shoes and drove from race to race, having runners try on the shoes, which at $60 were the highest-priced on the market. Though Reebok U.S.A.'s 1981 sales reached $1.5 million, Fireman had reason to be concerned. His company was struggling, and he was hard up for cash; that year he sold a majority stake to an investment group for $77,000, less than 1 percent of Nike's net annual income at the time.

A few short years later, Reebok's right-place, right-time development of aerobics shoes had helped catapult the brand to $1.79 billion in sales in 1988. Nike held the number two slot with $1.2 billion in sales.

Reebok's history shared several parallels with Nike's. Both companies gained a foothold in the industry by acting as the US hub for a foreign company, and both had risen to success by developing and marketing a new type of shoe. Their leaders, however, were different. Phil Knight still ran twenty miles a week, often hid behind wrap-around Oakley sunglasses, and removed his shoes before entering his office, as one would in Japan. Fireman worked with his office door open, and his sport of preference was golf.

The two sneaker titans met only once, at the 1993 U.S. Open, and exchanged pleasantries for about fifteen minutes. A colleague of Knight likened the meeting to the recent sit-down between Israeli prime minister Yitzhak Rabin and PLO chairman Yasser Arafat.

"I may be over the top on this," Knight said. "But I just don't want to like my competitors."

"At the end of a contest, I'd shake hands and walk away," Fireman said of Knight. "I think he would throw a shovel of dirt on the grave."

If there were ever to be a chance of peace, it probably ended in 1986, when Reebok overtook Nike as the US market leader. Nike had the consolation of its basketball renaissance, with Jordan and the Nike Air series, but the Reebok Freestyle and its successors had become a national phenomenon. The change in standings, which came just before Rob Strasser left the swoosh for Adidas, had a deep effect on Phil Knight.

Fireman, meanwhile, knew that Nike wouldn't quietly sit by as number two. The fitness craze had crested; Reebok would need another blockbuster basketball shoe to stay on top. In the late 1980s, Fireman ordered Paul Litchfield, who headed Reebok's "advance concept" group, to come up with that sneaker.

Litchfield's R&D team was a lean half-dozen members. His background working with Goodyear Rubber and DuPont placed him on the engineering side of shoe design—others would refine the look of the thing, but he would build it. The team's big idea came from a ski boot company Fireman had recently purchased, which made a boot that had an inflatable bladder inside to customize its fit, controllable with a pumping mechanism. Litchfield thought of Nike's success with the plastic air pocket in its running and basketball shoes. Air was light. Air was cushy. Air was visible (sort of). A new take on it, combined with eye-catching design and marketing, could be powerful.

It was hardly the first shoe to have an airbag. An 1892 patent had prefigured the Pump by nearly ninety years. But Litchfield's team built it from the ground up, taking inspiration on how to weave in the technology from Litchfield's days as a firefighter using blood pressure cuffs and inflatable bag–like air splints. Litchfield and his team applied the concept to an inflatable section wrapped around the midsole of the foot. Rather than using the plastic found in pool air mattresses, Reebok found a medical-grade equipment supply company that made intravenous and blood bags. The inflation mechanism was a hurdle: no one wanted to bring a separate pump to the court to air up his shoes; the pump had to be inside the Pump. Early prototypes inflated as you walked, but they didn't test well at local schools; kids wanted to pump up their shoes themselves. Another early design featured a pump on the heel of the shoe with a pressure release valve built into one side, but it was rejected for being too ugly. A designer on Litchfield's team came up with the ingenious idea of hiding the pump in plain sight as an orange basketball on the tongue of the shoe.

That was at the beginning of 1989. Litchfield had two marching orders: the shoe had to be on the shelves by Christmas, and they had to work. A Pump that wouldn't pump, especially at a price of $170 per sneaker, would be a PR fiasco. Litchfield and his team put layer upon layer of safeguards in place: the US-made pump bladders were tested three hours after they were made, then again twenty-four hours after they were made, before being shipped overseas to a shoe factory in South Korea. Once there, they were inflated and left for twenty-four hours. Another test was done when the bladders were stitched into the shoes and another when the completed shoe was on the line. Before the shoes were shipped from the factory, they were tested one last time.

Rather than inflate each shoe by hand over and over, one of

the Korean factory workers came up with the idea to adapt a sewing machine to inflate the thousands of shoes automatically. Unbeknownst to the factory workers, the makeshift solution bent the inflation mechanism on each sneaker; the final test was the last time their bladders would hold air.

When the shipment arrived at Reebok's distribution center in Massachusetts, a panicked employee phoned Litchfield to tell him that thousands of shoes were duds.

"Hey, Litch, these shoes don't inflate," Litchfield remembers him saying.

"What?"

"These shoes don't inflate."

"You're doing it wrong."

Litchfield headed down to the distribution center, convinced that the employee had just opened a bad batch. Box after box was opened, and the result was the same. Between 80 and 90 percent of the shoes didn't work.

"I about crapped myself," Litchfield remembers.

Litchfield and a half-dozen companions took over one of the stitching rooms and unstitched part of the sneaker's tongue enough to pull the pump mechanism out, replaced it with a new one, and hand-stitched the tongue back together. They did so for three or four thousand sneakers. The shoes made it to the shelves in time for Christmas.

What made the Pump so revolutionary, at least according to the ads, was that now you could *control* how much air was in your sneakers, giving *you* the power to choose the fit you wanted. Early Pump ads featured basketball stars of the day talking about how many pumps they preferred. Dominique Wilkins: 15, Danny Ainge: 20 to 25, Coach Pat Riley: 5 or 6. A magazine ad featuring the tennis star Michael Chang specified his preferred racket tension (64 pounds), grip size (4½), and shoe pumps (16 pumps for the left foot, 21 for the right). Paul Litchfield watched the 1991 Slam Dunk Competition at home, beer in hand. When he saw Dee Brown inflate his shoes on live national TV, something apparently no one at Reebok had known he would do, he knew it was the kind of advertisement you couldn't pay for.

It wasn't enough for Reebok to win; Nike also had to lose. The Pump's tagline, "Pump up and air out," had as much to do with the inflating and deflating mechanism as it did with Dominique Wilkins tossing a Nike Air shoe behind his shoulder at the end of every commercial. (Wilkins, nicknamed "The Human Highlight Reel," was the Nike Air's biggest name.) A particularly dark TV spot from 1990 featured two bungee jumpers, one wearing Nikes and the other pumping up his Reeboks before the pair make the leap. At the end of the ad, we see that the Reebok wearer is okay thanks to his snug-fitting shoes. All that's left of the other guy is a pair of Nikes dangling from the bungee cord. After one showing during the 1990 NCAA tournament, CBS refused to air it again. (Reebok withdrew the spot after complaints from parents.)

Nike countered with its own inflatable shoe, the Air Pressure. Though similar in concept to the Pump (and also a jaw-dropping $170), the Nike shoe lacked the internal inflation mechanism; you had to carry your Air Pressure pump with you. In every way that the various iterations of the Pump were a hit, the Air Pressure was not. It was quietly shuffled aside.

Nike did manage to regain a slight edge over Reebok in the $4 billion athletic shoe market, of which, in 1990, each company occupied nearly a quarter. Reebok lacked the media presence of the Jordan effect, but with Dee Brown's impromptu inflation it had shown it was capable of creating (or at least taking advantage of) a sensation. With a new class of shoe, new marketing strategies, and new athletes coming into play, the shoe wars were still anyone's game.

—

"YOU CAN'T BE SERIOUS, MAN!" protested John McEnroe. "You cannot be serious!"

During the first round of the 1981 Wimbledon tournament, the match umpire had ruled one of McEnroe's serves "out." Hands up and voice raised, McEnroe registered his displeasure the only way he knew how.

"That ball was on the line. Chalk flew up! It was clearly in! How can you possibly call that *out*?"

McEnroe was fined for his outburst (and for calling the umpire "the absolute pits of the world"). Not that it made much of a difference—the prize money from his eventual win in the singles tournament more than made up for it. He was young, he was talented, he was volcanic—just the combination Nike wanted in its athletes.

McEnroe had signed a deal with Nike in 1978. The "Super Brat" knew how to draw crowds and win matches. Nike played off his often profanity-laden outbursts by running ads with taglines such as "McEnroe swears by them" and "McEnroe's favorite four-letter word." After taking a hiatus for the birth of his first child, McEnroe was looking to dip back into tennis in 1986. He already had seven Grand Slam singles titles to his name and, at twenty-seven, was nearing the last stage of his competitive career. He contacted Nike to send him a range of shoes that wouldn't be so hard on his feet. He received several tennis shoes, as well as an experimental shoe that its designer, Tinker Hatfield, was unaware had even been sent to the player.

That shoe was different from the rest. It wasn't so much designed for tennis as it was a new class of all-purpose athletic shoe, the cross-trainer. The jogging and aerobics booms had given way to a more diversified exercise landscape, and since not many people were about to head to the gym with a bag full of sneakers, Nike's designers had reasoned that there was a need for a shoe suitable for many activities, from weight lifting to running to, sure, even tennis. The most distinctive feature of the prototype, later called the Air Trainer 1, was a Velcro strap that went across the toes, seemingly locking your foot in. The shoe's black, white, and gray patterning, with accents in green, was said to have been inspired by gym equipment.

"Once they were on, I was like, 'Sorry, guys, this is the one. We have to go with this, we have to reverse field here,'" McEnroe said. "This one felt really right." Against instructions to wear them in competition, he did anyway, winning his comeback tournament, 1986's Volvo International in Vermont, with doubles partner Peter Fleming. Watching McEnroe play, Hatfield was surprised to see his cross-trainer on TV.

"It was a jaw-dropping experience for me because I didn't know he was going to wear them," Hatfield said. "Nobody did." The sneaker had not been designed for tennis, nor, for that matter, was it ready to be seen. Following the tournament, McEnroe was asked to return the shoes, and, in his inimitable way, he refused. "These are the best tennis shoes you ass-holes have ever made," he said.

Given that foul-mouthed but sincere recommendation, the shoes were put into production and released to the public the following year.

ONE OF THE HALLMARKS OF the "Me Generation," baby boomers in the 1970s and 1980s, was a focus on self-improvement and health.

This attitude suggested a less obvious way to advertise than slapping a familiar athletic face on something: expanding the definition of "athlete." Along with the likes of Michael Jordan and Larry Bird, consumers themselves became the focus of ads for athletic products, sneakers in particular. The idea can be traced from Bill Bowerman's revelation while jogging in New Zealand decades earlier: runners weren't defined by how many Olympics they competed in but by the act of running itself. Many of the people who showed up at Bowerman's first clinics in Eugene were "ordinary" people; they weren't the Men of Oregon, but they were athletes nonetheless. As Bowerman would say, "If you have a body, you are an athlete."

In one 1987 Nike ad, sports stars and ordinary people are shown in a black-and-white montage of jogging, playing basketball, tennis, cycling, and just plain walking while the Beatles' "Revolution" plays in the background. Equal weight is given to shots of John McEnroe and a smiling toddler running down a sidewalk in a tiny pair of Nikes. The advertised product, the Air Max, is almost beside the point. Nike isn't selling a shoe so much as an idea: you can do it. Don't buy this shoe because a particular star wears them; buy it because you're already a star.

When Paul Fireman first saw the commercial, he said to himself, "*Good* night." The Pump wouldn't be released until 1989, and Fireman knew that without the right message, Reebok would be back behind Nike soon enough. If you weren't part of the revolution, you were one of the stodgy old-timers.

The "can-do" idealism hadn't sprung up in a vacuum. The television audience of the late 1980s had been primed by the growing sophistication of commercials. Emotion had begun to play a much larger role, whether in selling a product, a man, or an idea. During the 1980 Super Bowl a Coca-Cola advertisement ran featuring Pittsburgh Steelers defensive tackle "Mean" Joe Greene, in which the limping, dejected Greene heads to the locker room and is offered a Coke by a young boy. The player's mood lifts as soon as he drinks it, and he tosses the boy his jersey. Coca-Cola: it's about friendship.

Print advertisements changed as well. Images of jumping and running athletes were well and good, but the new consumer, companies decided, needed to know *why* he or she needed a gimmicky air cushion. A triptych of a disembodied foot wearing the Air Max showed a heel strike in one frame, the shock-absorbing air cushion in the second, and a shoe bouncing back for the next step in the third. Bar charts from the Nike Sport Research Lab purported to show the Nike Air's superior cushioning technology when stacked up against competitors such as the Converse Weapon. The quantifiable analysis made possible at the dawn of the digital age brought science into the appeal to the armchair athlete.

The admen of the 1960s had a name for the sum of all those parts: the "Big Idea." If a marketing campaign could be distilled down to a basic message, what would it be? What was a brand trying to say to the consumer?

Nike's "Big Idea" came from, of all places, the last words of a murderer about to be executed. Facing a Utah state firing squad in 1977, Gary Gilmore said, "Let's do it." Something about that phrase, especially the last two words, stuck with Dan Wieden, a cofounder of Wieden+Kennedy. When Nike solicited a new company slogan in 1988, the phrase Wieden had stored away all those years reappeared as "Just do it."

"Just do it" spoke to people in a way Nike's first tagline, "There is no finish line," hadn't. It was a direct call to action to anyone procrastinating about, maybe, going to the gym or taking up jogging. "People were applying it to just everything they were putting off or procrastinating about or avoiding dealing with," recalled

Liz Dolan, Nike's head of marketing at the time. "I had women writing to me saying, 'I finally left the bum.' They were getting divorces based on the 'Just do it' slogan."

IN MICHAEL JORDAN, Nike had one of the world's most popular athletes; in "Just do it," it had one of the most quotable slogans. What would happen if the two were combined?

Vincent "Bo" Jackson was the consummate athlete. He was capable of things you wouldn't believe had they not been filmed: things like breaking baseball bats over his leg (or helmeted head); plowing through linebackers as if they weren't there; running up the side, then along, the outfield wall to catch a baseball. If there were anyone who could equal or surpass Jordan's star power, it was the kid (the eighth of ten) from rural Alabama. He turned down being drafted by the New York Yankees in 1982 to attend Auburn University, where he not only played baseball but ran track and played football, for which he won the Heisman Trophy. After college he played outfield for the Kansas City Royals and running back for the Los Angeles Raiders, becoming the first athlete in the modern era to play two professional sports at the same time.

The same ad agency that had turned Jordan into a friendly, approachable household name would do the same for the superhuman Jackson. But Michael Jordan's basketball sneakers could seamlessly make the transition from court to street; what to do with Jackson, who played both his sports in cleats? Wieden+Kennedy paired Jackson's all-encompassing athleticism with Nike's newest experiment.

The 1989 TV ad campaign featured Jackson trying a range of sports while a stable of Nike athletes intoned "Bo knows basketball" (Jordan), "Bo knows tennis" (John McEnroe), "Bo knows running" (Joan Benoit Samuelson). The kicker came when Jackson attempted to play electric guitar, which prompted bluesman Bo Diddley to remark, "Bo, you don't know diddly." Nike's cross-trainers, the "Bo knows" ad campaign implied, were the only shoes he could use for every sport.

The shoe John McEnroe had sworn into public notice had found a market, and Nike was doubling down on cross-training. The cross-trainer was really just an amped-up version of the "fitness" sneakers Reebok was famous for, but Nike was canny about tying it to the sports-positive, everyone's-an-athlete wave of the "Revolution" ad and "Just do it" tagline. The Reebok Freestyle had been almost postsports—aerobics was, after all, fitness without the court, field, or track. Nike Air Trainers, on the other hand, were for a North American public who wanted to play *every* sport.

The "Bo knows" campaign was a hit, and in designing the Nike Air Trainer III, Tinker Hatfield took inspiration from Jackson himself. "The fun part about working on a shoe for Bo Jackson was that sometimes when you design athletic shoes," Hatfield said, "they're like caricatures of real shoes and here comes Bo Jackson, he was larger than life, he was faster than everybody else and stronger. Bo just seemed like a cartoon character to me." Jackson was, in fact, a cartoon character, at least on the 1991 Saturday-morning cartoon show *ProStars*, which cast Jackson, Michael Jordan, and Wayne Gretzky as crime-fighting superhero athletes. "Bo knows" puns appeared in nearly every episode, one of many, many places they showed up. The Chicago Symphony Orchestra used the phrase "Bow knows" in promotions.

Not to be left behind, other brands entered the cross-trainer market, some more successfully than others. Reebok, apparently missing the definition of the market segment, released a "cross-trainer for tennis" and a "cross-trainer for basketball."

As the "Bo knows" mania was at its zenith, Jackson's career

took a literal hit. In a January 1991 game, a seemingly routine tackle popped the twenty-eight-year-old running back's right hip out of its socket. The Raiders dropped him, the Royals dropped him, but Nike stood by him. Maybe it was that he'd always been half legendary, but even with a bum hip he could still move product. One ad featured him rehabbing in the gym while the comedian Denis Leary chided the audience, all us athletes with "two good hips," for watching TV.

THE 1992 OLYMPICS IN BARCELONA, Spain, would prove a perfect battleground for every major shoe brand. The "amateur only" requirement for Olympic athletes had finally begun to relax by the Barcelona games, in time for the inclusion of professional basketball players. As one might've expected, the United States was able to assemble the best possible "Dream Team" of players so talented and famous that many were already international household names. Each Dream Teamer came to the Olympics with his respective sneaker endorsement. Nike had Michael Jordan, Charles Barkley, and David Robinson. Larry Bird and Magic Johnson wore Converse. Though no one on the US team wore Reebok, Adidas, or Puma, smaller brands such as LA Gear, Avia, and Patrick Ewing's own signature brand had a piece of the action. Things had come a long way since basketball had been introduced during the Berlin Games in 1936, when the gold medal–winning US men's team had worn matching All Stars.

Knowing that most of the well-known Nike Olympians were on the basketball court, Reebok put the bulk of its pre-Olympic marketing efforts behind two then-unknown decathletes, Dan O'Brien and Dave Johnson. The two were cofavorites to win gold, and Reebok sensed that by creating media darlings out of two "track-famous" superathletes, it would have an advertising narrative able to trump the Dream Team—especially if one of them became the first American decathlete to win since Bruce Jenner in 1976. And if anyone knew about the shoes, surely it would be an athlete who had to be the best at running both fast (and long), jumping high (and long), throwing various objects as far as they would go, and so on. In other words, Nike has Bo Jackson? Big deal, Reebok has two Bo Jacksons.

The eight-month, $25 million "Dan & Dave" ad campaign featured the two going head to head to see who would be "the greatest athlete of all time." A typical TV spot featured home movies of O'Brien and Johnson while an announcer recited how far Dan could put a shot or how far Dave could long jump. Dan and Dave were endorsing the Reebok Pump Graphlite, the company's new crack at a multisport cross-trainer.

A month before the Olympics, Reebok's hope of one-upping Nike at the Games hit a snag: O'Brien failed to make the US Olympic team, totally undermining the ads' promise that the matter of who was the world's top athlete would be "settled in Barcelona." Reebok retooled the ads to focus on Johnson, who ended up competing through a foot injury to take bronze.

But Reebok had a consolation prize, or so it thought. It had designed the Dream Team's official Olympic warm-up outfits, meaning that the United States' inevitable gold-medal win offered the promise of seeing Michael Jordan, Charles Barkley, and the other marquee Nike players photographed wearing their rival's logo. The players couldn't simply refuse to wear the jacket; each Olympian had signed a document promising to wear the official uniform in the medal ceremony.

"I don't believe in endorsing my competition," Jordan said. "I feel very strongly about loyalty to my own company."

"Us Nike guys are loyal to Nike because they pay us a lot of money," Barkley put it more bluntly. "I have two million reasons not to wear Reebok."

Word spread that they were planning not to attend the medal ceremony at all. An angry public phoned Nike headquarters: America's biggest Olympic stars were going to skip the highest honor over wearing a logo? Press reports were also unsympathetic: "As for loyalty to his company, how loyal was Jordan to Coca-Cola when Gatorade offered him more money?" asked Dave Anderson in the *New York Times*. Phil Knight sensed a public relations disaster.

"This is getting serious," the Nike chief said. "We have to get to Michael."

After much negotiating, the entire team agreed to fold the collars of their jackets down over the Reebok logo and hold them in place with safety pins. Jordan and Barkley took the compromise a step further and draped American flags around themselves, Jordan even going so far as to safety-pin Old Glory to his warm-up pants to cover the tiny "Reebok" stitched into them.

For Reebok and Nike, it was just another day of the shoe wars.

What the rivals were only starting to realize was that there were other fights to be waged about sneakers—ones having nothing to do with sales but everything to do with how their products were made, who wore them, and what some people were willing to do to get them. The 1990s would bring a wake-up call.

15

SNEAKER CRIME AND PUNISHMENT

P hil Knight was pissed off.

Something was happening in the streets that he didn't like. He had just learned Reebok had released a Pump variation called the Blacktop, an absolute tank of a sneaker marketed as an outdoor basketball shoe, the first of its kind. Early one morning in 1991, Knight left a Post-it note on another exec's door saying, in typical Knight fashion, "What is our competitive response to this idea?" The exec took the note and stuck it on the drawing table of Tinker Hatfield, who, characteristically, had not arrived yet.

Reebok had beaten Nike to another overlooked market. Since the days of Chuck Taylor, basketball shoes had been made primarily with the indoor hardwood in mind, ignoring the real cauldron where great players were tested: blacktops and playgrounds. Missing a key demographic was one thing; having a rival, especially Reebok, get there first was something else.

Hatfield traveled to outdoor courts in New York and LA to see what streetballers, famous and nonfamous, wanted from a shoe. The game he saw was tighter, the fouls were rougher, and the crowds were closer. At New York's famed Rucker Park, a lone player might drive past defenders under the hoop to dunk the ball from the side opposite to the one he'd started on. Teamwork was still important, but moves that could get a cheer from the crowd ruled the day. Hatfield found that most players just wanted a tough shoe that would hold up on asphalt.

The "competitive response" Hatfield came up with featured a chunky midsole with a reinforced outsole that crept up the sides of the sneaker and a thick strap that crisscrossed the instep, as if locking the wearer's foot down for battle. Hatfield wanted to call the shoe the Air Jack, because other people would want it so much they'd steal the sneaker right off your foot. For obvious reasons, that name was rejected by Nike's executives. Instead, the Air Raid hit the street courts in 1992, complete with a Spike Lee commercial. The filmmaker was paired with another up-and-coming player, Tim Hardaway, then of the Golden State Warriors. In the ad, Lee (playing himself, not Mars Blackmon) stood in the middle of a colorful geometric-patterned outdoor court and told the audience to watch how Hardaway sank jump shots under windy conditions, a problem unique to outdoor basketball. The Air Raids Lee held up in the commercial, black with a gray X strap, coincidentally mimicked the stark poster for his forthcoming Malcolm X biopic, which, like *Do the Right Thing* before it, many would hail as a masterpiece.

Sports companies and marketers had finally woken up to a scene New Yorkers and Angelenos had known for decades. Suddenly Pizza Hut was offering a $4.99 "Streetball" basketball while movies such as 1992's *White Men Can't Jump* gave audiences across the country a taste of street-hustling asphalt-court California. But although sneaker companies were turning to the streets for new ideas, they were reluctant to see what else was going on.

ON THE AFTERNOON OF MAY 2, 1989, fifteen-year-old Michael Eugene Thomas left his high school in Fort Meade, Maryland, a small town outside Baltimore. Two weeks earlier, he had purchased brand-new Air Jordans for $115.50 with his allowance money and help from his father. Thomas cleaned his shoes every evening, displayed the box prominently in his room, and had even kept the receipt. His grandmother, sensing how sought after the shoes were, had told Thomas not to wear them to school.

"Granny," he said, "before I let anyone take those shoes, they'll have to kill me."

A few hours after heading home from school that Tuesday, Thomas's strangled and sodomized body was discovered in the woods, barefoot.

Not long after Thomas's body was found, investigators came upon seventeen-year-old James David Martin, who had been seen leaving school with Thomas. Martin was wearing a pair of red Air Jordans identical to the ones Thomas had purchased. After Martin told the police the shoes were his, officers discovered that they were not even his size. He was arrested for first-degree murder and robbery. Investigators suspected that the new Air Jordans had been the motive for the murder.

"I think it's a sign of our poor times," said Sergeant Thomas A. Suit, chief of the county homicide squad.

Some time later, before a workout at the Chicago Bulls' practice facility, Michael Jordan sat in a locked press room and read an account of Thomas's murder handed to him by a journalist.

"I can't believe it," he said quietly.

Martin served seven years in prison for the murder and was released in 1996, only to return behind bars for a string of other homicides. The 1989 case formed the basis of a *Sports Illustrated* cover story the following May about killings connected to sneakers and sports jackets. The provocative cover featured the back of a man wearing a maroon team jacket with a pair of white Air Jordans slung over his shoulder. A pair of hands of an unseen thief is grabbing the shoes and jamming a revolver into the man's back. The headline: "Your Sneakers or Your Life."

In the 1990s, *Sports Illustrated* held tremendous sway over the sports conversation. An athlete who managed to be featured had "made it." When an issue made it onto the cover, it set off a national conversation—this time, into violent crimes surrounding sneakers and other sports gear. The murder of Michael Eugene Thomas was hardly the first or the last of its kind; the article listed ten more instances of sneaker- or jacket-related attacks. News stations and newspapers chimed in to the debate: Who, they asked, was at fault? Was it the companies that made and advertised the products? Was it the celebrities who endorsed them? Was it the bleak desperation of the inner city? Was society itself to blame for letting a lust for materialism get this far?

"I never thought because of my endorsement of a shoe, or any product, that people would harm each other," Jordan was quoted as saying. "Everyone likes to be admired, but when it comes to kids actually killing each other . . . then you have to reevaluate things."

The *New York Post* columnist Phil Mushnick laid the blame on Jordan and filmmaker Spike Lee, who, in the columnist's eyes, had hyped the shoes too much. "It's murder, gentlemen," he wrote in a 1990 column. "No rhyme, no reason, just murder. For sneakers. For jackets. Get it, Spike? Murder."

By pointing the finger at two prominent black celebrities, Mushnick injected a racial element into sneaker crime. He believed that Lee and Jordan had betrayed their core audiences by selling a shoe too expensive for them—driving them to kill to get them. That was about as strong an argument as saying NBA basketball in the 1970s was "too black" to be popular.

Mushnick also, incidentally, ignored the very white ad agency that had come up with Lee and Jordan's campaign.

Lee was less than pleased by Mushnick's assessment.

"It's ridiculous to say that the blood of America is on the hands of Michael Jordan and [Georgetown University basketball coach] John Thompson and me," he said. "Are you going to blame killings on the sneakers?"

Asked about the column in an interview with *Playboy* the following year, Lee expanded: "Something is wrong where these young black kids have to put so much weight, where their whole life is tied up—their life is so hopeless—that their life is defined by a pair of sneakers. Or a sheepskin coat. The problem is not the coat or the sneakers. I mean, we tried to explore that with *Do the Right Thing* with the radio. These young black kids who are lost. Radio Raheem [a character killed by the police]—his life was that radio, he's invisible; people don't notice him. But with that radio blasting Public Enemy and 'Fight the Power,' you had to deal with him. It made people notice him. It gave him self-worth."

In the three years since the *Sports Illustrated* article more reports of sneaker crime had stoked a related debate: the connection between sportswear and gangwear. In 1993, Converse found itself in hot water for planning to name a basketball sneaker the "Run 'N Gun," after the fast-breaking, high-scoring style of play. After criticisms from youth and community groups, the sneaker's name was changed to the "Run 'N Slam."

Gang style had evolved in the two decades since the self-designed jean jackets of the South Bronx turf wars. Sportswear, with its range of logos, brands, colors, and markings, was more readily available and, in its own built-in way, more readily differentiated than 1970s street punk wear. In Boston, the Greenwood

Street gang preferred Green Bay Packers gear, while the Castle-gate gang wore Cincinnati Reds clothes and the Intervale gang wore exclusively Adidas hats, jackets, and shoes. Some apparel store owners in areas where gangs operated stopped selling jackets and sneakers that were popular with gangs and drug dealers.

"I always thought part of the whole deal was that kids might want to emulate me—to do what I do to get ready to play on the field," said Bo Jackson. "I always thought that if they emulated me instead of some street dealer—that was the idea."

To a middle America far removed from inner-city life, media speculation seemed to suggest that almost anyone wearing branded or team clothing could be gang affiliated. News reports broke down the street gang color lines: Crips wore blue, Bloods wore red. Having your shoes stolen by a stick-up boy was one thing; the scare du jour was wearing the wrong colors in the wrong neighborhood. But in a major city with gang activity, that warning carried a deadly grain of truth.

In May 1995, two teenagers went to buy gum in a southwest Detroit neighborhood. Both were wearing black-and-blue sneakers, the colors of a gang rivaling the dominant Latin Counts of the area, who wore red and black. Several Latin Counts approached the teenagers and started beating one of them up, saying he had the wrong shoes on. The confrontation escalated into a gunfight that left a gang member and a Detroit police officer dead.

ON THE WEST COAST during the 1980s, the crack cocaine epidemic ravaged areas of Los Angeles, fueling gang activity and the drug trade. Southern California's 1960s image of a laid-back "surf city" paradise was replaced by reports of a war zone of gangbangers targeting each other, and anyone else who happened to be in their way, to gain turf or to settle a score.

"South Central Los Angeles: a place where drugs, crime and violence rule the streets," intoned the actor Laurence Fishburne in the acclaimed 1991 movie *Boyz n the Hood*. Director John Singleton's film was one of the wider public's clearest looks at life in the predominantly black and poor LA neighborhood. A video of white police officers beating a black motorist, Rodney King, and the ensuing acquittal of the officers led to the six-day Los Angeles riots in 1992. That same year, Los Angeles County reported a record 2,589 homicides; July and August alone counted for more than 500.

Amid that backdrop, California's budding hip-hop scene took on a different flavor than that of the Bronx a decade earlier. Ice-T's seminal 1986 song "6 'N the Mornin'" begins with the lines "6 in the morning, police at my door / Fresh Adidas squeak across the bathroom floor" and goes on to detail a long tale full of police chases, shootings, stabbings, and sex. It was a far cry from the comparatively saintly "My Adidas" released by Run-DMC the same year. For many people, the violent lyrics found in the new West Coast rap were an indication that the music itself was to blame. But shootings, police brutality, drug use, and gang activity all found their way into the music less because the lifestyle was being glorified than because, as with "The Message," rappers were simply reporting what was happening in their own neighborhoods. Ice-T described their sound as "reality rap."

The label that ended up sticking was "gangsta rap," however, and "6 'N the Mornin'" ushered in its era—and with it a different sensibility, in fashion as well as music. The Compton-based hip-hop group N.W.A., another pioneer of gangsta rap, embraced black baseball hats from the LA Raiders or Kings as a kind of uniform, as if the group itself were a gang with its own colors. Raiders hats, jackets, and other gear were banned from many schools out of fear that they were gang-related. Sneakers, almost always black or white, were part of the group's look, too, though N.W.A. was not brand-loyal like Run-DMC. The group's members sported Nikes, Reeboks, Adidas, or the California brand K-Swiss, whatever was stylish at the time. The sensibility was in the same vein as Run-DMC's switch to the gold chains and leather jackets of their native Hollis, Queens: in order to be taken seriously by your fans, you had to look authentic, i.e., you had to look as though you came from where they came from. Rappers shouted out their neighborhood sneakers. "In L.A. we wearing Chucks, not Ballys," Tupac Shakur sang on his 1995 single "California Love." The Notorious B.I.G. namechecked Timberlands on 1994's "Suicidal Thoughts" when he said he preferred wearing "black Tims and black hoodies" to wearing white and "goin' to heaven with the goodie-goodies."

What you wore was tied closely to who you were and where you came from, for better or worse. At the beginning of the 1990s, few people were asking where sneakers themselves came from. That changed dramatically by the end of the decade.

In the movie *Forrest Gump*, the title character receives a pair of white Nike Cortezes and decides to go "for a little run" across the country. The scene takes place in the mid-1970s—Forrest starts the jogging boom—at which time Nike was making its shoes in factories in the United States and South Korea. By the time the movie was filmed in the early 1990s, many sneaker and garment companies had outsourced their labor; Nike had closed the last of its US shoe factories in the 1980s, with operations in South Korea picking up the slack. When workers at those independent producers gained the right to organize and strike near the end of the decade, Nike transferred its labor south to factories in Indonesia, China, and Malaysia, where wages were a fraction of what the company had been paying in South Korea. The prop shoes Tom Hanks was wearing in *Forrest Gump* likely came from the new factories. And as his character put it, "My mama always said you can tell a lot about a person by their shoes, where they going, where they been."

Most of the labor changes went under the nose of the general public until stories such as a 1992 article in *Harper's Magazine* started to appear, outlining the wide discrepancy between workers' wages and the price of the shoes they were assembling. The *Harper's* article, titled "The New Free-Trade Heel," mentioned that one Indonesian worker assembled midrange Nike sneakers for the equivalent of 14 cents per hour. Her monthly take-home pay, for ten and a half hours of work, six days a week, came to $37.46. To produce an $80 sneaker cost only 12 cents in labor.

In 1990, with $2.2 billion in annual revenue and about $243 million in annual profit, Nike finally claimed the top spot in the global athletic shoe and apparel market. A tight shot of Michael Jordan's face, eyes squinted shut in the midst of laughter, graced the cover of the annual report that year. As joyous as the moment may have felt, an existential crisis was brewing that would shake the entire clothing and footwear industry that relied on overseas labor. Though not the first to report on sweatshop conditions, the *Harper's* article proved to be the tip of the iceberg. Reports in *The Oregonian*, the *New York Times*, the *Los Angeles Times*, on CBS, in *The Economist*, and in many more outlets soon followed, detailing a labor situation in Southeast Asia that included low pay, abusive conditions, unfair terminations, intimidations, and more in the region's sweatshops. A typical sweatshop might feature a large room packed with workers hunched over rows and rows of sewing machines, often for many hours at a time, with few opportunities for even bathroom breaks and a never-ending stream of sneakers, jeans, other clothing, or toys to assemble.

At first, Nike wrote off the accusations by arguing that since it did not own the factories that made the shoes, only contracted with them, the conditions of the facilities were not its responsibility. In a globalized economy that relied on outsourcing labor, accountability had become at best hard to allocate, at worst easy to pass off down the line. "We don't pay anybody at the factories and we don't set policy within the factories; it is their business to run," Nike vice president of production Dave Taylor told *The Oregonian* in 1990.

In 1992, the company drafted a code of conduct that required each of its subcontractors and suppliers to conform with local regulations as well as allow regular inspections. Under that protocol, however, Nike would have to take subcontractors at their word that everything was within compliance. And for all Nike's assurances that it had cleaned up its act overseas, reports continued to surface throughout the decade that reality was another matter. In 1997, an accounting firm reported that 77 percent of workers in a Vietnam factory, mostly young women under the age of twenty-five, suffered respiratory problems from work-related exposure to toxins. Employees at the site, which was operated by a Korean subcontractor, were forced to work 65 hours a week, netting only $10 per week.

Nike wasn't alone in being called out for using cheap labor. Reebok, for instance, made a larger percentage of shoes in Indonesia than Nike did. For the antisweatshop movement, though, Nike was the big fish. In 1997, Nike reported more than $9 billion in global revenue, roughly triple what it was only three years earlier. Reebok had faded to $3 billion, relinquishing the number two slot to Adidas, at $5 billion in sales. For antisweatshop activists, singling out the globally recognized market leader was important.

"Without the single focus on Nike—with its bloated ad budget and multimillion-dollar endorsement deals," wrote the global labor activist Jeff Ballinger in the *New York Times*, "it would have been nearly impossible to draw the attention of consumers in the United States to the plight of Indonesians struggling against rapacious foreign contractors."

The conditions of sweatshop labor were reported more frequently as the 1990s wore on, and many products beyond sneakers were implicated. The Gap also contracted with South Asian factories accused of sweatshop practices and frequently had protesters outside its stores like those outside Niketowns. Celebrities were obvious targets, of course: the TV personality Kathie Lee Gifford came under fire in 1996 when it was revealed that her Wal-Mart clothing line was being made by thirteen- and fourteen-year-olds working long hours in Honduras. *Charlie's Angels* actress Jaclyn Smith's line for Kmart was implicated for using sweatshop labor the same year. Disney, Wal-Mart, Mattel, and Liz Claiborne also dealt with bad press. US newspaper coverage of sweatshops in the latter half of the decade, though, tended to focus on solutions rather than causes.

Though Nike took much of the heat, other sneaker brands sought to minimize any connection to overseas production. New Balance had long prided itself on its "Made in the USA" sneakers, and now it ran ads stating "If we can make great athletic shoes in America, why can't our competition?" Taking up the mantle of the "jogging president," Bill Clinton would often take early-morning runs around the capital and had swapped his Asics (formerly known as Onitsuka Tiger) for New Balance.

For Nike, adding to the public relations nightmare were numerous vilifications in pop culture. Beginning in May 1997, the comic strip *Doonesbury*, which was syndicated in hundreds of newspapers, ran a series of strips satirizing Nike's labor practices. In the strips one of the characters visits a distant relative who works in a Nike factory in Vietnam. The "Just do it" slogan is plastered on all the machinery, and the factory employees are allowed five minutes to worship a statue of not Buddha but Jordan. Upon meeting her relative, the underpaid, overworked distant cousin exclaims to a translator, "Has she come to free me from this hell-hole?"

In his 1998 documentary *The Big One*, director Michael Moore managed to land an interview with Phil Knight, a rarity for the filmmaker. Moore's well-received first documentary, *Roger & Me*, had revolved around his ultimately unsuccessful efforts to interview GM CEO Roger Smith about the company's closure of several auto plants in Flint, Michigan. Perhaps Knight and the PR team at Nike thought that speaking with Moore would give them a chance to address some of the labor reforms the shoe company had enacted in its Southeast Asian factories. Moore, in his typical gonzo style, presented Knight with a "gift" of two Singapore Airline tickets to Indonesia for him and Knight to tour Nike's factories in the country. The Nike chief declined the offer.

"I simply have a basic belief, having been burned on it once, and really believing this very strongly, that Americans do not want to make shoes," Knight told Moore. "They don't want to make shoes. That isn't what their ambition is." He had played right into the hands of Moore, who promptly offered to find five hundred people in his native Flint, Michigan, if Nike promised to build a factory there. Knight balked at the offer.

In May 1998, a month after *The Big One* hit theaters, Knight gave a speech to the National Press Club acknowledging his company's reputation problem. "The Nike product has become synonymous with slave wages, forced overtime and arbitrary abuse," he said. "I truly believe that the American consumer does not want to buy products made in abusive conditions."

He then made a number of promises, including ending child labor in Nike factories, increasing monitoring, and requiring the company's contractors to meet US health and safety standards. The company created a Corporate Responsibility Division and established a partnership with the Gap, the World Bank, and several nonprofits to improve conditions for factory workers. But shaking a bad image is easier said than done. Despite making improvements in line with Knight's promises (hundreds of factory audits, a 108-page report detailing the poor conditions in some of its factories), the sting of the sweatshop controversy never really left Nike. In 2001, Jonah Peretti, an MIT grad student and later cofounder of the Huffington Post and BuzzFeed, sent a request for a custom set of sneakers through NIKEiD, a service that lets you personalize your sneakers. Peretti requested that the word "sweatshop" be embroidered on his shoes. Nike denied the request on the grounds that the word was "inappropriate slang."

Regional trends, labor conditions, and criminal activity were all things sneaker companies learned, often the hard way, to pay attention to. How the public sees a brand's cultural footprint has a deep, wide-ranging impact. This focus on image has played a larger and larger role as brands have gotten better at determining why consumers want something, how much they are willing to pay for it, and how much trouble they are willing to go through to get it.

16

I, SNEAKERHEAD

On Tuesday, February 22, 2005, Jeffrey Ng turned the corner down Orchard Street on Manhattan's Lower East Side to open his shop for the morning. He was surprised to find hundreds of people, some of them carrying baseball bats and knives, waiting for him. They were after his sneakers.

"What the fuck is going on here?" he wondered. Ng, who also goes by his *nom de design* "jeffstaple," was twenty-six and bald, with a confident openness. His retail store/art gallery, Reed Space, had opened two years before and served as a lifestyle boutique for streetwear enthusiasts. Streetwear, a broadly defined fashion scene that came to prominence in the late 1990s/early 2000s, has its roots in southern California's 1980s and '90s surf culture but encompasses elements of hip-hop, pop art, skate wear, athletic gear, and boutique brands. Streetwear "hypebeasts," as its fans are sometimes derisively called, play into the personal-identity focus of early-twenty-first-century pop culture and often go to great lengths for the right look.

Sandwiched between a vacant space available for rent and a discount clothing store that hung jackets and shirts from its fire escape, Reed Space was easily the trendiest shop on the block. Ng got his start silk-screening T-shirts of his own design; in less than a decade he had gone from selling small orders of his shirts to having his own menswear line, design studio, and an offer from Nike to reimagine one of its signature sneakers.

The shoes in question were a special pair of Nike Dunk SBs—part of a limited-run series called Art of the Dunk, which commemorated four cities: Tokyo, London, Paris, and New York. The Dunk began life as a basketball shoe known for its many color combinations, often designed for college teams. Nike had rereleased the shoe in the late 1990s as a casual sneaker and, as a nod to the streetwear audience the shoe had found, as a skateboarding shoe called the Dunk SB.

To celebrate the shoe's twenty-fifth anniversary, one designer in each of the four cities was chosen to reimagine it as if the sneaker had been created for his or her hometown. The grays of the London edition were meant to evoke dreary weather; a small blue squiggle near the heel stood in for the River Thames. The Paris model used a sliced-up painting for the upper, and, as no two pairs featured the exact same swatch of the canvas, each one was unique. The germ of the sneaker-as-city-art idea had come from Nike's president after, a year earlier, he had commissioned a group of Japanese artists to create works using the Nike Dunk as inspiration. Few of the pieces were shoes themselves—one looked like a Transformer-esque robot able to fold itself into a shoe; another was a ghoulish, skeletonized sneaker featuring a boney swoosh; another a sculpted angel lacing up a tiny pair of the shoes. In a nod to that exhibition, the Tokyo Dunks in the City Pack were made of blank white canvas, as if waiting for the wearer to come up with his own design.

In designing a shoe to represent the Big Apple, Ng chose a symbol he felt represented the true nature of New Yorkers: the pigeon. To many the bird is one of the city's nuisances; to Ng it stood for something more empowering. "That street mentality of, like, just get it by any means necessary," he said. "That's what a pigeon does, right? If you look at a pigeon, it survives. It's not supposed to survive in a city. It succeeds in a city. It just manages a way to win." The two-toned gray shoes brought to mind the bird's filthy feathers; the sole was the same shade of orange as its foot. A tiny pigeon was stitched on an outer side. The people who lined up to buy jeffstaple's Dunks for $300 were probably buying the ritziest thing ever associated with the *Columba livia domestica*.

Only 150 of the Nike x Staple Design Dunk Low Pro SB Pigeon, the shoe's full name, were made. (In the taxonomy of sneaker collaboration names, an "x" separating the brand from the designer acts as a kind of multiplier, with the model of the shoe usually appearing at the end.) Five trendy boutique shops, including Reed Space, would have the privilege of selling them. The thirty pairs allotted to Reed Space had the added distinction of being laser-etched with an individualized number in a series, making them even more exclusive than the pairs at the other four stores.

No one lined up on Orchard Street had any idea what the shoe looked like. Ng hadn't released a picture, nor had one been leaked. The only clue that a shoe would even be available was a small graphic the designer had released featuring a tiny, drawn pigeon above a release date. The numerical month and year were visible, but the number 22 was mostly covered with a glob of bird droppings. Also not mentioned was that there were only thirty pairs available.

Ng had gotten an inkling that fans really, really wanted his shoe. A few days prior to the twenty-second, a line had begun to form outside of Reed Space. Those thoughtful enough to plan for the 40-degree weather tied lawn chairs and tents to the store's security gate or took refuge in nearby parked cars. In early 2005, the concept of camping out in line for a shoe was not entirely foreign—Foot Lockers often saw devotees come prepared to tough it out overnight for the latest Air Jordans. But this case seemed different. This was a limited-release shoe relying primarily on word-of-mouth marketing and, more important, it was winter. In New York City. Before Ng left work late the day before the launch, he bought pizza for some of his would-be customers, which was small comfort for braving a half inch of snow.

Major brands such as Nike, Adidas, and Reebok had succeeded in creating something high-fashion brands had been cultivating all along: a devoted following for an expensive, exclusive product. By offering hyperlimited runs, the brands created buzz for themselves and their collaborators and the consumer had the satisfaction of having a product few others had. In the largely male community that cared—really cared—about sneaker style, one could establish himself in the pecking order by having shoes that were pricey, difficult to find, or both. Of course, a killer sneaker had to be paired with the right outfit, much the same way owning a Birkin bag didn't mean much unless you looked good carrying it.

Ng returned the next morning at ten to find the block cordoned off, an even greater number of people—more than a hundred—now outside his shop, and NYPD officers and squad cars at the ready. Most worrying, an unsavory crowd with bats, knives, and even a machete lined the perimeter. The math was simple: if each person in line had at least $300 cash for the shoes, there were tens of thousands of dollars, or at least a fresh pair of kicks, ready for the taking.

"I think what escalated that was people knew they wouldn't

be able to get the shoes because of the demand so they brought weapons with them to mug the kids who could get them," Ng said.

Every once in a while a fight would break out and the police officers would pull someone out of the line, while others hung on to Reed Space's security gate to avoid losing their place. Ng sneaked in through the back entrance to figure out how his tiny store was going to handle such a demand by the time it opened at noon. Working with NYPD officers, he came up with a plan: customers would be let into the store in limited numbers, then shuffled out the back door, where a waiting taxi would take each lucky buyer home.

It took an hour to sell the thirty pigeon shoes, as customers were shepherded into the store and ushered out the back. Once it became clear that no more were on offer, the crowd and the cops dissipated. Then a new group descended on Ng's store: the news media.

Across the front page of the next morning's *New York Post*, a paper never known for its subtlety, an all-caps headline roared, "SNEAKER RIOT." Below was a photo of a mass of people crowding the sidewalk outside Reed Space, flanked by NYPD officers. After the local CBS News affiliate ran a story on its evening broadcast, the desk anchors bantered about the absurdity of a sneaker-obsessed subculture: "Parrotheads—sneakerheads, now?" asked one anchor, referring to the legion of Jimmy Buffett fans who self-identify with a different type of bird.

"Sneakerhead" actually dates to the 1990s as a term for sneaker enthusiasts, but with the "Riot," they were out in the open. Ng saw the effects of exposure almost immediately: the weekend after his shoe's release he noticed business-suited Wall Street types in his shop alongside his usual clientele of OG streetwear enthusiasts. Day traders now had another status symbol to flaunt along with high-end watches and imported cigars. A day after the Pigeon Dunk's release, the shoes were listed on eBay for a thousand dollars.

The Dutch professional skateboarder Wieger van Wageningen learned how much people wanted his shoes the hard way. When he was brought onto the Nike team, he would often receive boxes of shoes, especially SB Dunks. "I was never a sneaker freak," he said. "For me I just skated all of those shoes. Which I shouldn't have done."

To Wageningen, the Pigeon Dunk was just another sneaker he put through the rigors of kick flips and grinds while shooting a trick highlight reel.

"I had no clue they were so expensive," he said. "I was, like, 'Oh, cool,' mellow color shoe.' You know?"

A couple of days later, he was in line at an airport, wearing the same pair of Pigeon Dunks.

"There was a hole in the shoe already. Some Japanese guy behind me tapped me on the shoulder. He pointed at my shoes," he said. "He got angry at me for ruining the shoes. I got home and looked on the Internet, and they went for a lot of money. I had no clue!"

SNEAKER COLLECTING GOT ITS START the same way any other collecting did: the people who liked it simply did it. If you wanted a hot pair of shoes in the 1970s, first you needed to know they existed. Those lucky enough to live in a big city had the advantage of seeing hundreds of pairs of shoes walking around each day. Before the mid-1970s, there was only a handful of TV ads for athletic shoes; sneaker ads were more likely to be black-and-white newspaper spots. As far as the average consumer knew, if a local store didn't have red Chucks, they didn't exist. Early sneakerheads, on the other hand, knew where certain shoes could be obtained and sometimes traveled to different cities or traded with other collectors to get them. They might have a friend who worked in a sporting goods store. The Beastie Boys had their "sneaker pimp" to outsource the time-consuming process of hunting for particular models.

The phenomenon of lining up for a limited release was the culmination of decades of sneaker history. The fads around tennis, jogging, aerobics, and cross-training had introduced the public to a range of sneakers that could be worn casually. Megapopular brand pitchmen of the 1980s, including Michael Jordan, Run-DMC, and Bo Jackson, built a mystique around certain models. And the rise of shopping malls, with their Foot Lockers and the Athlete's Foot, meant that you no longer needed the hookup to get most kicks, you just needed to be within driving distance of any one of hundreds of stores.

The final catalyst of sneakerhead culture was, of all things, the Internet. It not only made everything much more available (for a price) but also connected like-minded collectors as never before. When chat rooms came into fashion in the 1990s, for the first time sneakerheads anywhere could easily debate styles, share industry gossip, or engage in an activity that would have seemed completely strange even half a decade earlier: buying and selling used sneakers. eBay made the practice even easier.

If any sneakers, new or old, were now easily obtainable with a click of the mouse, standing out meant having rarer pairs than the next collector. The state of the shoe itself became a major factor. As strange as it might seem that someone would want a pair of used shoes, stranger still was that many shoes were prized for never having been removed from their boxes. The worst thing you could do to a collectible sneaker was wear it. This "long tail" toward obscurer shoes seemed to extend infinitely—sale price was now no longer the upper limit of what a shoe was worth.

This new secondary market would change the sneaker industry in unexpected ways.

In the old days, there might've been a new Air Jordan each season through the 1990s with annual changes and a predictable fanfare. By the 2000s, a release date was an event, and the major sneaker brands faced a steep learning curve in managing realistic expectations of supply and demand. Reebok, taking a page from Run-DMC's Adidas deal in the 1980s, had signed two of the biggest hip-hop artists of the early 2000s, Jay-Z and 50 Cent. Titled after his birth name, Shawn Carter, Jay-Z's S. Carter sneaker, the first signature line for a musician, was launched in 2003 to much acclaim. The white, low-cut tennis shoe sold out within hours in many shops. In a week, the 10,000-pair initial run had sold out altogether. Reebok put more pairs into production and sold them at more places, still with success. Then the company again ramped up, but a funny thing happened: the shoes suddenly didn't sell so well. The market was too flooded; the shoes had to be marked down and liquidated. 50 Cent's G Unit shoe suffered a similar fate. The failure of both lines wasn't because of the lack of star power of the endorsers; it was because the shoes had lost their mystique the second they became too available. Reebok and its competitors were learning the lesson of sneakerhead culture: sometimes less is more.

THE STORY OF ONE OF the most expensive pairs of sneakers began eight years before the Pigeon shoe riot, on June 9, 1997, with a late-night pizza order. That season marked the twelfth entry in the Air Jordan line. The black sneaker featured lined stitching radiating out from the red sole, inspired by Japan's Rising Sun flag. Jordan wore the shoe as the Chicago Bulls were locked in an NBA finals battle with the Utah Jazz. The teams were tied at two wins apiece, and it was the third straight game in Park City, Utah. A loss in game five wouldn't sink the Bulls' chances, but it would give their opponents back-to-back wins, handing the critical momentum to his former Dream Teammates on the Jazz: Karl Malone, the current MVP, and John Stockton, whose signature move was a well-placed assist to his teammate's baskets. In other words, Jordan and the Bulls had better wrap the series up soon.

Two nights before the game and long after his Park City hotel's room service had closed, Jordan had a pizza delivered. At two the next morning, he phoned his trainer, who discovered him curled up on the floor in the fetal position. A day before a crucial game five, and Chicago's star was laid out with probable food poisoning.

The media speculated beforehand on what condition, if any, Jordan would be playing in. He'd been in bed the entire day, hooked up to an IV, rising only a few hours before the 7 p.m. tipoff. Before the game Jordan saw Preston Truman, a ball boy for the Jazz who had helped him find applesauce when the Bulls had been in Park City earlier in the season. For game five, Truman had made sure Jordan's locker had graham crackers and applesauce stocked, and he asked a favor: Could he have Jordan's shoes after the game? Jordan shot Truman a look that made him feel he had overstepped his bounds.

By the end of the first quarter, the Jazz comfortably led the Bulls, and Jordan's play seemed to match the rest of his team's performance: sluggish and not quite there. He slowly found his footing, though. During the game Truman again brought the grateful Jordan applesauce to counteract his dehydration. Even by nonsick standards, Jordan's second half was one for the books. He seemingly willed his team to a 2-point victory, thanks to a couple of late-second shots that capped off a 38-point, seven-rebound effort.

By Jordan's own admission, the Flu Game, as it came to be known, was the hardest he had ever played and would go down as one of his greatest performances. When the final buzzer sounded, Jordan collapsed in the arms of teammate Scottie Pippen as they headed off the court. In the locker room, the Bulls' equipment manager grabbed at the black-and-red Air Jordan XIIs, but Jordan brushed him away and pointed at Truman, saying the shoes were for him. He signed each sneaker for the ball boy, the socks still inside them. The Bulls went on to win game six and their fifth championship. Truman put the shoes into a safety deposit box, despite receiving an offer of $11,000 for them. In 2013, he finally put them up for auction, where they sold, socks and all, for $104,765.

It was a record-setting price. For comparison, a pair of game-worn black-and-white Air Jordan XIs from the previous season fetched slightly less than $5,000 in a 2013 auction. The "Flu sneakers" would remain an outlier, but within a few years some models would regularly fetch upward of $5,000—shoes that hadn't once had Jordan's foot in them and that might even appear unremarkable to the layman's eye.

How could that happen? The Internet, leveling up.

IN SOME WAYS, TECHNOLOGY HAS pushed the shoe industry through the same transformative changes as the music industry. Brick-and-mortar record stores were once the only way to get the album you were after. The MP3, whether downloaded at 99 cents a pop or illegally through any number of peer-to-peer networks, chipped away at the need to physically seek out music. Independent stores were the first to suffer. They couldn't keep up with the shelf space or margins that big-box stores such as Tower Records or Barnes & Noble could boast. But the titans, too, soon fell into trouble. How could any size store compete with the likes of Amazon or iTunes, home of virtually anything ever recorded?

Like independent record stores, mom-and-pop sneaker stores felt the first pinch of the industry moving online, as not just sneakerheads but everyone else discovered the perks of at-home shopping. A casualty of the business moving online wasn't just the loss of physical space in which to display and purchase a product, it was the disappearance of the physical space that had brought hobbyists into the same room to discuss their obsession. At Amazon and Zappos there were no knowledgeable shop owners passing on their enthusiasm to their clientele.

The endless diversity made possible by the Internet enabled ever more stratified pricing. On one level there was the basic inflation that had been happening for decades, similar to the way gentrification does: someone comes into a neighborhood and offers to pay a higher price for a house than everyone else, then that higher price becomes the norm, making it difficult for the longtime resident to afford to buy one. In 1985, $65 was the going rate for a hip shoe, until the Air Jordan II pushed the price beyond $100. A few years later the Reebok Pump raised the stakes to $170. Decades later, an off-the-shelf Nike LeBron costs $200, while a deluxe model is beyond that.

Factor in limited runs, store exclusives, and runaway demand from collectors, and the sky is now the limit on the price of a new shoe. That goes for the secondary market, too, which in the United States alone is estimated at $1.2 billion and in the $6 billion neighborhood globally, according to Josh Luber, cofounder and CEO of StockX, a website that calls itself "the stock market of things." Nike accounts for 96 percent of the secondary resale market. As Luber pointed out in a 2015 TED Talk, customers who buy and sell preowned Nikes make nearly twice as much overall profit as Skechers does in a year.

On the other end of the spectrum, what sells well and what doesn't often trickles down the line to cheaper sneakers. All the hype surrounding a new version of the Air Jordan elevates the status of the brand as a whole, but brands make their real money by selling not a few ridiculously expensive shoes but a lot of midpriced shoes. Design elements and color combinations from successful shoes will find their way into more affordable models. Adidas' knit NMD line of sneakers can retail for about $170, but the Adidas NEO subbrand sells a similar-looking (to the layman, anyway) mesh shoe for $80. Any discount store will sell a Converse All Stars doppelgänger for $15 or so, while the real McCoy is double the cost. In January 2017, a pair of the ultrarare Pigeon Dunks sold on the secondary market for $7,500. Around the same time, the fast-fashion retailer H&M was offering a children's sneaker in a nearly identical two-tone gray and orange. Its price: $15.

Not every brand has courted the sneakerhead market or even really the Internet. Shaquille O'Neal, once pursued by sneaker brands as if he were the next Jordan, broke off with Reebok in 1998 to sell his own brand of affordably priced Dunkman shoes to retailers such as Wal-Mart and Payless ShoeSource. At prices as low as $12.50, Shaq tweeted in 2016 that Dunkman had sold more than 120 million pairs at Wal-Mart.

In February 2016, the rapper Kanye West held a massive release party in Madison Square Garden in New York for his Adidas line of clothing and shoes titled Yeezy Season 3. Tracks from his long-in-the-works new album *The Life of Pablo* were streamed for the thousands of attendees. Thirty years after Run-DMC's Adidas deal and thirteen years after Jay-Z's S. Carter sneaker, hip-hop artists were still aligning with shoe brands and taking to their music to continue the brand war. In late 2015, the rappers Drake and Future released a track titled "Jumpman," a call to Drake's shoe deal with the Jordan brand; a month later, West released a track from the forthcoming *Pablo* called "Facts" with the chorus "Yeezy, Yeezy, Yeezy just jumped over Jumpman" and a slight against Nike's overreliance on Drake's endorsement. A later line adds, "Nike, Nike treat employees just like slaves."

Around the turn of the millennium, a new element was added to fuel the demand for high-priced sneakers: collaboration with luxury brands. Luxury brands had been dipping their toes into the sneaker market at least since 1984, when Gucci had introduced a high-cost tennis shoe; over time, more fashion designers, big and small, realized that the right partnership could expand their reach to new audiences. Fans of streetwear brands, large fashion houses, and completist collectors were now tempted by collaborations between Reebok and Chanel, Adidas and Moschino, or Vans and the skateboard brand Supreme.

Kanye West's foray into the design world was an unusual one for a world-famous celebrity. Previous collaborations with celebrity shoe "designers" amounted to the star in question selecting new colors and materials for a given shoe model (or "silhouette," in sneakerspeak). But since 2005, West had partnered with Nike, Louis Vuitton, and the boutique brand A Bathing Ape, producing collaborations that were both remixed versions of existing shoes and new models entirely, some of which retailed for close to $1,000 and sold for many times that amount on the secondary market. In 2013, West abruptly and publicly split with Nike to sign with Adidas, a move that Adidas' global director of entertainment said was because, though Nike had offered more money, "we offered him full creative reign [*sic*]."

The Madison Square Garden show was barely a month after West's diss track "Facts" dropped. Though the event was a massive advertisement for his new sponsor, West wasn't about to miss a chance to get in a few more digs at his old one. "I want to thank Adidas for paying for this and supporting me," he said, which prompted the crowd to chant, "Fuck Nike." When chants of "Fuck Michael Jordan" were heard, however, West quickly put a stop to it. "No, no, no," he said. "Not 'fuck Michael Jordan,' Michael Jordan is our boy. I wouldn't be here if it wasn't for Michael Jordan. Respect Jordan."

Much the same way a sports fan can admire the performance of a rival team's MVP, the reverence that West insisted his audience show Jordan was about acknowledging everything Jordan had accomplished and represented, both on and off the court. Showing respect to the ultimate pitchman was something that crossed the lines of brand loyalty.

KANYE WEST IS HARDLY THE most idiosyncratic personality in today's anything-goes sneakerhead world. Benjamin Kapelushnik, a go-to shoe consigliere known as "Benjamin Kickz" and "the Sneaker Don," got his start buying and selling sneakers to his friends, later graduating to paying people to wait in lines to get new releases and selling them on his website. Now high-profile musicians and athletes, including DJ Khaled, Drake, and NFL wide receiver Odell Beckham, Jr., seek out the Sneaker Don for his connections in getting shoes before they're released to the public. As of this writing, Kapelushnik is eighteen years old.

These days limited-edition shoes can take just about any form: chicken-and-waffle-inspired Nikes, a hamburger-themed Saucony (the takeout-themed box includes packets of "ketchup" and "mayonnaise" containing shoelaces), and stuffed-animal Adidas shoes with teddy bear heads sewn on top, to name a few. To navigate it all, sneakerheads have developed their own lingo. "OG" is an original model; "retro" is a slightly altered and updated rerelease. The most valuable variety are "deadstock" shoes, however old, never removed from their boxes. Almost as sought after are "NIBs," new in box, which may have been taken out but never worn. A "silhouette" is a particular model of shoe, which comes in many "colorways." For some people, a "grail" might be a rare Air Jordan version or a shoe from childhood they wanted but never owned.

Yet for all its eccentricities, sneaker culture is becoming more mainstream. It gained more exposure in 2013, when the first exhibition to examine the shoe's social history and influence opened in Toronto's Bata Shoe Museum, in partnership with the American Federation of Arts. "Out of the Box: The Rise of Sneaker Culture" has since traveled to New York, California, and Australia. According to the show's curator, Elizabeth Semmelhack, one major cultural contribution is the shift sneakers have sparked in encouraging men to participate in fashion in broader ways.

"The widespread interest in urban men's fashion allows for greater expressions of individualism and challenges or reinterprets traditional notions of masculinity—in particular, what masculine success now looks like," Semmelhack wrote.

This shift has been reflected in media. The men's fashion magazine GQ has a dedicated sneaker section. The pop culture magazine Complex regularly runs sneaker news, and its website features a show that takes celebrities sneaker shopping. Hypebeast, a streetwear and culture website, boats a social media reach of more than 800 million and 44 million visitors a month; three-quarters of the audience is in the 18–35 male demographic.

That last statistic illustrates an important missing element in sneaker culture: women. Though there is certainly a community of female sneakerheads, they have often had to fight for legitimacy and recognition by their male peers. Major brands often do not make dedicated sizes of their limited-run sneakers for women, who then have to settle for a child's or smaller men's size. In 2013, London sneaker fans Emilie Riis and Emily Hodgson started a fantasy sneaker site called Purple Unicorn Planet as part of a campaign to get Nike to make women's versions of its shoes. "Trainers are unisex shoes and have been for a while. But it seems we are still stuck in an outdated view on what kinds girls and boys, respectively, should wear," Riis said. "Girls don't just want pink, purple, or banana yellow trainers."

This feeling was echoed by Kiah Welsh, cofounder of a female sneakerheads blog, who once had to stuff a pair of $180 sneakers to make them fit.

"I had to settle for a [men's] size 9 and the guy at the store told me I had to double sole my shoes," said Welsh.

Sophia Chang, a designer and illustrator who has worked with Nike, Puma, and Jeffrey Ng's studio, Staple Design, holds out hope that these dispiriting examples, and the voices raised in protest, will lead to better representation. "With the internet and the ability to voice your creativity," she said, "there are plenty of confident, creative, and stylish women who are just like me, sharing their stories."

WHEN IT COMES TO UNDERSTANDING their customers' diversity, sneaker companies are still grappling with a steep learning curve. What they have realized is how badly some people want the right sneaker—and how to use that desire. Far from the days of Reebok flooding the market with S. Carters, major brands now strategize meticulously about their limited-run shoes, reading the tea leaves to keep supply just behind demand. Build the proper buzz around a new release, they know, and a given pair might have several owners before they're even tried on.

Nearly a decade after the "sneaker riot," the ability of a rare release to put on a good show hasn't changed. At 7 p.m. on Wednesday, April 2, 2014, a sea of about a thousand people had amassed outside the Supreme boutique in New York's SoHo neighborhood, waiting for the release of the Supreme x Nike Air Foamposite 1 collaboration. They had started lining up on Monday for the Thursday release; the $250 sneakers were expected to fetch $1,000 on the secondary market. When some people started to rush the store that night, police quickly dispersed the crowd and Supreme announced that the in-store launch would be canceled. The shoes were released online at 11 a.m. the next day. They sold out in five minutes.

BACK AT IT AGAIN

On October 21, 2015, a teenager named Marty McFly, looking to blend in to new surroundings, was given a fresh pair of Nike sneakers. After he put them on, the laces automatically tightened around his foot.

"Power laces, all right!" he said.

At least, that was what happened according to 1989's *Back to the Future II.* In the sequel to the popular 1950s-themed time-travel movie, McFly, played by Michael J. Fox, travels in a souped-up DeLorean from 1985 to the year 2015. The film's production design team was tasked with guessing what thirty years into the future might look like. Some of their imagined technology, such as video conferencing and handheld computers, ended up becoming a reality; flying cars and hoverboards, less so. Nike designer Tinker Hatfield was brought on board to imagine what a sneaker might look like in three decades. Rather than focus on the "magnetic levitation" shoe that had originally been storyboarded, Hatfield wanted to envision something that *could* potentially be developed. For the time being the special effect of the automatic lacing was merely a stagehand pulling the laces tight from below a fake floor.

Back to the Future II would go on to achieve cult status with the other films of the series. Though the sneaker scene seemed like a throwaway gag at the time, Hatfield and his Nike colleagues received endless requests to make the Air Mag real, a desire Nike would eventually encourage. The actor Christopher Lloyd reprised his time-traveling mad scientist "Doc" Brown role for a 2011 commercial in which he visits a Nike shop looking for shoes and realizes he hasn't traveled far enough into the future when a shoe store employee (Hatfield in a cameo) tells him that the power-lace version of the Nike Air Mag won't be available until 2015. The ad's end cards state that 1,500 replica pairs of the sneaker from the movie, though with ordinary laces, will be auctioned on eBay to benefit the Michael J. Fox Foundation for Parkinson's Research. The highest winning bid was for nearly $10,000.

On October 21, 2015, the same date his character had arrived in "the future," Michael J. Fox was given a pair of real-life self-lacing Nike Air Mag shoes—the culmination of years of effort by a skunkworks team that included Hatfield and Nike "senior innovator" Tiffany Beers. For as much as fans might be willing to pay for a piece of movie magic made real, a self-lacing sneaker could also solve a functional, performance-related problem.

"Go look at the feet of a pro athlete who's played basketball for ten years," Hatfield said. "They're trashed because their shoes are too tight. They tie their shoes so tight because they need them tight, but they stay that way throughout all their practices and all their games and their feet become deformed and damaged and sometimes it incapacitates them." In other words, a shoe that would automatically loosen up when a player was just standing around or on the bench and tighten up when he went back on the court would help the player's feet long term.

The result of years of research and product development was the late-2016 Nike HyperAdapt. For a cool $750, consumers could avoid the hassle of tying their shoes and instead rely on a sensor in the heel to tighten the shoe for them as they walk (two buttons can manually tighten or loosen the shoe). Online, the sneakers fetched several times that price only a few days after release.

"IT'S GOTTA BE THE SHOES." To get to the point where Mars could knowingly say that in a national commercial, and beyond, the sneaker had to come into its own on two parallel tracks. It's gotta be the shoes that make Jordan so *good*, the commercial tells us; at the same time, the reason Mars is there at all is that it's also gotta be the shoes, those Air Jordans he won't take off even in bed, that can make us *cool*.

So on the one side there's the focus on aesthetics and design, today exemplified by sneakerheads. But the performance side of sneakers has also advanced in leaps and bounds—and many tiny increments—over the years, with the implementation of vulcanized rubber, leather uppers, multisport shoes, waffle soles, sneakers that can be pumped up to hug your foot, and uppers woven from a single thread. Some people will wait in line for days to get kicks no one else has, but there are also people who will insist on trying on every shoe in a running store to find the most comfortable one to jog in. Sneaker companies have gotten smarter about marketing from a fashion side, but they haven't forgotten their product's essential identity: shoes for athletics.

Advances in shoe technology have helped the common person exercise more efficiently and with less danger of injury. They've also helped elite athletes push the boundaries. When

Roger Bannister broke the four-minute-mile barrier in 1954, the English medical student accomplished something few at the time thought a human body could do. Now that sub-four-minute miles are commonplace at the Olympics and on university tracks and are even seen at the high school level, only one running barrier has captured the imagination the same way: a marathon run in under two hours. Shaving almost three minutes off the world record, currently 2:02:57, would require every advantage that can be wrung from nutrition, training, race conditions, and, of course, the shoes. Since there would be an element of prestige (not to mention marketing gold) to the company that could make the shoes that break the record, Nike and Adidas both announced they had shoes in the works specially designed for the task.

In early 2017, former world record holder Wilson Kipsang wore the Adizero Sub2 shoe in the Tokyo Marathon; he won the race but missed the record. In May, it was Nike's turn. Three elite runners lined up on an empty Formula 1 track in Italy, all of them wearing custom-tailored grayish-blue-and-red Nike Zoom Vaporfly Elite 4% shoes for the event Nike's PR team called a "moonshot." The runners ran in a tight pack for about the first hour before stringing out, all the while beside pacers who cycled into and out of the race to keep them on target. When Kenyan Eliud Kipchoge, the strongest of the three, rounded the final corner, he was on pace to run faster than anyone had ever run 26.2 miles, but it was clear from his face that he knew he'd fall just short of two hours.

Since the effort involved the use of midrace pacers, among other measures, Kipchoge's time of 2:00:26 was not recognized as a world record by running's governing body. Also suspect: the shoes themselves. The Zoom Vaporfly Elite 4% contains a carbon-fiber plate embedded in the sole that supposedly makes runners 4 percent more efficient. Though Nike maintains that it meets international running regulations, some have called for the shoe to be banned from competition, arguing that the carbon-fiber plate creates an unfair advantage. This brings up a question: Exactly when are good shoes *too* good?

The subject of unfair "shoes" had come up before in international competition. In 2008, South African sprinter Oscar Pistorius was initially barred from qualifying for the Olympics because organizers believed he had an unfair advantage: Pistorius, a double amputee, ran in curved carbon-fiber running prosthetics that, as some argued, gave him a level of spring and flexion impossible with ordinary track spikes. His Össur Flex-Foot Cheetah running blades allowed him to compete at the Olympic level but opened a debate about what qualifies as an advantage as technology improves. Pistorius was eventually cleared for the 2012 London Games, where he competed in two events but did not medal.

For designers and advocates of running blades like the ones Pistorius wore, the controversy was dispiriting because it overshadowed the technical feats that had allowed disabled runners to do things never before possible. The model Pistorius wore worked well on an all-weather track because spikes could be incorporated into the blade, but Sarah Reinertsen, a Nike-sponsored athlete and former Paralympian, also used an Össur running leg to compete in triathlons. To provide better grip, she would strip off the outsole from a regular running shoe and attach it to the prosthetic, but she knew that was not a perfect solution. In 2006, Nike approached her to help develop a slip-on sole for the Össur Flex-Foot prosthetic that could be easily slid on and off like a sleeve when the tread wore down, as one could do with a conventional running shoe. The resulting Nike Sole, developed in collaboration with Össur, is available worldwide through prosthetists' offices.

Obvious technological advantages are only one ongoing debate in the performance sneaker world. A more common topic of controversy is when shoes may not be as revolutionary as their makers suggest, and some companies have learned the hard way to be careful about talking a big game.

Tony Post's big breakthrough came during one of his lowest points as a runner. Post, who had worked for Reebok and Rockport, was CEO and president of the US division of Vibram, an Italian company that first made rubber outsoles for boots in 1937. He had just come off knee surgery and was unable to run three or four miles without developing knee pain. He saw a concept shoe, the FiveFinger, on a trip to Italy and decided to give it a try. The FiveFinger was more glove than shoe—each toe had its own compartment, and the thin sole offered little in the way of cushioning. Post noticed that the shoe made him run with a quick, light stride and that after three miles, he didn't have any knee pain. He decided it was the cushioning in his old shoes that was causing the problem. "It caused me to remember, 'I've done this before.' When we were running cross-country in college, my coach had us do strides across the football field barefoot." Post was sold on his company's new shoe. He thought about the implications for the entire running industry: What if running shoes hadn't been built right all along? What if all you really need is a thin sole that mimics what it was like to be barefoot?

When the FiveFinger was released in 2008, Peter Sagal, the host of NPR's *Wait Wait . . . Don't Tell Me!* news quiz show, wrote a lighthearted column in *Runner's World* in which he described trying out the shoes for two weeks. "Day 11: Speedwork Day," he wrote. "Back in the FiveFingers I zip around the track as if I've been freed from eight-ounce ankle weights. I run pain-free and fast." He went on to mention the strange looks his running group and strangers gave him when they saw the shoes.

Evangelists swore that knee, shin, and other leg, hip, and back pains disappeared when wearing the shoes. "My knees were screaming. My ankles hurt. Then, a few minutes later, all the pain was gone," wrote a self-described Vibram convert on the website TechCrunch in 2009. That same year, Jon Snyder in *Wired* called them "plastic gorilla feet" that nevertheless force "a more efficient stride."

Vibram wasn't alone in seeking to upend the traditional chunky-shoe running experience. In 2005, Nike launched its Free line of lightweight trainers with flexible, segmented soles meant to encourage a more natural stride. Would-be Buildermen around the world were at work making idealized running shoes their own. A cofounder of Altra, a high school cross-country runner at the time, ripped open a pair of shoes to remove padding from a heel and then used a toaster oven and glue to reassemble the lighter shoes. A Swiss duathlete cut up pieces of his garden hose and glued them to the bottom of his running shoes in pursuit of better cushion and propulsion; he went on to cofound On AG, which makes running shoes with outsoles resembling squishy rubber packing peanuts.

What would most shake up the running shoe industry near the end of the 2000s wasn't a new sneaker but a book. Christopher McDougall's 2009 best seller *Born to Run* told the story of a tribe of Native Mexicans who were famous for running long distances, sometimes more than a hundred miles, without injury. McDougall posited that since members of the Tarahumara tribe run in thin sandals (sometimes made from discarded automobile tires), it must be modern, cushioned running shoes that cause us to run in injury-increasing ways.

Supporting this claim was the work of the Harvard professor and evolutionary biologist Daniel E. Lieberman. One of Lieberman's studies, in partnership with other researchers, suggests that humans evolutionarily developed to be great endurance runners, an anomaly in the animal kingdom, whose members in general rely on speed, not the gradual wearing down of a long chase, to catch their prey. Another Lieberman study looked at how wearing thicker shoes creates a different stride than walking barefoot or wearing minimal shoes and how a more "natural" approach may in fact prevent injuries. In other words, the human foot instinctively knows how to strike; blunting it with padding only interrupts this evolutionarily refined relationship with the ground.

Born to Run spent more than four years on the *New York Times* Best Sellers list, sold more than 3 million copies, and brought the niche barefoot running trend to mainstream attention. That was all the evidence many joggers (including myself) needed to justify switching to foot-shaped sneakers. In April 2011, however, Florida resident Valerie Bezdek purchased a pair of FiveFingers seeking, as the company's advertising claimed, "all the health benefits of barefoot running" and was less than satisfied. In a class action lawsuit filing, Bezdek argued that the "health benefits" such as strengthened foot muscles and improved range of motion supposedly provided by the shoes had no scientific basis and therefore falsely induced consumers to purchase the footwear.

Vibram argued that Bezdek had missed an important caveat of their shoes: you had to adjust your running style to strike the ground more with the ball of your foot, rather than the heel, in order to take full advantage of their potential. You couldn't, in other words, run the same way as you would in cushy sneakers. But that was all so much talk. Vibram came down hard on one side of the debate without scientific evidence to back up its claims. Studies such as Daniel Lieberman's had looked at barefoot running in general; they were not a rigorous scientific survey of Vibram's product. The company, denying any wrongdoing, agreed to a $3.75 million settlement in 2014 whereby nearly 150,000 claimants who had purchased the shoes could receive a refund and Vibram would discontinue making health claims about the shoes without further testing.

In practice, there's plenty of evidence on both sides of the minimalism debate. There have been elite barefoot runners in the past, such as the 1960 Olympic marathon winner Abebe Bikila and the middle-distance Olympian Zola Budd, but there have been many more who wore cushioned shoes. Bill Bowerman, a proponent of low-weight shoes, also recognized the benefits of well-placed padding as he tinkered with individualized shoes for his athletes. There may not be a one-size-fits-all approach to something as biomechanically complex as running technique.

Lieberman said as much in a 2012 study. "How one runs probably is more important than what is on one's feet, but what is on one's feet may affect how one runs," he wrote. So "plastic gorilla feet" might work for some people but not for others, as long as the way they run allows for them.

Other sneaker companies have also found themselves in trouble for unsupported performance claims. The sales of "toning" sneakers peaked at nearly $1 billion in the early 2010s. Unlike traditional fitness shoes that provide support, these trainers are intentionally made slightly unstable, the reasoning being that the instability will force leg and foot muscles to work harder. In 2011, an advertisement airing during the Super Bowl showed Kim Kardashian dismissing her personal trainer for a pair of Skechers Shape-ups, thick-soled sneakers that supposedly tone muscles and burn calories just by walking around in them. Other ads for the Shape-ups promised that you could "get in shape without setting foot in a gym." In a settlement with the Federal Trade Commission the following year, Skechers agreed to pay $40 million as penance for unsupported health claims behind its entire line of toning shoes. In a similar settlement, Reebok paid $25 million in customer refunds for its toning line. The posterior-centric ads for its EasyTone and RunTone sneakers promised "a better butt with every step."

When we have the "It's gotta be the shoes" idea in our minds, we're already asking a lot. We subconsciously want our sneakers to make us jump higher, run faster, or lose weight quicker, and when companies overpromise such things, the reality can be a (legal action–inducing) letdown. In the years following the Vibram settlement, the running public's interest swung in the exact opposite direction: toward brands such as the Hoka One One, whose soles are so thick you can hardly tell when you step on a curb.

OF COURSE, VIEWING SNEAKERS THROUGH the lens of form versus function creates a false dichotomy. There was a fashion element even to the Vibram FiveFingers—wearing them projected a crunchy granola vibe that paired much better with a hiking shirt and cargo shorts than with, say, a preppy polo shirt. Focusing on aesthetics versus technology also misses the multilayered journey sneakers have taken over the past two hundred years. Sneakers have become so many things that it's strange but believable that such disparate public figures as Mr. Rogers, Kurt Cobain, and Serena Williams wear the same type of footwear.

Even within the industry, opposites have shifted and merged over the years. Following a bankruptcy, Converse was purchased by Nike in 2003 for $309 million. In 2006, Adidas acquired Reebok for $3.8 billion, making the German brand started by Adi Dassler the second biggest sportswear company in the world after Nike. Vans, too, found new ownership when the Vanity Fair Corporation, not to be confused with the magazine of the same name, acquired the California skate shoe brand in 2004 for nearly $400 million.

Today sneaker trends seem to come ever thicker and faster. A new word, *microtrends*, has become useful to describe waves that might hit one segment of pop culture while others remain unaware. Normcore, a microtrend that surfaced in 2014, aimed to stand out by not standing out. Steve Jobs's "uniform" of a black mock turtleneck, jeans, and New Balance sneakers was the epitome of this purposely unfashionable unisex style. One designer summed up normcore's appeal: "Everyone's so unique that it's not unique anymore. Especially in New York." Fifteen years after *Seinfeld*, a "show about nothing," went off the air, comedian Jerry Seinfeld's wardrobe—notably his "dad jeans" and plain white Nike trainers—was being cited by *New York* magazine as an inspiration for the "fashion about nothing." As quickly as the microtrend came, it went, leaving the *New York Times* wondering if it had been a fashion in-joke all along. Everyone else noticed nothing at all.

In the age of ubiquitous smartphones and meme culture, it seems inevitable that a viral video would start a sneaker trend. On February 15, 2014, fifteen-year-old Joshua Holz uploaded a video to Twitter containing a short montage of his fourteen-year-old friend Daniel Lara. Each clip featured Holz saying, off camera, "Damn, Daniel," as a compliment to Lara's outfit. In one clip, Holz comments, "Back at it again with the white Vans," as Lara strides next to their high school's swimming pool. Within four days the tweet was liked nearly 150,000 times, and the video and its parodies traveled on Vine and YouTube. Three days after the original video was posted, Vans itself tweeted about it, along with other brands such as Clorox and Axe. An eBay seller posted white Vans sneakers claiming (falsely) to be the original "Damn, Daniel" shoes. Bids reached in excess of $300,000. A week later the two teens were on *The Ellen DeGeneres Show*, where they were told the video had received more than 45 million views. Lara was also presented with a lifetime supply of sneakers—courtesy of Vans, of course.

For the company, a few dozen shoes were a small price to pay for a viral marketing campaign. "Damn, Daniel" was just a more sophisticated—if less star-powered—version of Farrah Fawcett-Majors wearing Nikes on a poster or the young Sean Penn wearing Vans in a movie. How much did "Damn, Daniel" mean for Vans? On a sales report call with investors, the chief operating officer of Vans' parent company attributed a 20 percent bump in direct-to-consumer sales and a 30 percent bump in online sales to the video.

Viral videos are mere blips in the cultural memory. Today's "Damn, Daniel" quickly becomes tomorrow's "Where's the beef?" More sustained engagement comes from that old standby: celebrity association. Every week you can find stories on various sneaker and fashion websites about who wore what and where. Beyond advancing the fortunes of Nike, Adidas, or Puma, celebrities receive a boost to their own brand. Here's Drake wearing Air Jordans at a Toronto Raptors game. Here's Beyoncé walking down a New York City sidewalk in snakeskin-print All Stars. Here's Kanye wearing his Kanye-designed shoes everywhere he goes. The right shoe on the right star at the right moment can mean everything.

During President Barack Obama's final White House state dinner in October 2016, the rapper Frank Ocean attended in a tuxedo and checkered slip-on Vans. In his first interview in three years, Ocean stopped to chat with reporters, who immediately asked why he'd chosen to wear sneakers. "First time doing it, probably because it's my first time here," he said. "You can't think, you just have to do things." Besides the exposure, Vans had additional reason to be happy. That same week the company reported a 6 percent sales increase for the quarter, capping off a period of growth that had seen the once-troubled brand go from $320 million twelve years prior to more than $2 billion—in other words, a perfect storm that played equally well in social media, in entertainment news, and on Vans' balance sheet.

As easily as today's media landscape can help a brand, it can also do massive damage. Under Armour, a Maryland-based apparel company, grew its budding sneaker division in couplike fashion by luring megastar Golden State Warrior Stephen Curry away from the bigger brands. But in a February 2017 interview with CNBC, Under Armour founder and CEO Kevin Plank called President Donald Trump "probusiness" and a "real asset for the country," adding "I'm a big fan of people that operate in the world of publish and iterate versus think, think, think, think." The day after Plank's "asset" comments aired, Under Armour's biggest athlete joined the flood of negative reactions against his own brand by tweeting "I agree with that description if you remove the 'et.'" Curry later stated that despite his opposition to his sneaker boss's statement, he would stick by the company. Two other high-profile Under Armour signees, actor Dwayne "The Rock" Johnson and ballerina Misty Copeland, also publicly came out against the pro-Trump statements but wouldn't part ways with the company.

Plank should have known what might happen if he threw his support behind Trump; a nearly identical incident had happened just three months prior. Less than twenty-four hours after the 2016 US presidential election, New Balance's vice president of public affairs told the *Wall Street Journal* that president-elect Trump would move things "in the right direction." The shoe exec was speaking about Trump's opposition to, and the outgoing Obama administration's support for, the Trans-Pacific Partnership trade agreement, which New Balance opposed. The privately held company still makes some of its athletic shoes in the United

States and had argued that the trade agreement would help its overseas-sourced competitors. Social media largely overlooked the remark's context and took the statement as one of general support for Trump's policies. On Twitter, users posted that they had bought their last pair of New Balance shoes; some people uploaded videos of themselves throwing their sneakers away, flushing them down a toilet, or lighting them on fire.

New Balance posted the usual boilerplate statements in an attempt to clean up the PR mess, saying that the company "accepts all walks of life," but the snafu was not yet over. A neo-Nazi blogger hailed the "right direction" comments as a sign that New Balance was "the official brand of the Trump Revolution" and made the "official shoes of white people." (A 2013 *Saturday Night Live* sketch agreed on the latter point—the fake ad begins with a runner dashing up stadium steps as a voice-over asserts, "Comfort. Support. Stability. New Balance. Shoes made for running ..." before the camera cuts to cast member Tim Robinson dressed in khakis and dorky glasses, who adds, "... but worn by chubby white guys.") The incident wasn't even the first time New Balance was embraced by an unsavory element. In Germany in the 1990s, neo-Nazis preferred the sneakers because the *N* could stand for "Nazi." Other brands faced a similar ordeal: The British boxing and mixed martial arts clothing and equipment company Lonsdale was embraced by neo-Nazis because the middle part of the name on a partially covered T-shirt or jacket resembled part of the German initials of the Nazi Party, NSDAP. To distance themselves from the association, Lonsdale sponsored antiracist events and a campaign in 2003 featuring models of color.

Unlike the sweatshop controversy, which stretched the whole of the 1990s, public outrage over the Trump statements blew over. If Twitter hashtags are any indication, only a smattering of users were still using the #boycottnewbalance hashtag in the months after the controversies. This has something to do with the severity of each case—one dealt with rampant unfair labor practices, the other with ill-chosen corporatespeak—but no doubt also with Internet users' attention span.

Still, the boycotts hit New Balance harder than they did Under Armour. Perhaps it was because there just weren't the same numbers of people trashing, burning, or flushing their Under Armour merchandise away. But Under Armour's youthful, connected fan base was also receptive of Curry, the face of the brand, defusing the situation. New Balance had no endorsers close to the star wattage of Curry or even Misty Copeland—no trusted faces who could assure Americans that it was still okay to stand by their brand, even if it had made some mistakes.

An athlete slighting his sponsor is, in itself, a new phenomenon. Would Michael Jordan or Charles Barkley ever have risked bad-mouthing Nike at the height of their careers? But the century-long trajectory that started with athletes simply wearing brands and proceeded to their endorsing them, and to having brands built around them, has culminated in a new relationship between those who play sports and those who sell them. Stars, at least ones who are household names, no longer need sponsors to make them famous or shape their image. With social media they've become brands themselves, with or without something to sell; endorsers want the audience they've already curated. Stephen Curry's 36 million social media followers are more than the number of people who tuned in to watch Curry and the Warriors win the 2017 NBA finals. The greatest risk to a brand, it would seem, isn't so much a star who won't toe the company line but a star who isn't cut loose quickly enough once a true scandal breaks. Nike dropped Michael Vick (dogfighting), Manny Pacquiao (homophobic comments), Adrian Peterson (child abuse), and Oscar Pistorius (murder charges) after their respective scandals broke.

The Curry episode marked the first time the face of a sneaker brand acted like its conscience. His fans would expect nothing less. Today, our shoe celebrities—whether athletes, musicians, or others—are almost members of our social circle, appearing alongside our friends and family in Instagram feeds. Curry's tweet ended up doing more for the company than the apologetic, PR-approved full-page ad Under Armour took out in the *Baltimore Sun*. Why? Because it seemed authentic.

FOR EVERYTHING SNEAKER BRANDS HAVE done to get us to notice, choose, and stay loyal to them, our relationship to sneakers is still defined, ultimately, by what we do with them once we buy them. Sneakers might be worn every day or only for special occasions. They might be for sport or for style. They might be kept pristine in a box to be resold. They might be burned in a garbage can for social media to see. They might be loved or barely thought about.

Even a single shoe can have innumerable meanings depending on the wearer. Consider a pair of simple Chuck Taylor All Stars. On one pair of dancer Gene Kelly's Chucks, the laces themselves were tied together wherever they happened to break. That the normally dapper Kelly never bothered to buy new laces would disqualify him by even the loosest standards of a sneakerhead today. Yet the shoes were as well loved, or at least well worn, as sneakers could be. Chuck Taylor wore his while conducting basketball seminars. Kurt Cobain and the Ramones made them cool by wearing them onstage. LeBron James wore them on the red carpet. Michael J. Fox wore them in *Back to the Future* as an indicator that he had traveled back to the 1950s. Taylor Swift wore them while photographed by the paparazzi. Sylvester Stallone wore them on a training run in *Rocky*. First Lady Michelle Obama wore them in the White House vegetable garden. Thousands of years from now, future archaeologists will likely unearth pair after pair of identical Converse All Stars and wonder how, while so much else changed, a single sneaker was worn for so long by so many people.

Or maybe they'll still be wearing them.

EPILOGUE

New York's SoHo neighborhood is home to trendy art galleries and one-bedroom apartments that go for thousands of dollars a month. Cafés, restaurants, and boutique shops line nearly every inch of its downtown streets. If the Big Apple is one of the sneaker capitals of the world, SoHo is its stock exchange; no other place on the planet can boast so many high-end, well-known sneaker shops as the few dozen acres south of Houston Street. The sneaker's entire history is on display, if you know where to look.

On this typical Friday in August, the line outside the A Bathing Ape store was maybe a dozen people deep but moving steadily for an average day. BAPE, as the Japanese brand is also known, is essential streetwear, though more attainable than some brands. Outside the store several graffiti stencils featured BAPE's gorilla logo with the words "RIP Harambe." A layman might mistake many of its shoes for a generic-looking Nike or New Balance or Adidas, but for a sneakerhead shop like BAPE that's kind of the point. Those in the know will recognize them, and everyone else won't.

"If it's more than ten minutes, there's no way I'm standing in that line," said a father with a thick New Jersey accent to his teenage son, who had just begun waiting. The father stood outside a rope separating the line from the rest of the sidewalk, seemingly as a protest against his son's waste of time. Anyone who "pays $500 or $600 for a pair of sneakers needs to have their head examined," said the father, who wore black Nikes with an orange swoosh.

A few blocks away was a much longer line. A couple hundred people have come to 274 Lafayette Street for a chance to shop at Supreme, the superexclusive boutique where, in 2014, a thousand people hoped for a chance to flip a rare pair of Nikes on eBay. Were it not for the small army of teenage skater types waiting to get in and the team of tough-looking but generally friendly security guards directing a line wrapping around two blocks (the wait on each block, the guard says, lasts about an hour), it might be difficult to see what the fuss is about. There's not much to the store besides a wall of skateboard decks neatly arranged next to the cash register, sneakers lining one wall, and shirts racked nonchalantly against the other. After all, there's no line outside the Prada store a couple blocks to the west.

But today, like pretty much every other day, the small store was packed with a swarm of hands and arms. The shoppers looked as though they were tearing the place apart; every item was touched and handled as if it were the last available (which, in some sense, it was). Supreme makes its name on offering limited-edition runs of everything it stamps its distinctive Futura Heavy Oblique typeface logo on. T-shirts, skateboards, and sneakers are all exclusive collaborations with artists, designers, musicians, skateboarders, and companies. They run the gamut from minimalist to garish, inspired to kitschy. The brand's Fall/Winter 2016 collection included a brick with the Supreme logo stamped on it that retailed for $30. Recent collaborators include Louis Vuitton and Vans—high fashion and teen cool, together again.

Down at 21 Mercer Street is NikeLab, once a speakeasy-esque location known only by its street address, not to be confused with the company's high-tech development institute, the Nike Sports Research Lab. On the racks at NikeLab this particular afternoon were the sandal-like sneaker Nike Chalapuka ($220); the Air Footscape ($180), which resembles a baseball with the seams coming undone; and the limited-edition retro Air Jordan VII ($200), like the ones he wore on the 1992 Olympic Dream Team at the height of the Nike-Reebok war. Also available were Team USA and Team Brazil Rio Olympic jackets as well as a garish paisley-like print training outfit endorsed by the decathlete Ashton Eaton, and a running singlet that boldly displayed the name Gyakusou, a capsule collection from Japanese designer and Undercover founder Jun Takahashi. Running, Nike's original lifeblood, has made it into its street fashion, too.

And that's just SoHo. Reed Space, of "sneaker riot" fame, is only a couple neighborhoods to the east. To the north is Flight Club, where a wall of rare basketball shoes sold on consignment are wrapped in plastic to discourage poking and prodding of the many Air Jordans on display. A five-minute walk away is Designer Shoe Warehouse, where sneakers such as the Converse All Star and the Vans Sk8-Hi share shelf space with a Nike Air Monarch IV, a basic $60 cross-trainer that managed to sell more pairs than any other Nike model in 2013. Just down Fourth Avenue is a Kmart, where you can buy a bagful of sneakers from companies such as Everlast, Risewear, and Athletech for the same price as a single Air Jordan from Flight Club.

Cheap or expensive, rare or inescapable, stylish or nondescript, there are a million reasons we reach for sneakers, again and again. The Kmart shoppers might be buying for price or comfort; the teenagers standing in line at Supreme, to have something no one else has; the customers handling the shrink-wrapped shoes at Flight Club, to fulfill a dream of owning something they couldn't afford while younger.

Some reasons are more intangible still.

Not long ago a sneaker store in my neighborhood was having a seasonal "extra stock" sale. There wasn't anything I was looking for in particular, which is both the best and worst mentality when one is about to buy something. The shoe that caught my eye was a Nike Air Presto Essential, a technical-looking running shoe whose most distinctive feature is a stretchy neoprene upper that mimics the feel of a sock. The second I put it on, I was transported back to a version of the Presto I had in college, which was quite literally run into the ground when the miles I put on it wore holes in the sole. This was the shoe I'd walk out of the store in. The only thing left to do was choose the color. My four-year-old daughter was with me, and I put the question to her, hoping she'd pick the green ones I was leaning toward. Kids, though, have other plans.

"I don't like the green one," she said.

"How come?"

"It's ugly, I don't like it."

"Why do you like the gray one more?"

"I dunno."

"I'll get the green one."

"Pleeeease no. I don't like it."

Reader, I bought the green ones. By the next day my daughter had gotten over it. But even at four years old, we have strong opinions on matters of taste. I couldn't justify why I preferred green over gray any better than my daughter could; my argument could be boiled down to that universal "I dunno, I just do." A few months later, my apartment was broken into. The burglars left the TV, Nintendo, and passports, but they took my laptop, some watches . . . and those green sneakers. Strangely, they didn't take a pair of orange suede Nikes sitting right next to them. Even crooks have their sneaker preferences.

One annoying tic I've developed through the course of writing this book: I immediately look at what shoes people are wearing. My completely nonscientific, one-man sociological survey has reached several conclusions. First, the people at Converse have nothing to worry about. I live near a large shopping street in Vienna, Austria, where I've seen Chuck Taylor All Stars on kids, teenagers, moms, and even grandmothers. Second, classic designs, especially in white, will always be popular. Teenagers, college students, and hipsters (called "bobos" here) tend to gravitate toward the All Star, the Adidas Superstar, and the Adidas Stan Smith, though the last is becoming less common. As with Chuck Taylor, I wonder how many Adidas owners know that Stan Smith is a real person, despite the fact that the tennis player's picture appears on each pair. Finally, the sneaker ecosystem is different everywhere you go. In New York, Air Jordans are still the shoe to rock; in Vienna, less so. In Paris, the biggest sin is to look as though you're trying too hard, while in Tokyo, anything seems to go. In Budapest, the hottest thing is still the Communist-era brand Tisza Cipő.

After all this, do I consider myself a sneakerhead? Sneaker fan, yes. Sneaker fanboy, not so much. I appreciate craftsmanship, but I'd still feel a little self-conscious spending more than $100 on a pair. Including running shoes, I have a pair for every day of the week—enough of a range to make it seem as though I've put thought into my outfit. But the sneakers I wear the most aren't the most expensive I own, or the flashiest, or even the ones in the best condition. They're a pair of beat-up black Adidas so nondescript I can't even find out what model they are.

I like them because they fit me.

NOTES

This book is a work of nonfiction. There are no composite characters or invented re-creations. Attributed quotes in the text is actual dialogue from interviews, documentaries, and media articles or else is a citation from a book, memoir, magazine or newspaper article, letter, academic study, archive material, or other document, as cited below.

vii **"You cannot be comfortable":** Christian Louboutin, interview with Sara Sidner, *Talk Asia*, CNN, Aug. 10, 2012; http://www.cnn.com/TRANSCRIPTS/1208/10/ta.01.html.

vii **"In L.A. we wearing Chucks, not Ballys":** Tupac Shakur and Andre Love, "California Love," Death Row Records/Interscope, 1996.

PROLOGUE

4 **found to be a near constant:** Brian Fidelman, "The Roving Runner Goes Barefoot," *New York Times*, Oct. 5, 2009; https://well.blogs.nytimes.com/2009/10/05/the-roving-runner-goes-barefoot/?mcubz=3&_r=0.

1

THE FATHER OF INVENTION

8 **eight tons of overshoes:** Charles Slack, *Noble Obsession: Charles Goodyear, Thomas Hancock, and the Race to Unlock the Greatest Industrial Secret of the 19th Century* (New York: Theia Books, 2002), 31.

8 **"bag of wind":** Charles Goodyear, *Gum-elastic and Its Varieties, With a Detailed Account of Its Applications and Uses, and of the Discovery of Vulcanization* (New Haven, CT: self-published, 1853), 267.

8 **"Forget your valve":** Slack, *Noble Obsession*, 28.

9 **"perhaps as good a resting place":** Ibid., 107. These prisons trapped debtors in a vicious catch-22: they could leave once they repaid their debt, but they couldn't make money to repay it while in prison. Often an inmate would be released only because the creditor tired of paying the prisoner's daily bread fee.

10 **"Here is something":** Ibid., 42.

10 **population grew from 340,000 to 1.4 million:** "Population and Housing Unit Counts, New York: 2000," U.S. Census Bureau, September 2003; https://www.census.gov/prod/cen 2000/phc-3-34.pdf, 31.

11 **with a cork:** Elizabeth Semmelhack, *Out of the Box: The Rise of Sneaker Culture* (New York: Skira Rizzoli Publications, 2015), 23.

11 **Wait Webster:** Ibid., 26.

11 **the Liverpool Rubber Company:** Ibid., 23. Semmelhack goes on to mention that though the company is commonly cited as introducing a rubber-soled sand shoe, hard evidence has yet to surface.

12 **popularized by Union troops:** Matthew Algeo, *Pedestrianism: When Watching People Walk Was America's Favorite Spectator Sport* (Chicago: Chicago Review Press, 2017), 18.

12 **large buildings for public events:** Ibid., 21.

13 **The winner covered:** By 1900, pedestrianism had fallen out of favor. Crooked walking matches, inaccurate courses, and a lack of standardized measurement shifted the public's interest away from walking and toward running, where there could be more uniformity of rules, distances, and records.

13 **British public houses and taverns:** Edward S. Sears, *Running Through the Ages* (Jefferson, NC: McFarland & Company, 2015), 52.

13 **leather strap across the instep:** Semmelhack, *Out of the Box*, 201.

13 **heavy lead insoles:** Sears, *Running Through the Ages*, 85.

16 **5 million pairs a year:** Slack, *Noble Obsession*, 195.

17 **had eaten up most of the money:** Ibid., 165.

17 **seven hundred or so spectators:** Ibid., 184.

18 **"It would be painful":** Daniel Webster, *The Writings and Speeches of Daniel Webster*, vol. 15 (Boston: Little, Brown & Company, 1903), 443.

18 **"patent pirates":** The modern-day equivalent of the "patent pirate" is the "patent troll," a company that buys up as many patents as it can and then sues, claiming infringement. Whether there are any grounds for the suit is almost immaterial. Patent trolls make their money off of settlements; it is almost always cheaper to settle a patent infringement case to make it go away than bring it to trial.

19 **"I took the [rubber] cloak":** Webster, *The Writings and Speeches of Daniel Webster*, vol. 15, 442.

19 **widespread popularity:** Croquet first exploded as a game in the 1850s, when the patent of the lawn mower ran out and there were more versions of the machines available to trim a suitable lawn for playing.

19 **for the first time in generations:** Patricia Campbell Warner, *When the Girls Came Out to Play: The Birth of American Sportswear* (Amherst: University of Massachusetts Press, 2006), 29.

19 **Women's magazines noted:** Ibid., 29.

19 **"croquet sandal":** Semmelhack, *Out of the Box*, 23.

20 **hopped the pond:** "New Kind of Sport Shoe; The Sole Is Made of Unvulcanized Crepe Rubber," *New York Times,* Nov. 6, 1921; https://timesmachine.nytimes.com/times machine/1921/11/06/107031542.html. The article goes on to mention how shoes with a blanket crepe rubber sole are more resilient but also more expensive than plimsolls made with cheaper rubber, which last only two or three weeks.

21 **hundreds of thousands of dollars in debt:** Reflecting on his patent woes, Goodyear did take comfort in the fact that so many people were using his discovery. "Man has just cause for regret when he sows and no one reaps," he once wrote; see *A Centennial Volume of the Writings of Charles Goodyear and Thomas Hancock* (Boston: Centennial Committee, American Chemical Society, 1939), 97.

2
PEACH BASKETS AND TENNIS SETS

23 **"This new generation":** Richard Davies, *Sports in American Life: A History* (New York: Wiley-Blackwell, 2007), 76.

25 **Naismith recorded:** James Naismith, *Basketball: Its Origins and Development* (Lincoln: University of Nebraska Press, 1941), 109.

27 **"A man is not necessarily a sneak":** advertisement, *The Sacred Heart Review,* Aug. 3, 1895, 2 (as cited in Semmelhack, *Out of the Box,* 33, who also notes the similarity between this and the Run-DMC lyric "I wear my sneakers but I'm not a sneak" nearly ninety years later).

28 **"call 'em 'sneakers' now":** Quoted in Dale Coye, "The Sneakers/Tennis Shoes Boundary," *American Speech* 61, no. 4 (Winter 1986): 366.

28 **Calling them "gym shoes":** Google Books Ngram Viewer comparison among the terms "sneakers," "tennis shoes," "gym shoes," and "plimsolls," Aug. 15, 2017.

28 **"strong canvas rubber sole shoes"**: Elizabeth Semmelhack, *Out of the Box: The Rise of Sneaker Culture* (New York: Skira Rizzoli Publications, 2015), 40.

28 **"The first suction-sole"**: Naismith, *Basketball*, 90 (as cited in Semmelhack, *Out of the Box*, 40).

29 **"Tennis shoes are preferred"**: Patricia Campbell Warner, *When the Girls Came Out to Play: The Birth of American Sportswear* (Amherst: University of Massachusetts Press, 2006), 49.

29 **the customs agent didn't know**: Sam Roberts, "On Staten Island, the Earliest Traces of American Tennis," *New York Times*, Aug. 20, 2010; https://cityroom.blogs.nytimes.com /2010/08/20/on-staten-island-the-earliest-traces-of-american -tennis/?mcubz=3.

29 **her brother set up**: Incidentally, her brother, Eugenius Harvey Outerbridge, was the first chairman of the Port of New York Authority and the namesake of the Outerbridge Crossing, which connects New York with New Jersey.

30 **By the end of the summer**: Warner, *When the Girls Came Out to Play*, 44.

30 **"As for the participation"**: Pierre de Coubertin, *Olympism: Selected Writings*, ed. Norbert Müller (Lausanne: International Olympic Committee, 2000), 604.

31 **"appropriate for tennis"**: Davies, *Sports in American Life*, 106.

32 **"Unless a game"**: Ibid.

3

JOHNNY BASKETBALLSEED

35 **Taylor issued a simple challenge**: Abraham Aamidor, *Chuck Taylor, All Star* (Indianapolis: Indiana University Press, 2006), 64.

36 **"world champion" Original Celtics and "Olympic champion" Buffalo Germans**: Though the two teams were long linked with Taylor's name, there is little evidence to support his claim that he played for them. Further, because the "world

championship" involved only a handful of white-only teams in the Northeast, the title must be taken with a grain of salt. As for the "Olympic champions," some members of the team played at the already sparsely attended 1904 Games, when basketball was a demonstration sport. Besides, only nations, not city teams, could be Olympic champions.

37   **ankle patch:** Elizabeth Semmelhack, *Out of the Box: The Rise of Sneaker Culture* (New York: Skira Rizzoli Publications, 2015), 202.

38   **became one such salesman:** Aamidor, *Chuck Taylor, All Star,* 45. Taylor's embellished personal history extended to when exactly he started at Converse. Taylor himself mentioned the year as 1921, but further research makes 1922 more plausible.

38   **Madison Square Garden:** The current MSG, as it's known, opened in 1968 and is the fourth arena to hold that name. The first two opened in 1879 and 1890, respectively.

38   **dress shoes, cars, and fishing poles:** John Beckman, *American Fun: Four Centuries of Joyous Revolt* (New York: Vintage, 2014), 166.

39   **a semipro team:** Aamidor, *Chuck Taylor, All Star,* 30.

39   **Akron Wingfoots:** In a nice bit of historical symmetry, the Cleveland Cavaliers started wearing the Goodyear Wingfoot logo on their uniform during the 2017–18 season, making them an heir, of sorts, to the basketball of Chuck Taylor's day. Taylor, the most famous player of his era, wore Converse. Cleveland's LeBron James, the most famous player of his era, wore Nike, which now owns Converse.

40   **New York Renaissance:** The connection between the New York Rens' talent and Harlem was so significant that when naming his new all-black basketball team, owner Abe Saperstein decided on the Harlem Globetrotters, despite the fact that the team was from Chicago.

40   **which Taylor claimed:** No doubt to boost his credibility when visiting a new town. Then, as now, there was little way to verify his claims.

40 **a harbinger of controversies:** The Boston Celtics' place in basketball's black versus white dynamic would be further explored in Spike Lee's *Do the Right Thing.*

40 **"Who needs the shoes?":** Aamidor, *Chuck Taylor, All Star*, 68.

42 **Purcell had lost:** Semmelhack, *Out of the Box*, 49.

43 **switched his team's shoes:** Aamidor, *Chuck Taylor, All Star*, vii–viii.

43 **keeping dribbling in the game:** Prior to dribbling, as it's known today, players were only allowed to bounce the ball once and had to rely on passing to move the ball up the court.

43 **"In one of the games":** Aamidor, *Chuck Taylor, All Star*, 48.

44 **"The more you pay":** *Popular Mechanics,* April 1929.

45 **a feat only recently surpassed:** As of September 2017, Williams had won twenty-three Grand Slam tournament singles titles, second only to Margaret Court, who won twenty-four.

4

WAR AND BROTHERS

49 **"painted Adolf Hitler":** Richard Corliss, "All-TIME 100 Movies: *Olympia*, Parts 1 and 2," *Time*, Jan. 14, 2010; http://entertainment.time.com/2005/02/12/all-time-100-movies/slide/olympia-parts-1-and-2-1938/.

50 **wear your shoes:** According to Semmelhack, *Out of the Box*, 54, Owens wore the Dassler brothers' shoes only in practice, not in competition. This stands in contrast with the oft-repeated story that Owens won his medals in the shoes. In reality, the shoes Adidas said Owens wore do not appear to match photos of the ones he wore in competition.

50 **makeshift workshop in his mother's washroom:** Barbara Smit, *Sneaker Wars: The Enemy Brothers Who Founded Adidas and Puma and the Family Feud That Forever Changed the Business of Sport* (New York: Harper Perennial, 2009), 5.

52 **"encouragement of physical fitness":** Office of United States Chief of Counsel for Prosecution of Axis Criminality, "Program of the NSDAP: Document No. 1708-PS," *Nazi Conspiracy and Aggression,* vol. 4 (Washington, DC: U.S. Government Printing Office, 1946), 210.

52 **"impeccably trained bodies":** Office of United States Chief of Counsel for Prosecution of Axis Criminality, *Nazi Conspiracy and Aggression,* vol. 5 (Washington, DC: U.S. Government Printing Office, 1946), 931. A slightly varied translation is also cited in Semmelhack, *Out of the Box,* 54.

52 **joining the Hitler Youth:** Barbara Smit, *Pitch Invasion: Adidas, Puma and the Making of Modern Sport* (New York: Penguin, 2007), 14.

53 **"Here are the *Schweinehunde* again":** René Hofmann, "Kängurus an den Füßen," *Süddeutsche Zeitung,* Dec. 11, 2008 (author's translation); http://www.sueddeutsche.de/sport /fussballschuhe-kaengurus-an-den-fuessen-1.784197.

54 **"I will not hesitate":** Smit, *Sneaker Wars,* 19.

55 **trademarked three parallel white stripes:** Decades later, the two companies would still be fighting over branding. In 2017, Adidas sued Puma when the latter company produced a soccer cleat with four parallel stripes running down the side, arguing that the extra stripe was an attempt "to free-ride on Adidas' fame as a preeminent soccer brand."

56 **In Herzo, your shoe affiliation:** Kate Connolly, "Adidas v Puma: The Bitter Rivalry That Runs and Runs," *The Guardian,* Oct. 19, 2009; https://www.theguardian.com/sport/2009 /oct/19/rivalry-between-adidas-and-puma. Not even death could stop the brothers' animosity toward each other; they were buried at opposite ends of the cemetery in Herzogenaurach.

57 **"You are only a small king":** "Die feindlichen Stiefel," *Der Spiegel,* June 24, 1959 (author's translation). Original quote: "Sie sind nur ein kleiner König; wenn Sie nicht spuren, wählen wir einen anderen Bundestrainer"; http://www.spiegel.de/spiegel /print/d-42625840.html.

57 **"First comes Herberger, then the Lord God!":** Ibid. Original quote: "Erst kommt Herberger, und dann der Herrgott!"

58 **Herberger, recognizing the shoes' contribution:** Smit, *Sneaker Wars*, 36.

59 **Adidas reportedly refused:** "Streifen gewechselt," *Der Spiegel*, July 15, 1964.

59 **wearing Puma spikes:** Gunnar Meinhardt, "Ich hasste Deutschland, ich wäre zerbrochen," *Welt*, March 22, 2017; https://www.welt.de/sport/leichtathletik/article163054207 /Ich-hasste-Deutschland-ich-waere-zerbrochen.html.

59 **an attempt to play:** Tom Lamont, "Frozen in Time: Armin Hary Wins 100m Olympic Gold, Rome, 1960," *The Guardian*, Jan. 10, 2010; https://www.theguardian.com/sport/2010 /jan/10/frozen-in-time-olympics-100m. David Maraniss, "How Rome 1960 Changed the Olympics," *Newsweek*, July 25, 2008; http://www.newsweek.com/david-maraniss-how-rome-1960 -changed-olympics-93157. Hary, according to both articles, took sponsorship money from both Adidas and Puma.

5

BUILDERMAN

61 **Builderman:** Bill Bowerman's surname is Anglicized from the German Bauermann, which, given the track coach's hobby of tinkering with shoes, appropriately translates to "Builderman."

61 **"Mr. Moore, I'm going to ask you":** "Bill Bowerman," *Oregon Experience*, Oregon Public Broadcasting, prod. Nadine Jelsing, 2006.

62 **"Farmer can't get his mule to plow":** Kenny Moore, *Bowerman and the Men of Oregon: The Story of Oregon's Legendary Coach and Nike's Cofounder* (New York: Rodale, 2006), Kindle location 84.

62 **"Fundamentally, that was the proof":** "Bill Bowerman," *Oregon Experience*.

62   **"You will lay before me"**: Moore, *Bowerman and the Men of Oregon*, Kindle location 2737.

64   **"Did you hear me?"**: Ibid., Kindle location 656.

64   **"exhilarated, not exhausted"**: Ibid., Kindle location 1359.

64   **"If you work hard"**: "Bill Bowerman," *Oregon Experience*.

65   **"inexplicably warm water"**: Geoff Hollister, *Out of Nowhere: The Inside Story of How Nike Marketed the Culture of Running* (New York: Meyer & Meyer Sports, 2008), 24.

65   **heat up his set of keys**: "Bill Bowerman," *Oregon Experience*.

68   **"I was giving"**: Bill Bowerman, "The Kitchen-Table Shoemaker," *Guideposts*, May 1988.

70   **"sticky mess"**: notebook, Bill Bowerman papers, University of Oregon Libraries, Special Collections and University Archives, box 38.

71   **"All will not be fun and frolic"**: letter, Bill Bowerman papers, University of Oregon Libraries, Special Collections and University Archives, box 14.

71   **"white, white, shoes,"**: Moore, *Bowerman and the Men of Oregon*, Kindle location 1871.

72   **Stitching added too much weight**: J. B. Strasser and Laurie Becklund, *Swoosh: The Unauthorized Story of Nike and the Men Who Played There* (New York: HarperBusiness, 1993), 30.

6

SWOOSH

75   **He had tanked an interview:** J. B. Strasser and Laurie Becklund, *Swoosh: The Unauthorized Story of Nike and the Men Who Played There* (New York: HarperBusiness, 1993), 14.

76   **green Brooks Brothers two-button suit:** Stanford Graduate School of Business, "Stanford Graduate School of Business Graduation Remarks by Phil Knight, MBA '62," YouTube, July 7, 2014; https://www.youtube.com/watch?v=nRN9Fw WQY8w.

77 **"During the autumn track season":** Phil Knight, *Shoe Dog: A Memoir by the Creator of Nike* (New York: Scribner, 2016), 87.

78 **the solution to building communities:** Hiroshi Tanaka, *Personality in Identity: The Human Side of a Japanese Enterprise* (New York: Bloomsbury Academic, 2013), 21.

78 **"Onitsuka made the lasts":** Knight, *Shoe Dog*, 86.

78 **When his dinner arrived:** Jeremy Bogaisky, "Farewell to the Father of the Octopus Shoe," *Forbes*, Oct. 1, 2007; https://www.forbes.com/2007/10/01/onitsuka-asics-obit-face-markets-cx_jb_1001autofacescan01.html.

79 **the creator's initials:** Generally speaking, in Japan initials, like names, are written with the surname first.

79 **When perforated holes were added:** "All You Need to Do After Falling Down Is to Stand Up Again"; https://www.asics.fi/about/mr-onitsuka/.

81 **"kicked the shit out of the Aztecs":** Knight, *Shoe Dog*, 111. Kenny Moore's *Men of Oregon* reports Bowerman's question as, "Who's that Spaniard responsible for 400 years of Montezuma's revenge?"

81 **killing at least forty-four:** "The Dead of Tlatelolco," National Security Archive Electronic Briefing Book No. 201, Oct. 1, 2006; http://nsarchive2.gwu.edu//NSAEBB/NSAEBB201/index.htm. It should be noted that there are many estimates for how many people died during the Tlatelolco Massacre. By combing through records in archives, the National Security Archive documented forty-four confirmed deaths. Other estimates say that hundreds were killed.

82 **"Niggers need to go back to Africa!":** "The Man Who Raised a Black Power Salute at the 1968 Olympic Games," *The Guardian*, March 30, 2012; https://www.theguardian.com/world/2012/mar/30/black-power-salute-1968-olympics.

82 **"If I win I am an American":** "1968: Black Athletes Make Silent Protest," BBC, Oct. 17, 2008; http://news.bbc.co.uk/onthisday/hi/dates/stories/october/17/newsid_3535000/3535348.stm.

83   **"Well Mr. Owens":** Dave Zirin and John Carlos, *The John Car-los Story: The Sports Moment That Changed the World* (Chicago: Haymarket Books, 2011), 114.

83   **supposedly nonpolitical event:** During the 1972 Olympics, Puma hired John Carlos to hand out gear to the athletes. Avery Brundage and the IOC believed it was just a cover to "ruin another Olympics." In his 2011 memoir, Carlos recounted a bizarre incident in which the Palestinian terrorists who mur-dered eleven Israeli Olympic team members and a German po-lice officer had obtained the Puma gear worn during the attack from his stand.

83   **"militants" and "nonmilitants":** Arthur Daley, "Sports of the Times; The Incident," *New York Times*, Oct. 20, 1968; https://timesmachine.nytimes.com/timesmachine/1968/10/20/91236784.html?pageNumber=323.

83   **"made my heart jump":** "Olympics a Stage for Political Con-tests, Too," *Talk of the Nation*, Feb. 28, 2008; http://www.npr.org/templates/story/story.php?storyId=87767864.

85   **"It was just amazing":** Barbara Smit, *Sneaker Wars: The Enemy Brothers Who Founded Adidas and Puma and the Family Feud That Forever Changed the Business of Sport* (New York: Harper Perennial, 2009), 75.

86   **more than 80 percent of the athletes:** Melvyn P. Cheskin, *The Complete Handbook of Athletic Footwear* (New York: Fairchild Publications, 1987), 16 (as cited in Semmelhack, *Out of the Box*, 74).

86   **"poured them into the waffle iron":** "Bill Bowerman," *Oregon Experience*, Oregon Public Broadcasting, prod. Nadine Jelsing, 2006.

88   **"something that evokes":** Knight, *Shoe Dog*, 180.

88   **he wasn't going to let it go easily:** "Nike's Fiercely Competi-tive Phil Knight," *CBS Sunday Morning*, April 24, 2016; https://www.cbsnews.com/news/nikes-fiercely-competitive-phil-knight/. In that interview, Knight explained the origin of the Dimen-

sion Six name: "Well, there was a 5th dimension right? So we wanted it to be an extra dimension."

88 **"I guess we'll go":** Strasser and Becklund, *Swoosh*, 116.

7

COURTING STYLE

89 **Almost every night:** Walt Frazier and Ira Berkow, *Rockin' Steady: A Guide to Basketball & Cool* (Chicago: Triumph Books, 2010), 13.

90 **"Hey, get Clyde":** Ibid.

90 **"Just before going":** Ibid., 109.

91 **Converse had sold 400 million pairs:** Abraham Aamidor, *Chuck Taylor, All Star* (Indianapolis: Indiana University Press, 2006), 13.

92 **"Pelé pact":** Jason Coles, *Golden Kicks: The Shoes That Changed Sport* (New York: Bloomsbury, 2016), 72. Puma offered Pelé $25,000 to wear the brand during the World Cup, $100,000 for the next four years, and 10 percent in royalties.

93 **120 stations across the country:** Ron Rapoport, "Inside and Outsized," *Los Angeles Times*, Jan. 20, 2008; http://articles.latimes.com/2008/jan/20/sports/sp-uclahouston20.

94 **"They had played in canvas":** Barbara Smit, *Sneaker Wars: The Enemy Brothers Who Founded Adidas and Puma and the Family Feud That Forever Changed the Business of Sport* (New York: Harper Perennial, 2009), 93.

95 **squeaky clean dress code:** Elizabeth Semmelhack, *Out of the Box: The Rise of Sneaker Culture* (New York: Skira Rizzoli Publications, 2015), 88.

96 **Horst and Smith met at a nightclub in Paris:** "Der Mann mit dem Schuh," *Süddeutsche Zeitung*, Oct. 14, 2016; http://www.sueddeutsche.de/wirtschaft/stan-smith-der-mann-mit-dem-schuh-1.3205443.

96 **So had tennis's popularity:** Matthew Futterman, *Players: The Story of Sports and Money and the Visionaries Who Fought to Create a Revolution* (New York: Simon & Schuster, 2016), 106. In 1972, about 22 million people in the United States played tennis; three years later that number had jumped to about 41 million.

96 **half of the Wimbledon field:** Alex Synamatix, "Interview: Stan Smith," The Daily Street, Jan. 14, 2014; http://www.thedailystreet.co.uk/2014/01/interview-stan-smith/.

96 **"I got really annoyed":** Smit, *Sneaker Wars*, 96.

97 **New York had more public parks:** Alexander Garvin, *The Planning Game: Lessons from Great Cities* (New York: W. W. Norton & Company, 2013).

97 **"more physical":** *#Rucker50*, dir. Robert McCullough, Jr., Maryea Media, 2016.

98 **"If we played the Lakers":** "When the Garden Was Eden," *30 for 30*, dir. Michael Rapaport, ESPN Films, Oct. 21, 2014.

99 **"If you didn't dress":** Ibid.

99 **"After the game":** Ibid.

100 **the same model used:** Semmelhack, *Out of the Box*, 79.

101 **the Puma Clyde was the first:** Bobbito Garcia, *Where'd You Get Those?: New York City's Sneaker Culture* (New York: Testify, 2013), 52.

101 **"We'd see a snowstorm and get happy":** Ibid., 61.

8

EVERYONE IS DOING IT

104 **"I went about a hundred yards":** Kenny Moore, *Bowerman and the Men of Oregon: The Story of Oregon's Legendary Coach and Nike's Cofounder* (New York: Rodale, 2006), 146.

106 **"something weirdos did":** Phil Knight, *Shoe Dog: A Memoir by the Creator of Nike* (New York: Scribner, 2016), 76.

106 **South Carolina senator Strom Thurmond:** Phil Edwards, "When running for exercise was for weirdos," *Vox*, Aug. 9, 2015, https://www.vox.com/2015/8/9/9115981/running-jogging -history.

106 **"It blew my mind":** Pat Putnam, "The Freshman and the Great Guru," *Sports Illustrated*, June 15, 1970; https://www.si.com /vault/1970/06/15/611398/the-freshman-and-the-great-guru.

106 **"run next week":** *Fire on the Track: The Steve Prefontaine Story*, dir. Erich Lyttle, Chambers Productions, 1995.

107 **they became friends again:** Frank Shorter, *My Marathon: Reflections on a Gold Medal Life* (New York: Rodale, 2016), 230.

108 **"Next year, I'm going to do it":** Interview, Norbert Sander, September 8, 2016.

108 **"The park became":** *Run for Your Life*, dir. Judd Ehrlich, Flatbush Pictures, 2008.

108 **jogging outfit for children:** Eleanor Nangle, "Jogging in Fashion," *Chicago Tribune*, Oct. 15, 1968; http://archives .chicagotribune.com/1968/10/15/page/37/article/jogging-in -fashion.

109 **"Violent movements of the body":** Gertrud Pfister, "The Medical Discourse on Female Physical Culture in Germany in the 19th and Early 20th Centuries," *Journal of Sport History* 17, no. 2 (Summer 1990); http://library.la84.org/SportsLibrary /JSH/JSH1990/JSH1702/jsh1702c.pdf.

109 **"Women aren't allowed":** Roy M. Wallock, "How Bobbi Gibb Changed Women's Running, And Finally Got Credit For It," ESPN, Jan. 6, 2016; http://www.espn.com/sports/endurance /story/_/id/15090507/endurance-sports-bobbi-gibb-first-woman -run-boston-marathon.

110 **a range of half-inch widths:** New Balance website, https:// support.newbalance.com/hc/en-us/articles/212729638-What -Are-The-Widths-That-Are-Available-In-New-Balance-Shoes-. A Tribe Called Quest's 1991 track "Buggin' Out" includes the line "I sport New Balance to avoid a narrow path."

110 **"Do I need a new name?":** "Brands That Stand the Test of Time"; http://hecklerassociates.com/about/. Terry Heckler, the designer who assured the New Balance chief that the name was fine, would go on to create the Starbucks logo.

111 **best running sneaker:** Dave Kayser, "Shoes of Our Youth," *Runner's World,* July 18, 2009; https://www.runnersworld.com/barefoot-running/shoes-of-our-youth.

114 **"kind of demystifying it":** "Episode 18: Shalane Flanagan and Frank Shorter," *The Runner's World Show,* podcast, Aug. 11, 2016.

114 *Runner's World* **saw its circulation jump:** Jonathan Black, *Making the American Body: The Remarkable Saga of the Men and Women Whose Feats, Feuds, and Passions Shaped Fitness History* (Lincoln: University of Nebraska Press, 2013), 77.

116 **He has featured heavily:** "40 Years of Prefontaine," June 1, 2015; https://news.nike.com/news/40-years-of-prefontaine.

116 **"You can bet":** Richard Goldstein, "Bill Bowerman, 88, Nike Co-Founder, Dies," *New York Times,* Dec. 27, 1999; http://www.nytimes.com/1999/12/27/sports/bill-bowerman-88-nike-co-founder-dies.html?mcubz=3.

9

MEANWHILE, ON THE WEST COAST

117 **circulation of more than 7 million:** A. J. Zuilen, *The Life Cycle of Magazines: A Historical Study of the Decline and Fall of the General Interest Mass Audience Magazine in the United States During the Period 1946–1972* (Uithoorn, Netherlands: Graduate Press, 1977), 89, 99.

118 **The group's first four out of five singles:** From November 1961 through July 1963, the Beach Boys released "Surfin'," "Surfin' Safari," "Surfin' U.S.A.," and "Surfer Girl." A fifth single during that period, "Ten Little Indians" didn't reference the sport, but the cover featured the five bandmates carrying a surfboard.

118 **"sidewalk surfing"**: Google Books Ngram Viewer analysis of the term "sidewalk surfing," Aug. 17, 2017. "Sidewalk surfing" was first used in the 1960s, reaching its peak usage around 1975.

119 **"associated with conformist"**: Emily Chivers Yochim, *Skate Life: Re-imagining White Masculinity* (Ann Arbor: University of Michigan Press, 2010), 27.

119 **"Is skateboarding going"**: "Few Youths Entering Skateboard Contests," *Los Angeles Times*, August 14, 1966.

119 **first US skate shop:** Daniel Schmid, Dirk Vogel, and Jurgen Blumlein, *Made for Skate: The Illustrated History of Skateboard Footwear* (Berlin: Gingko Press, 2008), 27.

119 **"Being the first to wear"**: Ibid.

119 **"We're going to be fine"**: Interview, Steve Van Doren, Sept. 5, 2017.

120 **third largest manufacturer:** "The History of Vans: Steve Van Doren Interview," April 27, 2015; http://stage.sneakerfreaker .com/articles/the-history-of-vans/.

121 **"there's a fabric store"**: Interview, Steve Van Doren, Sept. 5, 2017.

122 **The canvas used for the first Vans:** The canvas on the #44 was also stronger than the kind used on other sneakers of the time. Duck canvas is more tightly woven and durable than conventional canvas used in sneakers like the Converse All-Star. Duck comes on a scale of 1 to 12, 12 being the lightest and 1 usually reserved for heavy-duty products such as hammocks and sandbags. The Van Dorens used #10 duck and kept it in place with nylon instead of canvas thread, which other companies avoided because it was more expensive.

123 **"Rat Patrol"**: G. Beato, "The Lords of Dogtown," *Spin*, March 1999; http://www.angelfire.com/ca/alva3/spin.html.

123 **"We'd sit up on the pier"**: Ibid.

124 **"You could get impaled"**: *Dogtown and Z-Boys*, dir. Stacy Peralta, Agi Orsi Productions, 2001.

124 **"To a 12-year-old kid"**: Beato, "The Lords of Dogtown."

124 **faster rides and sharper corners:** In addition to polyurethane wheels, extra foot protection meant more elaborate, risky tricks could be attempted, leaving the rubber, canvas, suede, and nylon to take most of the beating. Better board technology also facilitated better tricks, pushing the need for tough shoes even further. Sandpaper affixed to the top of the board to increase shoe traction (a necessity when trading up from the feel of bare feet on hardwood) gave way to adhesive grip tape that provided a rough, uniform surface that still ground down a shoe's sole. Finally, there was the damage created by a botched trick. Low-top shoes may offer better movement and board control, while high-tops give more protection.

125 **"Trashed shoes are like a war wound":** Schmid et al., *Made for Skate*, 1.

125 **"Where's our trophies?":** Beato, "The Lords of Dogtown."

125 **"It was like Ferraris versus Model-T's":** Ibid.

126 **"My father was also wearing":** Schmid et al., *Made for Skate*, 80.

127 **Per design trends:** One of the unlikeliest contributors to the design of today's sneaker is the Modernist Finnish architect Alvar Aalto. In the 1930s, Aalto created something revolutionary at the time in swimming pool design: curves. His kidney-shaped pools were a sharp contrast to the traditional rectangular pools of the time. The architect's 1939 Villa Maira residence in Noormarkku, Finland, contained the first kidney-shaped pool whose organic arcs, smooth drop-offs, and lack of sharp angles made vertical skateboarding possible decades later. Aalto's design might have remained a curious landscape architectural flourish were it not for his friend and fellow architect Thomas Church, who used the kidney-shaped pool in designing the Donnell Garden in Sonoma, California, a decade later. The oft-photographed pool was widely copied across the state, and having a pool of a similar design was a way of owning your own slice of the California high life.

128 **referring to the moment:** Robert Klara, "After 51 Years, Vans Is Finally Explaining What 'Off the Wall' Means," *Adweek*,

Feb. 20, 2017; http://www.adweek.com/brand-marketing/after
-51-years-vans-is-finally-explaining-what-off-the-wall-means/.

128 **Universal Studios asked Vans' PR rep:** Robert Klara,
"From *Ridgemont High* to 'Damn, Daniel,' Vans Is Still Kicking It at 50," *AdWeek*, March 15, 2016; http://www.adweek
.com/brand-marketing/ridgemont-high-damn-daniel-vans-still
-kicking-it-50-170130/. *Fast Times at Ridgemont High* was
filmed in November and December 1981.

129 **"We were about":** Adam Tschorn, "How Vans Tapped Southern California Skate Culture and Became a Billion-Dollar Shoe
Brand," *Los Angeles Times*, March 12, 2016; http://www.la
times.com/fashion/la-ig-vans-turns-50-20160312-story.html.

129 **"The price stickers":** Schmid et al., *Made for Skate*, 70.

130 **five-star rating from *Runner's World*:** Holger von Krosigk,
ed., "Interview: Steve Van Doren," *Sneakers Magazine*, Feb. 10,
2014, 103; http://sneakers-magazine.com/sneakers-magazine
-issue-21-free-digital-edition/.

130 **140 undocumented workers:** Chris Woodyard and Michael
Flagg, "Vans Factory Back on Line After Raid," *Los Angeles
Times*, Jan. 16, 1993; http://articles.latimes.com/1993-01-16
/business/fi-1320_1_illegal-immigrants. The 1984 raid wasn't
the last time federal immigration authorities visited the company; federal agents arrested 233 workers in 1993, about 10
percent of Vans' workforce.

130 **the Serios were only semisuccessful:** von Krosigk, "Interview: Steve Van Doren," 103.

10

LET'S GET PHYSICAL

133 **90 million worldwide viewers:** Jesse Greenspan, "Billie Jean King Wins the 'Battle of the Sexes,' 40 Years Ago,"
Sept. 20, 2013; http://www.history.com/news/billie-jean
-king-wins-the-battle-of-the-sexes-40-years-ago.

134 **"I can't play for money":** Gerald Eskenazi, "$100,000 Tennis Match. Bobby Riggs vs. Mrs. King," *New York Times*, July 12, 1973; http://www.nytimes.com/1973/07/12 /archives/100000-tennis-match-bobby-riggs-vs-mrs-king-its -mrs-king-against.html?mcubz=3&_r=0.

134 **Senorita Cortez:** Sometimes also called Lady Cortez.

135 **"any education program or activity":** United States Education Amendments of 1972, Public Law No. 92-318, 86 Stat. 235, Title IX, 1972.

135 **"This is going to save us":** lagarchivist, "New York City Mayor Edward I. Koch on the 1980 Transit Strike," YouTube, June 25, 2010; https://www.youtube.com/watch?v=w5XuOJLta5Y.

136 **The strike lasted eleven days:** Grandmaster Flash's seminal 1982 track "The Message," which cataloged the city's ills, included a reference to the strike.

136 **carrying tote bags:** Sewell Chan, "25 Years Ago, Subways and Buses Stopped Running," *New York Times*, April 4, 2015; http://www.nytimes.com/2005/04/04/nyregion/25-years-ago -subways-and-buses-stopped-running.html?mcubz=3.

136 **"It looked a little weird":** Joanne Wasserman, "How City Rode Out Strike," *Daily News*, Dec. 12, 2002; http://www.nydaily news.com/archives/news/city-rode-strike-article-1.499686.

136 **sneakers outside sports:** Elizabeth Semmelhack, *Out of the Box: The Rise of Sneaker Culture* (New York: Skira Rizzoli Publications, 2015), 117.

137 **"Her class was a revelation":** Jane Fonda, *My Life So Far* (New York: Random House, 2005), 387.

138 **one of the top-selling:** Judy Klemesrud, "Self-Help Video-tapes, from Cooking to Car Repair," *New York Times*, Aug. 3, 1983; http://www.nytimes.com/1983/08/03/garden/self-help -videotapes-from-cooking-to-car-repair.html?mcubz=3.

139 **well-received running shoes:** Reebok's early US models received a five-star rating from *Runner's World* magazine, which was a big selling point for distributors looking to place their shoes in running stores.

139 **many exercised barefoot:** Glenn Rifkin, "Does This Shoe Fit? Reebok Marketing Ace Stamps His Style on Rockport," *New York Times*, Oct. 14, 1995; http://www .nytimes.com/1995/10/14/business/does-this-shoe-fit-reebok -marketing-ace-stamps-his-style-on-rockport.html?page wanted=all&mcubz=3.

139 **carpeted floors, hardwood, or concrete:** Angel Martinez interview, *The School of Greatness* podcast, Jan. 30, 2015.

139 **"Aerobic shoes":** Rifkin, "Does This Shoe Fit?"

139 **"Shoes must allow for sideways movement":** "Jacki Sorensen: Whirlwind Middle of Movement," *Sarasota Herald-Tribune*, Oct. 14, 1981.

139 **sketched a sneaker on a napkin:** Rifkin, "Does This Shoe Fit?"

140 **Judy Delaney . . . repeatedly brought up:** J. B. Strasser and Laurie Becklund, *Swoosh: The Unauthorized Story of Nike and the Men Who Played There* (New York: HarperBusiness, 1993), 398.

140 **"make shoes for those fags":** Donald Katz, "Triumph of the Swoosh," *Sports Illustrated*, Aug. 16, 1993; https://www .si.com/vault/1993/08/16/129105/triumph-of-the-swoosh -with-a-keen-sense-of-the-power-of-sports-and-a-genius-for -mythologizing-athletes-to-help-sell-sneakers-nike-bestrides -the-world-of-sport-like-a-marketing-colossus.

141 **Nike's designers at one factory:** Strasser and Becklund, *Swoosh*, 398.

141 **two free weeks:** Rifkin, "Does This Shoe Fit?"

141 **"If on Monday":** Angel Martinez interview, *The School of Greatness* podcast, Jan. 30, 2015.

141 **"pyramids to the boom years":** Joan Didion, *The White Album* (New York: Farrar, Straus and Giroux, 1979), 180.

142 **walking by its display:** The origin of this particular concept can be traced to an Austrian architect named Victor Gruen. After fleeing to the United States in 1938, Gruen hit upon the idea that in order to get people into stores, the window displays had to be interesting. In the lean Great Depression years,

Gruen knew that every advantage needed to be taken in the design of the store, both inside and out. The more time a customer spent in a space, the more likely he or she was to spend money. Gruen wasn't content to design just storefronts. The rise of the suburbs and automobiles in postwar America removed the presence of "third places," spaces separate from home and work that are meant to build community. A proponent of communal urban spaces, Gruen imagined great indoor mixed-use facilities where people could live, work, and play, replicating the public, shop-lined streets of his native Vienna. He finally received a commission to build an indoor, climate-controlled shopping center in Edina, Minnesota, in 1952.

142 **sell 20 percent:** "Foot Locker, Inc. History"; http://www.fundinguniverse.com/company-histories/foot-locker-inc-history/.

143 **"We made shoes":** Angel Martinez interview, *The School of Greatness* podcast, Jan. 30, 2015.

144 **"It wasn't about tennis":** Dan Lovett with K. C. Endsley, *Anybody Seen Dan Lovett?* (Bloomington, IN: Balboa Press, 2014), 135.

<h1 style="text-align:center">11</h1>

<h1 style="text-align:center">STYLE AND FLOW</h1>

145 **the teenage DJ himself:** Jeff Chang, *Can't Stop Won't Stop: A History of the Hip-Hop Generation* (New York: Ebury Press, 2005), 70.

145 **its linoleum floors:** Will Hermes, *Love Goes to Buildings on Fire* (New York: Farrar, Straus and Giroux, 2012), 27.

145 **Herc would soak off:** Chang, *Can't Stop Won't Stop*, 79.

146 **Forty percent of the South Bronx:** Gary Hoenig, "Execution in the Bronx," *New York Times,* June 17, 1973; http://query.nytimes.com/mem/archive-free/pdf?res=980DEFD6173BE533A25754C1A9609C946290D6CF&mcubz=3.

147 **lost 97 percent of their buildings:** Joe Flood, "Why the Bronx Burned," *New York Post,* May 16, 2010; http://nypost.com/2010/05/16/why-the-bronx-burned/.

147 **"Give us money!":** "Carter Takes 'Sobering' Trip to South Bronx," *New York Times*, Oct. 16, 1977; http://query.nytimes.com/mem/archive-free/pdf?res=9C07E3D9153DE034BC4E53DFB667838C669EDE&mcubz=3.

147 **"There it is":** Flood, "Why the Bronx Burned."

147 **expanding territory and attracting recruits:** Chang, *Can't Stop Won't Stop*, 95.

147 **"When I did become a DJ":** Ibid.

148 **Grand Funk Railroad:** Ibid., 97.

148 **"I had never heard sound":** Joseph Saddler, *The Adventures of Grandmaster Flash: My Life, My Beats* (New York: Crown/Archetype, 2008), 47.

148 **"I was a scientist":** Chang, *Can't Stop Won't Stop*, 112.

149 **five for anyone wearing sneakers:** Hermes, *Love Goes to Buildings on Fire*, 259.

150 **track suits, Kangol hats:** Greg Foley and Andrew Luecke, *Cool: Style, Sound and Subversion* (New York: Rizzoli, 2017), 101.

150 **As sneaker brands released:** Bobbito Garcia, *Where'd You Get Those?: New York City's Sneaker Culture* (New York: Testify, 2013), 59.

150 **"We liked [the Adidas Superstars]":** Ibid., 93.

150 **Each New York City borough:** *Fresh Dressed*, dir. Sacha Jenkins, Cable News Network, 2015.

150 **were known as "Uptowns":** The definition of "Uptowns" would later change to include the Nike Air Force One basketball shoe.

151 ***Oh! Oh! Obesity!:*** Sherri Day, "Jamaica Journal; An Old-Fashioned Country Doctor Finishes His Last Rounds in the Big City," *New York Times*, Oct. 29, 2000; http://www.nytimes.com/2000/10/29/nyregion/jamaica-journal-old-fashioned-country-doctor-finishes-his-last-rounds-big-city.html?mcubz=3.

151 **hold young black men back:** Elizabeth Semmelhack, *Out of the Box: The Rise of Sneaker Culture* (New York: Skira Rizzoli Publications, 2015), 143.

153   **"What we wear onstage":** *Fresh Dressed*, dir. Sacha Jenkins.

153   **"We're going to flip the stereotype":** *Just for Kicks*, dirs. Thibaut de Longeville and Lisa Leone, Caid Productions, 2006.

155   **"Everybody had on new Adidas":** *Evolution of Hip-Hop*, Episode 3: "The New Guard," dir. Darby Wheeler, Banger Films, 2016.

155   **From his vantage point:** *Just for Kicks*, dirs. Thibaut de Longeville and Lisa Leone.

156   **"played out":** Garcia, *Where'd You Get Those?*, 146.

157   **"We have a certain respect":** "Summer Edition '92," *House of Style*, MTV, 1992.

157   **lengths some people would go to:** Anyone doubting that the Beastie Boys were fashion influencers need only to look when, in 1987, Mike D wearing a compact disc–size VW hood ornament on his gold chain inspired a rash of hood ornament thefts.

12

HIS AIRNESS

160   **Akeem "The Dream" Olajuwon:** He would add an *H* to his first name in 1991.

161   **"Individual athletes, even more than teams":** Randall Rothenberg, *Where the Suckers Moon: The Life and Death of an Advertising Campaign* (New York: Vintage, 1995), 205.

162   **"If you had gone to a playground":** David Halberstam, *Playing for Keeps: Michael Jordan and the World He Made* (New York: Broadway Books, 2000), 142.

162   **"Am I getting fucked on this deal?":** David Falk, *The Bald Truth: Secrets of Success from the Locker Room to the Boardroom* (New York: Pocket Books, 2009), 44.

163   **"Oh, Buck, Buck":** Phil Knight, *Shoe Dog: A Memoir by the Creator of Nike* (New York: Scribner, 2016), 319.

163   **"The question is":** John Papanek, "There's An Ill Wind Blowing For The NBA," *Sports Illustrated*, Feb. 26, 1979.

164 **more than 120:** J. B. Strasser and Laurie Becklund, *Swoosh: The Unauthorized Story of Nike and the Men Who Played There* (New York: HarperBusiness, 1993), 424.

165 **push hard for Jordan:** "Sole Man," *30 for 30*, dirs. Jon Weinbach and Dan Marks, Electric City Entertainment, 2015.

167 **"Michael," she said:** Strasser and Becklund, *Swoosh*, 433.

167 **"From what I understood and perceived":** "Error Jordan: Key Figures Still Argue over Who Was Responsible for Nike Deal," *USA Today*, Sept. 30, 2015; https://www.usatoday.com /story/sports/nba/2015/09/30/error-jordan-key-figures-still -argue-over-who-responsible-nike-deal/72884830/.

167 **"I can't wear that shoe":** David Halberstam, *Playing for Keeps: Michael Jordan and the World He Made* (New York: Broadway Books, 2000), 145.

168 **Meetings with Converse and Adidas:** Incidentally, Jordan's Converse sneakers worn in the 1984 Olympics fetched more than $190,000 at auction in 2017, well beyond the $100,000 Converse offered Jordan for his endorsement in 1984.

171 **fifty pairs of sneakers:** "Lou Reed, Alan Alda, Michael Jordan," *Late Night with David Letterman*, NBC, May 19, 1986.

171 **"Well, neither does the NBA":** Ibid. The ugly red-and-blue track suit Jordan wore on Letterman's show even inspired a similarly colored edition of the Air Jordan I in 2016.

13

MARS AND MIKE

174 **$7 million at the box office:** "1986 Domestic Grosses," Box Office Mojo, http://www.boxofficemojo.com/yearly/chart/?yr =1986.

174 **"There's something genuinely different":** Michael Wilmington, "Movie Review: Nola's Jazzy Love Life in 'She's Gotta Have It,'" *Los Angeles Times*, Aug. 23, 1986; http://articles.la times.com/1986-08-21/entertainment/ca-17460_1_spike-lee.

174 **"These characters are well-grounded":** Spike Lee, *Spike Lee: Interviews*, ed. Cynthia Fuchs (Jackson: University Press of Mississippi, 2002), 4.

174 **"Mr. Lee has said":** D.J.R. Bruckner, "Film: Spike Lee's 'She's Gotta Have It,' " *New York Times*, Aug. 8, 1986; http://www.nytimes.com/1986/08/08/movies/film-spike-lee-s-she-s-gotta-have-it.html?mcubz=3.

176 **"we can take Michael":** J. B. Strasser and Laurie Becklund, *Swoosh: The Unauthorized Story of Nike and the Men Who Played There* (New York: HarperBusiness, 1993), 526.

177 **Hatfield was grateful:** "Tinker Hatfield: Footwear Designer," *Abstract: The Art of Design*, dir. Brian Oakes, Tremolo Productions, 2017.

178 **designing office spaces and showrooms:** *Respect the Architects: The Paris Air Max 1 Story*, dir. Thibaut De Longeville, ThreeSixty, 2006.

178 **"the perfect shoe":** "Tinker Hatfield: Footwear Designer."

179 **When Spike Lee received a call:** David Halberstam, *Playing for Keeps: Michael Jordan and the World He Made* (New York: Broadway Books, 1999), 181.

179 **"Do I get to work with Michael Jordan?":** Ibid.

179 **Jordan hadn't seen:** Reserve Channel, "Spike Lee: Michael Jordan and Mars Blackmon | Ep. 9 Part 2, Segment 2/4 ARTST TLK | Reserve Channel," YouTube, 2013; https://www.youtube.com/watch?v=SGzKlUxQhx0.

180 **"If Michael had said":** Spike Lee, *Best Seat in the House* (New York: Three Rivers Press, 1997), 135.

180 **On their first meeting:** Halberstam, *Playing for Keeps*, 182.

181 **(twice what his first film had):** *School Daze* earned more than $14 million domestically; "1988 Domestic Grosses," Box Office Mojo; http://www.boxofficemojo.com/yearly/chart/?yr=1988&p=.htm.

181 **"I thought it was important":** Lee, *Spike Lee: Interviews*, 53.

183 **cameo by Nola:** In the commercial for the new Air Jordan IV, Lee again appeared as Mars Blackmon, this time questioning

Nola (played by Tracy Camilla Johns), his love interest in *She's Gotta Have It*, why she preferred Jordan to him. After a string of Mars's "Is it because . . . ?" questions, Nola gives her answer: "It's because he's got the new Air Jordans, Mars."

183 **product placement in Lee's next film:** That particular model of shoe would make an appearance in Lee's 1989 film, *Do The Right Thing*, in which a pair of scuffed Jordans instantly triggers a heated confrontation about race, gentrification, and regional sports allegiances. The white character who runs the shoes over with a bicycle in the scene not so subtly wears a Boston Celtics Larry Bird T-shirt.

14

BATTLE OF THE BRANDS

186 **"If I run up there":** "Sneaker Wars," *Dunkumentaries* podcast, ESPN Radio, 2016.

187 **brought his arm over his eyes:** Brown's gesture of shielding his eyes in his elbow while extending the other arm would later be known as a dance move called the "dab." As the origin of the dance move is traced to the Atlanta hip-hop scene of the early 2010s, the Celtics player could not credibly be called "the first dabber."

187 **"Hey, you did a great job":** "Sneaker Wars," *Dunkumentaries* podcast, ESPN Radio, 2016.

188 **"My goal was to have":** Associated Press, "The Man Who Made Reebok Jump High," *Los Angeles Times*, Aug. 15, 2005; http://articles.latimes.com/2005/aug/15/business/fi-reebok15.

189 **Nike's net annual income:** Nike's annual income was $26 million that year; Nike Inc., 1981 Annual Report, 13.

189 **$1.79 billion in sales:** Douglas C. McGill, "Nike Is Bounding Past Reebok," *New York Times*, July 11, 1989; http://www.nytimes.com/1989/07/11/business/nike-is-bounding-past-reebok.html?mcubz=3.

190   **"I may be over the top":** Kenneth Labich, "Nike vs. Reebok: A Battle For Hearts, Minds, and Feet," *Fortune,* Sept. 18, 1995.

190   **"At the end of a contest":** Ibid.

191   **air splints:** Brian Betschart, "Pump Designer Paul Litchfield Interview," SneakerFiles, Nov. 20, 2009; https://www.sneakerfiles .com/paul-litchfield-steve-kluback-reebok-pump-interview/.

192   **"Hey, Litch, these shoes don't inflate":** "Ep107-OSD-Paul Litchfield x Reebok PUMP," *Obsessive Sneaker Disorder* podcast, Nov. 19, 2009.

194   **"You can't be serious, man!":** Wimbledon, "Share the Moment: John McEnroe coins 'You cannot be serious,'" YouTube, July 3, 2015; https://www.youtube.com/watch?v=t0hK1wyrrAU.

195   **"Once they were on":** Tim Newcomb, "The evolution of tennis shoes: From plimsolls to Stan Smiths and Nikes," *Sports Illustrated,* Nov. 18, 2015; https://www.si.com/tennis/2015/11/18 /tennis-shoes-stan-smith-john-mcenroe-pete-sampras.

195   **"It was a jaw-dropping experience":** Jason Coles, *Golden Kicks: The Shoes That Changed Sport* (New York: Bloomsbury, 2016), 127.

195   **"These are the best tennis shoes":** Ibid., 127.

196   **"If you have a body, you are an athlete":** Nike mission statement; https://help-en-us.nike.com/app/answer/a_id/113.

196   **"*Good* night":** J. B. Strasser and Laurie Becklund, *Swoosh: The Unauthorized Story of Nike and the Men Who Played There* (New York: HarperBusiness, 1993), 510.

197   **"People were applying it":** *Art & Copy: Inside Advertising's Creative Revolution,* dir. Doug Pray, The One Club, 2009.

199   **"The fun part":** "You Don't Know Bo: The Legend of Bo Jackson," *30 for 30,* dir. Michael Bonfiglio, RadicalMedia, 2012.

199   **Saturday-morning cartoon show *ProStars*:** Though the show ran for only thirteen episodes, it was enough to merit a special edition of the Air Jordan 5 in 2015 that subtly featured a green color accent similar to the cartoon's title card, seemingly proving that nearly anything can merit a limited sneaker colorway.

199 **"Bow knows"**: Donald Katz, *Just Do It: The Nike Spirit in the Corporate World* (New York: Adams Media, 1994), 12.

201 **"settled in Barcelona"**: O'Brien would get his turn on the medal stand by winning gold in the decathlon at the 1996 Olympics in Atlanta, the first American to do so since Bruce Jenner's win in 1976.

201 **"I don't believe"**: Dave Anderson, "Sports of The Times; On Loyalty to Company, or Country?," *New York Times*, Aug. 2, 1992; http://www.nytimes.com/1992/08/02/sports/sports-of -the-times-on-loyalty-to-company-or-country.html?mcubz=3.

202 **Word spread:** Not every Dream Team athlete objected to skipping the awards ceremony. John Stockton, a Nike endorser, was quoted as saying "In a million years there's no way I'm not going up there."

202 **"As for loyalty to his company"**: Anderson, "Sports of The Times; On Loyalty to Company, or Country?"

202 **"This is getting serious"**: Katz, *Just Do It*, 21.

15

SNEAKER CRIME AND PUNISHMENT

203 **Phil Knight was pissed off:** "Ep198-OSD-Tinker Hatfield," *Obsessive Sneaker Disorder* podcast, Oct. 20, 2011.

203 **"What is our competitive response"**: Ibid.

205 **"I think it's a sign"**: Ed Bruske, "Police Theorize Arundel Youth Was Killed For His Air Jordans," *Washington Post*, May 6, 1989; https://www.washingtonpost.com/archive/local/1989/05/06 /police-theorize-arundel-youth-was-killed-for-his-air-jordans /f5dc8ea5-376e-44bc-9ee2-19dff47c514b/?utm_term=.ba7c2c c58ed4.

205 **Martin served seven years:** A few years after being released, Martin strangled and stabbed a seventeen-year-old relative, who miraculously survived. In 2005, three months after being released from prison for that crime, he strangled yet another

victim, his wife, and hid her body in a garbage bag. In 2012, DNA evidence linked Martin with the rape and murder of a fourteen-year-old Bronx girl.

206 **"I never thought"**: Rick Telander, "Senseless," *Sports Illustrated,* May 14, 1990; https://www.si.com/vault/1990/05/14/121992/senseless-in-americas-cities-kids-are-killing-kids-over-sneakers-and-other-sports-apparel-favored-by-drug-dealers-whos-to-blame.

206 **"It's murder, gentlemen"**: Phil Mushnick, "Shaddup, I'm Sellin' Out . . . Shaddup," *New York Post*, April 6, 1990.

207 **"too black" to be popular**: Matthew Schneider-Mayerson, "'Too Black': Race in the 'Dark Ages' of the National Basketball Association," *The International Journal of Sport and Society* 1, no. 1 (2010): 223–24.

207 **"It's ridiculous to say"**: Ira Berkow, "Sports of The Times; The Murders over the Sneakers," *New York Times*, May 14, 1990; http://www.nytimes.com/1990/05/14/sports/sports-of-the-times-the-murders-over-the-sneakers.html?mcubz=3.

207 **"Something is wrong"**: Spike Lee, *Spike Lee: Interviews*, ed. Cynthia Fuchs (Jackson: University Press of Mississippi, 2002), 52.

208 **wore exclusively**: Telander, "Senseless."

208 **stopped selling jackets**: Ibid.

208 **"might want to emulate me"**: Donald Katz, *Just Do It: The Nike Spirit in the Corporate World* (New York: Adams Media, 1994), 269.

208 **had the wrong shoes on**: Roger Chesley, Jim Schaefer, and David Zeman, "Violence Began with Sneakers Police Say Setup May Have Led Officer to Neighborhood, Death," *Detroit Free Press*, May 27, 1995; http://www.crimeindetroit.com/documents/052795%20Violence%20began%20with%20Sneakers.pdf.

209 **"reality rap"**: "Straight Outta L.A.," *30 for 30*, dir. Ice Cube, Hunting Lanes Films, 2010.

210 **"In L.A. we wearing Chucks, not Ballys":** Tupac Shakur and Andre Young, "California Love," Death Row Records/Interscope, 1996.

210 **"black Tims":** Christopher George Latore Wallace and Robert Hall, "Suicidal Thoughts," Bad Boy Records, 1994.

211 **14 cents per hour:** Jeffrey Ballinger, "The New Free-Trade Heel," *Harper's Magazine*, August 1992, 46; https://harpers .org/archive/1992/08/the-new-free-trade-heel/.

211 **$2.2 billion in annual revenue:** Nike Inc., 1990 Annual Report, 23.

212 **"We don't pay anybody":** Bob de Wit and Ron Meyer, *Strategy: Process, Content, Context: An International Perspective*, 4th ed. (Hampshire, UK: Cengage Learning EMEA, 2010), 950.

212 **forced to work 65 hours a week:** Steven Greenhouse, "Nike Shoe Plant in Vietnam Is Called Unsafe for Workers," *New York Times*, Nov. 8, 1997; http://www.nytimes.com/1997/11/08 /business/nike-shoe-plant-in-vietnam-is-called-unsafe-for -workers.html?mcubz=3.

212 **"Without the single focus on Nike":** Jeff Ballinger, "Nike's Role in the Third World," letter to the editor, *New York Times*, March 18, 2001; http://www.nytimes.com/2001/03/18/business/l -nike-s-role-in-the-third-world-443425.html?mcubz=3.

213 **tended to focus on solutions:** Josh Greenberg and Graham Knight, "Framing Sweatshops: Nike, Global Production, and the American News Media," *Communication and Critical/Cultural Studies* 1 (2004): 151–175; http://www.tandfonline.com /doi/abs/10.1080/14791420410001685368.

214 **"synonymous with slave wages":** "Nike Pledges to End Child Labor And Apply U.S. Rules Abroad," *New York Times*, May 13, 1998.

215 **108-page report:** Nike FY04 Corporate Responsibility report, April 13, 2005.

215 **"inappropriate slang":** "Jonah Peretti and Nike," *The Guardian*, Feb. 19, 2001; https://www.theguardian.com/media/2001 /feb/19/1.

16

I, SNEAKERHEAD

217 **"What the fuck is going on here?":** Sole Collector, "10 Years Later: The Nike Pigeon Dunk Riot," YouTube, Feb. 20, 2015; https://www.youtube.com/watch?v=PmHQCFAT6XY.

217 **southern California's 1980s and '90s surf culture:** Bobby Hundreds, "'It's Not About Clothes': Bobby Hundreds Explains Why Streetwear Is a Culture, Not Just Product," *Complex*, Feb. 16, 2017; http://www.complex.com/style/2017 /02/what-is-streetwear-by-bobby-hundreds.

219 **"That street mentality":** KarmaloopTV, "Jeff Staple Explains the Meaning of the Pigeon Logo - Making the Brand - Episode 1," YouTube, Oct. 30, 2013, https://www.youtube.com /watch?v=3wDoQz7aLLk.

219 **The people who lined up:** Tom Sykes, "Sneak Attack," *New York Post*, March 3, 2005; http://nypost.com/2005/03/03 /sneak-attack/.

220 **high-fashion brands:** Reebok collaborated with Chanel around 1997, Adidas with designers Jeremy Scott and Yohji Yamamoto in 2002, and Nike with Supreme in 2002, to name a few early collaborations with exclusive brands and designers.

220 **"I think what escalated":** "The Classics 10: Jeff Staple," *The Monocle Weekly* podcast, Aug. 2, 2015.

222 **"I was never a sneaker freak":** VICE Sports, "15 Years of SB Dunk: Stories from the Inside Out," YouTube, March 9, 2017; https://www.youtube.com/watch?v=K4Jsmg2oYH4.

223 **kicks:** The *Oxford English Dictionary* dates the usage of "kicks" for "shoes" to 1904.

224 **"long tail":** Chris Anderson, "The Long Tail," *Wired*, Oct. 1, 2004; https://www.wired.com/2004/10/tail/.

224 **Jay-Z's S. Carter sneaker:** Tim Arango, "Reebok Running Up Sales with New Jay-Z Sneakers," *New York Post*, April 23, 2003; http://nypost.com/2003/04/23/reebok-running-up-sales -with-new-jay-z-sneakers/.

224 **marked down and liquidated:** Matt Powell, "Sneakernomics: Will Kanye West Help Adidas Sales?" *Forbes*, May 1, 2014; https://www.forbes.com/sites/mattpowell/2014/05/01/sneakernomics-will-kanye-west-help-adidas-sales/#2ad8841131ae.

224 **most expensive pairs of sneakers:** That record was eclipsed in 2017 when another pair of Jordan's shoes, a signed pair of Converse sneakers he had worn in the 1984 Olympics, sold at auction for $190,373.

226 **fetched slightly less than $5,000:** A pair of Air Jordan XI shoes attributed to the 1996 NBA All Star Game sold at auction for $4,915.20 in April 2013.

227 **In 1985, $65 was to be the going rate:** That was the price of the original Air Jordan. See Matt Burns, "Dan Gilbert and Campless Founder Launch a Marketplace for Sneakers," TechCrunch, Feb. 8, 2016; https://techcrunch.com/2016/02/08/dan-gilbert-and-campless-founder-launch-a-marketplace-for-sneakers/.

227 **"the stock market of things":** The seed of this idea began when Luber started working at IBM in 2010. After doing a lot of data work, he had become curious about getting ahold of sneaker data to see if he could get anything out of it. He ended up creating Campless, a kind of Kelly Blue Book price guide for sneakers that rested on mounds of data to assign a fairer value for shoes than what the wild eBay auctions were charging. Campless morphed into StockX by selling only verified deadstock, in other words, brand-new, unworn shoes that have been declared authentic much the same way an art dealer might vouch for a rare vase or old painting.

228 **twice as much overall profit:** Josh Luber, "Why Sneakers Are a Great Investment," TED, October 2015; https://www.ted.com/talks/josh_luber_why_sneakers_are_a_great_investment.

228 **sold on the secondary market for $7,500:** StockX.com.

229 **"full creative reign":** Jon Wexler, status update, Twitter.com, Sept. 22, 2015.

231 **"The widespread interest"**: Elizabeth Semmelhack, *Out of the Box: The Rise of Sneaker Culture* (New York: Skira Rizzoli Publications, 2015), 197.

231 **44 million visitors a month:** Hypebeast.com, About page.

232 **Purple Unicorn Planet:** Semmelhack, *Out of the Box*, 189.

232 **"Trainers are unisex shoes":** "Sneaker Envy Motivated These Two Women to Create a Nike Fantasy Shop," *Fast Company*, July 25, 2013; https://www.fastcompany.com/1683462/sneaker-envy-motivated-these-two-women-to-create-a-nike-fantasy-shop.

232 **"I had to settle for a [men's] size 9":** "Meet the Female 'Sneakerheads' of Toronto and See Why They Are Calling for Shoe Companies to Step Up," *CBC News*, July 10, 2017; http://www.cbc.ca/news/canada/toronto/women-sneakerhead-blog-1.4197330.

232 **"With the internet":** Semmelhack, *Out of the Box*, 189.

232 **"At 7 p.m.":** Frank Rosario and Aaron Fels, "Sneaker Release Nearly Causes Riot at Soho Store," *New York Post*, April 3, 2014; http://nypost.com/2014/04/03/sneaker-release-nearly-causes-riot-at-soho-store/.

233 **They had started lining up:** Albert Samaha, "NYPD Shuts Down Foamposite Sneaker Release Because of Big Crowd," *Village Voice*, April 3, 2014; https://www.villagevoice.com/2014/04/03/nypd-shuts-down-foamposite-sneaker-release-because-of-big-crowd/.

233 **expected to fetch $1,000:** Rosario and Fels, "Sneaker Release Nearly Causes Riot."

233 **sold out in five minutes:** Samaha, "NYPD Shuts Down Foamposite Sneaker Release."

17

BACK AT IT AGAIN

235 **imagine what a sneaker might look like in three decades:** The highest-grossing movie of 1989, Tim Burton's *Batman*, also featured a custom-designed Hatfield sneaker. Nike had a deal with Warner Bros. to feature its shoes in its movies. "Eighties sportswear is not going to fit in with our 1940s look," the lead costume designer, Bob Ringwood, said to his assistant designer, Graham Churchyard. Instead of forcing sneakers into the movie, the pair came up with the idea of just letting Nike design the Batboot. Using plaster casts of Michael Keaton's calves, Hatfield made more than a dozen pairs of leather and polyurethane boots using the Air Trainer SC as a base. Keaton and the stuntmen reportedly loved how comfortable the Batboots were. Though the swoosh is hard to spot, the sneaker's distinctive forefoot strap can be seen in several shots of the movie. The sequel, *Batman Returns*, the third-highest-grossing movie of 1992, also featured a repurposed Nike shoe, this time the Air Jordan IV. The *Batman* and *Back to the Future* movies were hardly the first to feature sneaker product placement; 1986's *Aliens* featured Sigourney Weaver's Ripley character wearing a pair of futuristic Velcro Reebok sneaker boots.

236 **"Go look at the feet":** *Abstract: The Art of Design*, Episode 2: "Tinker Hatfield: Footwear Design," dir. Brian Oakes, RadicalMedia Production, 2016.

239 **some have called for the shoe to be banned:** For an interesting look at the technology and implications of a performance-enhancing shoe, see Ross Tucker, "Ban the Nike Vaporfly & Other Carbon Fiber Devices for Future Performance Credibility," *The Science of Sport*, March 21, 2017; http://sportsscientists .com/2017/03/ban-nike-vaporfly-carbon-fiber-devices-future -performance-credibility/.

240 **first made rubber outsoles for boots in 1937:** Solving sole problems was a Vibram focus that went right back to the company's founding in the 1930s. At the time, mountaineering

boots were made with leather soles with metal hobnail cleats. They were not well insulated and became slippery when they froze. The boots would be worn during the beginning of climbs before being exchanged for flat-bottomed climbing shoes closer to the summit. In 1935, Vitale Bramani led an expedition up Mount Rasica in the Italian Alps. The group was struck by a heavy snowstorm and fog; six of the climbers died from frostbite and exposure. Bramini thought that his friends might have survived if their shoes had been better suited to extremely cold weather. Once again, Charles Goodyear's invention provided the solution to Bramani's problem. Using vulcanized rubber for the boot's outsole provided protection from the water and the cold. By developing a specialized hiking sole pattern he called the *carrarmato*, or tank tread, Bramani found a way to increase traction over a wide variety of surfaces. The mountaineering sole, with its distinctive "plus-sign" ridges running up the middle of the forefoot, proved to be so effective that the pattern became standard.

240 **"It caused me to remember"**: Jonathan Beverly, "50 Years of (Mostly) Fantastic Footwear Innovation," *Runner's World*, Nov. 18, 2016; https://www.runnersworld.com/running-shoes /50-years-of-mostly-fantastic-footwear-innovation.

240 **"Day 11: Speedwork Day"**: Peter Sagal, "Foot Loose," *Runner's World*, Aug. 15, 2008; https://www.runnersworld.com /road-scholar/vibram-five-finger-running-shoes.

240 **"My knees were screaming"**: John Biggs, "Review: Vibram Five Fingers Classic," TechCrunch, Aug. 10, 2009; https://tech crunch.com/2009/08/10/review-vibram-five-fingers-classic/.

241 **"plastic gorilla feet"**: Jon Snyder, "Review: Vibram FiveFingers KSO and Classic Running Shoes," *Wired*, July 10, 2009; https:// www.wired.com/2009/07/pr_vibram_fivefingers_kso/.

241 **squishy rubber packing peanuts**: "Olivier Bernhard Talks About On-Running Shoes and the 'Cloud' Technology," Lets-Run, Jan. 31, 2013; http://www.letsrun.com/news/2013/01 /on-running-shoes-1231/.

242 **more than four years:** Brian Metzler, "Six Years Later: The Legacy of 'Born to Run,'" *Competitor,* Jan. 5, 2017; http://running.competitor.com/2014/05/news/the-legacy-of-born-to-run_72044.

242 **sold more than 3 million copies:** Ben Child, "Matthew McConaughey Born to Run in Upcoming Native American Drama," *The Guardian,* Jan. 29, 2015; https://www.the guardian.com/film/2015/jan/29/matthew-mcconaughey-native -american-born-to-run-gold.

243 **"How one runs":** Daniel E. Lieberman, "What We Can Learn About Running From Barefoot Running: An Evolutionary Medical Perspective," *Exercise and Sport Sciences Reviews,* 2012, 64.

245 **"Everyone's so unique":** Fiona Duncan, "Normcore: Fashion for Those Who Realize They're One in 7 Billion," *New York* magazine, *The Cut* blog, Feb. 26, 2014; https://www.thecut .com/2014/02/normcore-fashion-trend.html.

246 **20 percent bump:** "'Damn, Daniel!' You Sold a Lot of White Shoes," *Bloomberg,* April 29, 2016; https://twitter.com /business/status/726490120052985856.

246 **"First time doing it":** Alex Ungerman, "Frank Ocean Gave His First Interview in 3 Years and Was Asked About . . . His Shoes—Watch!," *Entertainment Tonight,* Oct. 20, 2016; http://www.etonline.com/music/200873_frank_ocean_first _interview_three_years.

246 **6 percent sales increase:** "VF Reports Third Quarter 2016 Results," Oct. 24, 2016; http://www.vfc.com/news/press-releases/detail/1603/vf-reports-third-quarter-2016-results.

248 **lighting them on fire:** Katie Mettler, "We Live in Crazy Times: Neo-Nazis Have Declared New Balance the 'Official Shoes of White People,'" *Washington Post,* Nov. 15, 2016; https://www.washingtonpost.com/news/morning-mix/wp /2016/11/15/the-crazy-reason-neo-nazis-have-declared-new -balance-the-official-shoes-of-white-people/.

248　**"Comfort. Support. Stability":** *Saturday Night Live*, May 4, 2013.

248　**the *N* could stand for "Nazi":** Thomas Rogers, "Heil Hipster: The Young Neo-Nazis Trying to Put a Stylish Face on Hate," *Rolling Stone*, June 23, 2014; http://www.rollingstone.com /culture/news/heil-hipster-the-young-neo-nazis-trying-to-put -a-stylish-face-on-hate-20140623.

249　**36 million social media followers:** Total of Curry's Facebook, Twitter, and Instagram followers as of November 1, 2017.

249　**the number of people who tuned in:** According to Sports-MediaWatch.com, 24.47 million people watched game five of the 2017 NBA Finals.

250　**the laces themselves were tied together:** Henry Leutwyler, *Document* (Göttingen, Germany: Steidl, 2016).

EPILOGUE

253　**one of the sneaker capitals:** With Madison Square Garden, playground basketball courts, the home of American fashion publishing, the birthplace of hip-hop, and 8 million people making the sidewalks their own personal catwalks, a strong case can be made for New York being the sneaker capital of the world. Other cities that can make a strong plea for that title include Paris, Tokyo, Los Angeles, Boston, and Portland, Oregon.

255　**brick with the Supreme logo:** A few months later, the bricks would be going for two to four times that amount on eBay.

255　**more pairs than any other Nike model:** Russ Bengtson, "10 Reasons You Should Own Nike Air Monarchs," *Complex*, Oct. 21, 2013; http://www.complex.com/sneakers/2013/10 /reasons-you-should-own-nike-air-monarchs/.

ACKNOWLEDGMENTS

Like running, my other hobby, writing this book was a largely solitary, sometimes lonely, activity. Far from being a solo effort, however, this book would not have existed without the support of many coaches, trainers, pace setters, mentors, and managers to whom I owe a great debt.

I would first and foremost like to thank Samuel G. Freedman, who conducts the book seminar at the Columbia University School of Journalism. Without his encouragement and guidance from the very beginning, this book never would have happened. The invaluable lessons learned in his class have been a constant and welcome presence throughout the researching and writing process, probably none more applicable than the oft-repeated "Time is hurrying us."

I owe a debt of gratitude and thanks to my editor, Meghan Houser, and the rest of the wonderful team at Crown. Meghan's sharp eye for detail and big picture view of what this book could be shaped a lumpy first draft into what you now hold in your hands.

I'd like to thank my excellent agent, John Rudolf, of Dystel & Goderich Literary Management, for his patience and suggestions for whipping the proposal into shape, and for taking a chance on this writer.

I'm also grateful for the help and support of Carey Reed, Ainissa Ramirez, and Hilary Brueck, who slogged through very early, very rough portions of this book, and their input and suggestions have been invaluable and much appreciated.

A special thanks to the Lynton family, whose generous Lynton Fellowship in Book Writing was a critical vote of confidence in the project and provided important research support.

My research assistant, Stacey Szewczyk, provided indispensable help in securing photo permissions.

I would like to thank Jennifer O'Neal and the rest of the staff at the University of Oregon Libraries, Special Collections and University Archives, for their assistance in helping me sift through the Bill Bowerman Papers. Thanks also to Rebekah Burgess, New York City Parks photo archivist, who provided valuable help in searching for images of sneakers in the city's playgrounds, courts, and gyms. I am also grateful to the countless staff of the Columbia University Libraries who helped me track down all manner of documents over the life of this project.

I am indebted to the fine work that came before on shoes and the sports industry, in particular Elizabeth Semmelhack's *Out of the Box: The Rise of Sneaker Culture,* Barbara Smit's *Sneaker Wars,* J. B. Strasser and Laurie Becklund's *Swoosh,* Donald Katz's *Just Do It,* Abraham Aamidor's *Chuck Taylor, All Star,* Charles Slack's *Noble Obsession,* and Bobbito Garcia's *Where'd You Get Those?*

I'm also thankful for the friends and family who put up with listening to arcane sneaker facts and who looked at early, often excruciating, portions of the book. I am likewise grateful for all the people who granted their valuable time for interviews, follow-up questions, and general assistance throughout the life of this project.

Finally, an extra-special thanks goes to my wife, Ghadeer, to whom this book is dedicated. She was responsible for making the behind-the-scenes stuff happen that often doesn't getting discussed in the book-writing process. Things such as handling more than the usual share of parenting responsibilities, making sure I had enough time to write in the evening hours and on the weekends, lending a kind ear to my near-constant kvetching about "shoe-this or sneaker-that," and having the keen sense of knowing the best time when a hot pizza is called for in between long writing sessions. It's an old cliché, but partners really are the unsung heroes of large undertakings; their names may not be on the front of the final product, but credit for their oft-unseen efforts and struggles deserves equal recognition.

PHOTO INSERT CREDITS

PAGE 1: (*top*) Collection of the Bata Shoe Museum. Image copyright © 2017 Bata Shoe Museum, Toronto (photo: Ron Wood); (*middle*) Smith College Archives; (*bottom*) Maurice-Louis Branger/Roger Viollet/Getty Images

PAGE 2: (*top*) This photo originally appeared in *Chuck Taylor, All Star: The True Story of the Man Behind the Most Famous Athletic Shoe in History*, published by Indiana University Press and written by Abe Aamidor; (*middle*) Keds; (*bottom*) New York City Parks Photo Archive

PAGE 3: (*top*) Adidas AG; (*middle*) Nike; (*bottom*) Nike

PAGE 4: (*top*) Neil Leifer/*Sports Illustrated*/Getty Images; (*middle*) New York City Parks Photo Archive; (*bottom*) Warren Bolster/Courtesy Concrete Wave Editions

PAGE 5: (*top*) ABC Photo Archives/ABC via Getty Images; (*middle*) New York City Parks Photo Archive; (*bottom*) Reebok

PAGE 6: (*top left*) Ebet Roberts/Redferns/Getty Images; (*top right*) SI cover/*Sports Illustrated*/Getty Images; (*middle*) Walter Iooss Jr./*Sports Illustrated*/Getty Images; (*bottom*) Danita Delimont/Alamy Stock Photo

PAGE 7: (*top*) Dale Algo/@daleknows; (*middle*) Craig Sillitoe/Fairfax Media via Getty Images; (*bottom*) Brooklyn Museum. Digital Collections and Services: Exhibition. *The Rise of Sneaker Culture* [07/10/2015–10/04/2015] installation view

PAGE 8: (*top*) Paa Joe (Ghanaian, born 1945). *Coffin in the Form of a Nike Sneaker*, mid-1990s. Wood, pigment, metal, fabric, 29 × 80 × 221/2 in. (73.7 × 203.2 × 57.2 cm). Brooklyn Museum, gift of Lynne and Robert Rubin in honor of William C. Siegmann, 2000.71; (*middle*) image courtesy of Össur, Inc.; (*bottom left*) Nike; (*bottom right*) Adidas AG

INDEX

ABOUT THE AUTHOR

Nicholas Smith has covered a range of topics as a reporter, including stolen World War II art, melting glaciers, Austrian indie gamers, and the New York City mayoral election. He is a 2014 graduate of the Columbia University School of Journalism, where he was awarded the Lynton Fellowship in Book Writing. A native of Arizona, Nick now lives in Vienna, Austria, with his wife and their two children.